LEARNING

MAKING LEARNING ENVIRONMENTS
MORE EFFECTIVE

Editor:
DeWayne J. Kurpius, Ed.D.
Associate Professor of Education
Indiana University
Bloomington, Indiana

Contributors:
Samuel J. Christie, Ph.D.
Charles Jerry Downing, Ed.D.
Geraldine Ball, M.S.
Uvaldo Hill Palomares, Ed.D.
Carl E. Hollander, M.A.
Thomas C. Froehle, Ph.D.

INCORPORATED

Accelerated Development Inc.
P. O. Box 667
Muncie, In 47305
Tel. (317) 284-7511

49697

Library of Congress Catalog Card Number: 77-80964

International Standard Book Number: 0-915202-12-3

Corporate Editor: Linda K. Davis

Graphic Artist: Mary J. Blizzard

Printed in the United States of America, May 1978

For additional copies order from

Accelerated Development Inc.
2515 W. Jackson Street
Muncie, In 47305
Tel. (317) 284-7511

Cost: $11.95 plus postage and handling
—in U. S. and Canada add 50 cents
—in other countries, postage depends upon
prevailing rates

Price is subject to change without notice.

PREFACE

Creating effective, efficient, and relevant learning environments in schools has long been a goal for most education practitioners and trainers. This Book concentrates on the multiple ways that teachers, counselors, psychologists, social workers, parents, administrators, and students themselves can improve the quality of the school learning environment.

Research findings and practical experience have moved us far beyond the point of believing that learning should be made difficult and that learning "should" occur for the sake of knowledge acquisition. We know that most learning occurs because of the natural human incentive to improve one's self. That is, students desire to grow and to develop and tend to experience this growth as a positively reinforcing consequence. These same principles of growth and development apply toward educators. Observing growth producing environments, educators feel positively about themselves and about their students. Also, in such nurturing and supportive environments students too have a strong desire to excel in performance.

Given the proven importance of a positive learning environment, how then do we establish such a situation? What are the ingredients? And how do we recognize one already in existence? To answer the last question first, when observing a positive learning environment, one will see: (1) students and teachers smiling; (2) people exploring and inquiring about scientifc, artistic and human issues; (3) staff and students giving and receiving feedback which is objective, timely and growth producing; (4) students and staff sharing leadership responsibilities; (5) individuals giving positive reinforcement for desired behaviors and sparingly using negative reinforcement for improper behaviors which violate clearly defined and agreed-upon goals; (6) participants exhibiting spontaniety and naturalness, being confident that a mistake will be perceived as growth producing rather than wrong-doing; (7) learners judging the quality of their work and recognizing where special help might be needed; (8) parents viewing the school as a community organization where open communication and collaboration are demonstrated between school and community, and (9) task performance objectives and interpersonal relationship objectives operating.

Offering alternative methods on how to improve the quality of learning environments is the goal of this Book. Each chapter presents a different set of factors which influence the creation of effective, efficient and relevant learning environments. These factors are followed by operational definitions of how to implement plans for improvement.

In Chapter 1 the school is viewed as a social system. By definition, this means potentially an unlimited number of forces working both for and against the development of a positive learning environment. These forces are linked to the human interaction dynamics experienced via the goals, values, roles, rewards, leadership structure and problem-solving capabilities of the social system. Many of the existing positive forces can be accelerated to become even more impactful while the forces defined as negative can be adjusted, modified or changed to become positive vectors.

We begin the Chapter by building a rationale for establishing positive learning environments as a high priority for education. We give reasons why such an environment is important and what can be done at organizational and classroom levels to create a learning environment which would meet the criteria described. For example, we describe the importance of being inquiry and collaboratively oriented individual and group problems solvers, the significance of open versus closed systems, the importance of shared leadership, and the necessity of recognizing human interaction as the key to change.

Lastly, we present a systematic and collaborative problem-solving model which can be applied at several levels such as the classroom, the school, and the family. Along with this model is a description of tools and techniques which are commonly used by

iv

educators to enhance learning environments. Giving and receiving feedback, force-field analysis, efficient leadership of small group meetings, and conflict utilization are a few of these tools.

In Chapter 2 are succinctly described the needs, concepts, goals, practices, and evaluation procedures for developing a positive classroom learning environment. Research has long verified the importance of learners experiencing a supportive and cohesive classroom environment, one in which both teachers and peers care about each other and in which both content objectives and interpersonal relationship objectives are valued and appropriately integrated into the school curriculum.

The methodology followed to create such a positive learning environment centers around the use of small group procedures. The authors refer to these small groups as the "Magic Circle." The term was created during the early development of this model by a student who had had a very positive experience in his group and thus later referred to it as the "magic circle."

A step-by-step description of each phase of the group program is provided in the Chapter so that all members of a school, such as teachers, support staff, paraprofessionals, administrators and students themselves, can participate both as leaders and as followers. In addition, special lessons are set out for a series of group meetings with special guidelines for each group.

Chapter 3 is also based upon the importance of establishing a supportive learning environment. However, Chapter 3 differs in that it introduces a third member—the parent—into the learning environnment. Thus, the Chapter describes a triadic working relation between learner, teacher, and parent. While most of the learners' values and behaviors can be understood by direct observation in school, and many of the teachers' and parents' values and behaviors can be communicated via the learner, much more can be accomplished for inducing positive learning. The Chapter includes descriptive examples to help teachers and parents work more interdependly and to develop and maintain the best possible learning situation both at home and in school.

Chapter 4 is more psychologically based than the preceding Chapters. Emphasis is placed on role playing, sociodrama and psychodrama which stem from psychological theories. However, these theories are rapidly becoming meaningful components of the normal educational process. Psychodrama was originally created as a highly personal technique based on the hyphotheses that humans could act out feelings and thoughts in such a way as to increase one's understanding of self and others. While the use of this technique may require special training, role playing has followed psychodrama as a very useful and impactful process. Often while students are playing the role of teacher, counselor or principal, they may discover new insights about the lives of these professionals. Other role-playing techniques are also included to help school staff to become more creative in establishing the best possible learning environment. Sociometry, also introduced in this Chapter, is a tool for assessing the interpersonal network within a classroom. Appreciation of such techniques can greatly enhance the use of positive forces already existing in a given classroom and in most cases can be instrumented by the classroom teacher.

In many ways Chapter 5 is the most universal of all. The general focus is on perceiving, defining and valuing accountability as a positive force in education. Helping education professionals and their learners to recognize that the application of certain assessment procedures will actually make the task of learning an easier and more enjoyable experience is the primary intent of this Chapter.

While the content of the Chapters is directed toward the classroom, the school and the family, most of the concepts and techniques can be generalized to many other situations. The materials are very applicable for in-service and continuing education programs. If used at the pre-service and entry levels, college and university students could be better prepared for student field experiences and subsequent entrance into an educational profession. The information presented is applicable to any learning environment.

DeWayne Kurpius
Bloomington, Indiana
April, 1978

TABLE OF CONTENTS

Chapter   **Page**

PREFACE iii

LIST OF FIGURES xv

1. A SYSTEMATIC AND COLLABORATIVE APPROACH
   TO PROBLEM SOLVING by Samuel G. Christie and
   DeWayne J. Kurpius 1

   About the Editor, DeWayne J. Kurpius 2
   Editor's Notes 3
   About the Author, Samuel G. Christie 5

   Seeking Answers through Active Inquiry 8
       Inquiry as a Response to a Basic Need 8
       Problem Solving through Inquiry 9
   The School as a System 10
       The School as a Biological System 11
       The School as a Social System 11
   Social System Norms and Role Expectations 12
   Existing Conditions in School—A Built-in
       Resistance to Change 13
       Low Interdependence of Staff 13
       High Vulnerability 14
       Goal Ambiguity 15
       Individual Orientation 16
   The Systematic and Collaborative Approach
       (S-C) 17
   The Key to Change—Human Interaction 17
   An Introduction to the S-C Model 18
       Systematic Group Problem Solving 19
       Collaborative Group Problem Solving 20
   Implementing the Systematic and
       Collaborative Approach—A Group
           Problem-Solving Approach 21
       Sensing the Problem, Step 1 21
       A Suggested Tool Skill to be used for
           Step 2 23
           Assessment 23
           Analysis 24
           Synthesis 24
           Decision Making 24

49697

Selecting a Strategy to Solve the
    Problem, Step 3 24
    Force Field Analysis 25
    Brainstorming 29
Planning for the Implementation of
    the Chosen Strategy, Step 4 29
Implementing the Plan and Evaluating
    the Process, Step 5 31
Other Considerations in Problem Solving 33
    The Individual in Relation to the
    Group 33
Understanding and Utilizing Conflict 33
Giving and Receiving Feedback 36
Hints to Establishing a Beginning
    Point for Group Problem Solving 38
    Access 39
    Linkage 39
    Acceptance 40
    Termination 41
Organizing and Conducting Better
    Meetings 41
    The Delphi Technique for Future
    Planning 43
Conclusion 45
Bibliography 46

2. ADULT AND CHILD: IMPROVING LEARNING
ENVIRONMENTS THROUGH BETTER COMMUNICA-
TIONS by Charles J. Downing 47

Editor's Notes 48
About the Author, Charles J. Downing 50

Theoretical Framework 53
Environmental Conditions of Optimal
    Learning 54
Needs Assessment and Formulation of
    Objectives 55
Ways of Looking at Children and Their
    Behaviors 57
The Goals of Children's Behaviors 59
Learning About Children and Their
    Behaviors 63

Listener Involvement 66
    Paraphrasing 67
    Checking Out a Perception 67
    Admission of Confusion 68
    Questioning 69
    Summarizing 69
    Exercising for Increasing Listener
       Involvement 70
How to Get Children to Listen to Parents
   and Teachers 72
    Exercises in Clarifying Objectives 75
Sources of Information 77
Some Ideas About Changing Children's
   Behavior 78
    Planning for Behavior Change   79
    Environmental Change 80
      Exercise for Environmental Change 81
Cognitive Change as a Behavior Change
   Strategy 81
    Goal Orientation 81
    Exercise for Goal Orientation 83
    Bolstering the Child's Esteem 83
    Exercise for Bolstering the Child's
      Esteem 84
    Improving the Child's Decision-
      Making Skills 84
    Providing Access to Alternative
      Behavior by Direct Instruction 85
Reinforcement Model 85
    Successive Approximations 88
    Contingency Contracting 88
    Exercise on Contingency Contracting 90
Resolution of Conflict 90
    Problems in Using Punishment 92
    Alternative to Punishment 93
Evaluation Systems 96
References 97

3. THE HUMAN DEVELOPMENT APPROACH—A PRE-
    VENTIVE MENTAL HEALTH CURRICULUM by Uvaldo
    H. Palomares and Geraldine Ball 101

Editors' Notes 103
About the Authors, Geraldine Ball and Uvaldo
  H. Palomares 105
The Magic Circle and Innerchange
  Programs—Alternatives in Education 108
  Theoretical Bases and Objectives 110
Who Can Benefit? 112
  Prevention—Not Therapy 113
Topics Relating to Awareness, Mastery,
  And Social Interaction 116
  Awareness 117
      Sample Magic Circle Awareness
        Topics 119
      Warm Fuzzy Awareness Topics 120
      Sample Innerchange Awareness Units 120
  Mastery 121
      Sample Magic Circle Mastery Tasks 122
      Sample Magic Circle Mastery Topics 126
      Sample Innerchange Mastery Units 123
  Social Interaction 124
      Sample Magic Circle Social
        Interaction Topics 126
      Sample Innerchange Social
        Interaction Units 127
The Teacher's Role Brought into Focus 127
      Leading the Circle Session 129
  Transcript of a Minimally Edited
      Tape Recording of an Actual Circle Session with
      Fifth and Sixth Graders Led by Their
      Teacher 131
  Critique of the Session by Ms.
      Blakemore 147
  Critique by Geraldine Ball of the
      Session 148
  Evaluation 149
      Evaluating the Session 149
      Analyzing the Session 150
  Evaluating the Human Development
      Program 152
  Developmental Profile 153

Articulating the Program in the Self-
Contained Classroom 156
Group Size and Composition 156
Time and Space 157
How Often Should Circle Sessions
be Held? 158
Why Student Leadership Is
Important 162
Parents and Community 163
A Final Word to the Reader 163
References 164

4. PSYCHODRAMA, ROLE PLAYING AND
SOCIOMETRY: LIVING AND LEARNING
PROCESSES by Carl E. Hollander 167

Editor's Notes 168
About the Author, Carl E. Hollander 170

PART ONE—Learning Is a Creative Process 177
PART TWO—Psychodrama 182
Language of Psychodrama 183
The Psychodramatic Process 185
The Curve 186
The Warm-up 189
The Psychodrama Enactment 191
Integration with Audience 203
Psychodramas in Summary 206
PART THREE—Role Playing 206
Role-playing Structure and
Implementation 213
PART FOUR—Sociometry 218
Sociemetry and Learning 219
The Psychological Social Atom 220
Collective Social Atom 221
Individual Social Atom 223
Sociometric Networks 227
Teacher Interventions to
Facilitate Learning 229
Tele-Transference—Empathy 232
PART FIVE—Life Process Curve 233
PART SIX—Conclusion 236
References 240
Recommended Readings 241

5. LEARNING HOW TO ACCESS HUMAN GROWTH
   THROUGH SYSTEMATIC APPROACHES by Thomas
   Froehle 243

   Editor's Notes 245
   About the Author, Thomas Froehle 247

   The Why for Writing This Chapter 249
   Chapter Overview: Some Objectives 252
   PART ONE—Goal Analysis 254
     Hawd-1, How Are We Doing? 255
   Analyzing Goals Description in Terms
     of Performance 257
     Abbreviations 258
     Performance 259
     Hawd 2, How Are We Doing? 259
     Hawd 3, How Are We Doing? 262
     Hawd 4, How Are We Doing? 262
     Hawd 5, How Are We Doing? 263
   Classification of Criteria-Referenced
     Objectives 263
     Hawd 6, How Are We Doing? 265
       Cognitive-Based Objectives 265
       Affective-Based Objectives 265
       Performance-Based Objectives 265
       Consequence-Based Objectives 266
     Hawd 7, How Are We Doing? 267
   Describing Goals in Terms of Criteria-
     Referenced Objectives 269
     Objectives 269
     Hawd 8, How Are We Doing? 273
     Hawd 9, How Are We Doing? 276
   PART TWO—Assessment Procedures 277

   Assessment: Some Distinctions 278
     Pre-Assessment 278
     Process Assessment 280
     Post-Assessment 280
     Hawd 10, How Are We Doing? 280
   Evaluative Assessment Versus Diagnostic Assessment . 281
   End-Point Assessment Versus Periodic Assessment 281
     Hawd 11, How Are We Doing? 282

Criterion-Referenced Assessment Versus
    Normative-Referenced Assessment 283
    Hawd 12, How Are We Doing? 286
Systematic Observation and Assessment 286
What to Assess 286
    Measurable Attributes of Human Performance 287
    Derived Indices of Frequency,
        Duration and Intensity 288
    Hawd 13, How Are We Doing? 289
        Low-rate and High-rate Performance   290
Where to Assess 291
When to Assess 291

Reporting Data with Graphs 292
    Hawd 14, How Are We Doing? 293
        Advantages of Graphic Representation 293
        Baseline Measures 296
    Hawd 15, How Are We Doing? 297
        Why Baseline? 291
        Baseline Reliability 297
        The Obtrusive Baseline 297
    Hawd 16, How Are We Doing? 298
        The Baseline Treatment 298
    Hawd 17, How Are We Doing? 300
        Success Gradients 300
Monitoring and Evaluating the Intervention
    Strategy 303
    Hawd 18, How Are We Doing? 303
Summary 304
References 306
INDEX 309

LIST OF FIGURES

Number		Page
1.1	Illustration of Forces Supporting and Blocking Change from Present Situation to Desired Goal	26
1.2	Supporting and Blocking Forces Identified When Force Field Analysis was Applied to a Committee ...	28
1.3	The Systematic and Collaborative Group Problem-Solving Model	32
2.1	Post-Meeting Reaction Form	56
2.2	Classification of Behavior Systems	58
2.3	Ways of Looking at Children and Their Behaviors ..	63
2.4	Sequence of Individual Internal Processes	74
2.5	Sequence of Internal Processing During an Interpersonal Encounter	75
2.6	Environmental Change Worksheet	82
3.1	Teacher Meets with One Group in a Single Circle at a Time	159
3.2	All Students Are Involved in Each Session, Either as a Member of the Inner or Outer Circle	160
3.3	Three Groups Led by Students Meet at Once	161
3.4	Three Groups Are Divided into Six Smaller Groups Led by Students	161
3.5	Another Student Leadership Variation: Dyads	162
4.1	Illustration of How New Experiences Create New Lenses for Viewing Life	175
4.2	Triad of Vertical and Horizontal Dimensions	187
4.3	The Three Divisions of the Warm-Up Period	192
4.4	Reality-Climax-Surplus. Reality in Psychodramatic Enactment	200
4.5	Integration Steps	204
4.6	The Hollander Psychodrama Curve	208
4.7	Important Affiliations and Collective Social Atoms of a Nine-year-old Male	224
4.8	Diagram of a Sociometric Network Linkage	228
4.9	Life-Process Curve	235
5.1	Need Definition	250
5.2	Systematic Problem Solving	251
5.3	Solution Definition	252

5.4   Focus for Evaluation for Experimental Objectives and for Outcome for Objectives 256

5.5   Observable Components of the Behavioral Abbreviation: Depressed 261

5.6   Assessment Focus for Criteria-Referenced Outcome Objectives and Criteria-Referenced Experimental Objectives 268

5.7   Components of Performance—Term Objectives 272

5.8   Performance Objectives Components Classified According to Criteria Specified by Mager (1962) 274

5.9   Assessment Functions and Questions Associated with Each Function 279

5.10   Normal (Bell-shaped) Grading Curve with Percentages of Students Receiving Different "A" to "F" Letter Grades 284

5.11   Negatively Skewed Grading Curve with Percentages of Students Receiving Different "A" to "F" Letter Grades 284

5.12   Positively-Skewed Grading Curve with Percentages of Students Receiving Different "A" to F" Letter Grades 285

5.13   Measurement Dimensions of Three Attributes of Performance 287

5.14   Observation Record of Hand Gesturing Behavior ... 290

5.15   Trips Tony Takes to the Restroom 294

5.16   Kim's Tattling Episodes Over a Three-Week Period . 294

5.17   The Effects of Two Intervention Strategies Upon the Number of Target Behaviors Observed Each Day ... 295

5.18   Time Days Sampling of Sam's Out-of-Seat Behavior Over a Two-Week Period 299

5.19   Baseline and Intervention Data on Trips Tony Makes to the Restroom 302

1

A SYSTEMATIC AND COLLABORATIVE
APPROACH TO PROBLEM SOLVING

DeWayne J. Kurpius
Samuel G. Christie

DEWAYNE KURPIUS

DeWayne J. Kurpius, presently an associate professor of education at Indiana University, has worked as a consultant with a wide variety of situations and organizations such as mental health clinics, universities, medical schools, public schools, state departments of public instruction and the U. S. Office of Education.

In early 1977 Kurpius co-authored *Family Counseling: A Systems Approach* with Laura Sue Dodson and published by Accelerated Development, Inc., Muncie, IN. In addition to this book, which incudes chapters contributed by other authors, Kurpius is co-authoring two other books to focus on influencing the school learning environment supervision of applied training and psychoeducational consultation.

At Indiana University Kurpius is currently teaching and conducting research in the areas of counselor training and consultation. Kurpius' present research thrust is directed toward explicating the interaction variables which influence human and organizational change.

Editor's Notes:

The first Chapter, A Systematic and Collaborative Approach to Problem Solving, looks at the total school. In this context the Chapter has three goals. The first goal is to conceptually describe the school as both an organization system and as a social system. The second goal is to present a field-tested model for systematic and collaborative problem solving. Third, is to provide the reader with a series of techniques and tool skills for creating and activating a problem-solving culture within the school.

As an organzational system many schools are still trying to make the transition into post-industrial society. School managers and teachers are recognizing that old forms of management and teaching are no longer effective given the new values, issues, goals and demands placed on today's schools. Recognizing that change is needed is only the first step. Thus, the Chapter describes the multiple factors that feed into organizational effectiveness and ineffectiveness. Issues such as goal ambiguity, low staff interdependence, conflict avoidance, reliance upon tradition, and linear organizational structures are discussed.

The school as a social system is also presented. Social system factors which influence the learning environment are communication patterns, feedback styles, work climate, norms, boundaries, rewards, punishment and role models. When operationalized into member behavior these factors become the forces for social influence. That is, those factors are those supporting and resisting forces which occur in a given school or classrooms that influence the values and behaviors of both students and staff.

While the first part of the Chapter is focused on conceptual issues, the remaining space is directed toward action issues. A step-by-step model for systematic and collaborative problem solving is described. Each step is presented in outline form followed by an operational

3

definition. Lastly, the common tool skills and techniques for developing and implementing an effective problem-solving program which is both systematic and collaborative are included. These techniques are described in such a way that they can be easily utilized by students, staff, para-professionals and parents.

ABOUT

THE

AUTHOR

SAMUEL CHRISTIE

Samuel Christie is currently program evaluator with the Stockton Unified School District in California, a capacity in which he works directly with school adminitrators and school staffs helping them to develop their own evaluation and problem-solving skills. For the past two years Dr. Christie has also worked as an evaluation consultant for three different external degree programs at Sonoma State College in California. Dr. Christie's redesign of the evaluation plans for these programs served as a model for changing the evaluation of all external degree programs in California. Following the evaluation of the 1975-76 programs for Master of Arts in Humanistic Psychology and Early Childhood Education Dr. Christie and a colleague were retained by the commission on External Degrees of the California State Colleges and Universities to write new guidelines for all external degree programs. From 1972-75 Dr. Christie was on the faculty of Indiana University with a joint appointment in School Administration and Counseling and Guidance.

While at Indiana University Dr. Christie was an evaluation consultant to a National Science Foundation project on curriculum development in social studies. In this capacity he designed evaluation instruments to measure classroom and school climate, and made site visits in high schools nationally to evaluate field trials, interview students, teachers, and administrators.

Prior to his experiences at Indiana University Dr. Christie worked with Dr. John Goodlad at the Institute for the Development of Educational Activities, Research Division, in Los Angeles, California. At IDEA Dr. Christie was the coordinator of a project to develop guidelines that would help school staffs to become more effective problem solvers.

Dr. Christie co-authored *The Problem Solving School,* 1972, and is the author of "Beyond Student Militancy" (in *The Power to Change*). He has also conducted workshops and symposia on organizational development, problem solving, and evaluation at both regional and national conferences, including the Association for Supervisors of Curriculum Development and the American Educational Research Association.

A SYSTEMATIC AND COLLABORATIVE
APPROACH TO PROBLEM SOLVING

DeWayne J. Kurpius and Samuel G. Christie

The purpose of this Chapter is to present and explain a strategy that concerns two basic aspects of group problem solving; being *systematic and collaborative* in attacking problems. We will call this strategy the *Systematic and Collaborative approach* (S-C). However, before elaboration and support for these two concepts are made more fully, we will examine the nature of the school as a system and the existing characteristics of schools.

By considering the *conditions* of the educational establishment, the personal *value systems* that must be met, and the potential *discrepancy* that may exist between goals and reality, the initial stages of problem solving will be recreated according to the S-C model. Actually one "problem solves" on an individual basis every time a position paper of any kind is read. For example, the "problem" to be solved is that of finding a better way to solve problems, a way that will lead to satisfying changes within the school system. One solution to this is offered by S-C presented later in the Chapter.

The personal, social, and economic challenges faced as citizens of a modern technological society grow more complex each year. It is not necessary to dwell on those challenges in this Chapter because there is a general awareness of such challenges. While predicting with any certainty the kinds of events that will shape the future cannot be done, educators can and should, nonetheless, direct efforts to preparing those individuals who will create and have to cope with, the problems of the twenty-first century.

7

Eric Trist (1973), believed the theory that in our time, in the post-industrial society, the old forms of adaptation, both personal and organizational, will no longer suffice to meet the higher levels of complexity now coming into existence. No longer will old problem-solving methods provide solutions to new problems. Creative change requires new ways of thinking and new ways of organizing. To meet this challenge of change as an educator, one must develop more adaptable educational systems which encourage participants to seek answers through *active inquiry* rather than through docile acceptance of old answers.

SEEKING ANSWERS THROUGH ACTIVE INQUIRY

Most professionals in education actually support the principle of inquiry and agree with the hypothesis that one should strive to utilize that principle. Why however do so many educators who believe in the inquiry process rarely practice the technique? Traditional pedagogy has apparently bypassed inquiry in favor of direct dispensing of knowledge in predigested form. The source of such resistance to inquiry is deeply rooted in the traditional structure of the educational establishment. One aim in this Chapter is to suggest organizational changes that will allow and advance greater usage of the inquiry principle.

Inquiry as a Response to a Basic Need

In Maslow's (1971) theory of motivation, he identified five sets of goals for man which, if not satisfied, Maslow said become basic needs. These goals are physical well being, safety, love, esteem, and self-actualization.

Maslow suggested another need; however, he does so tentatively, for he wrote that this need may apply only to the intelligent person. This need is "to satisfy curiosity by using knowledge and facts so to test reality from an informed point of view." Desire to know ultimately leads to attempts to collect information, to analyze it by looking for relationships and meanings, to synthesize findings and make decisions based on information gathered.

An assumption was made when writing this Chapter, that professional educators at elementary, secondary and university levels have this need, this concern, and desire for seeking understanding, for seeking knowledge, and for developing sound judgment. Realistically however one recognizes that some teachers, counselors, and administrators in both elementary and secondary schools and universities have a limited commitment to these concerns. A challenge is seen for educational leaders to work toward raising the priority of inquiry by changing those conditions which inhibit the implementation of inquiry in teaching.

A strong plea is made for teachers to rely more on the inquiry process in the classroom. However, one should make the fact clear that the main subject of discussion in this Chapter is not *teaching* through the inquiry process, although the discussions will be related to that issue. Primarily, advocation is that the inquiry approach as a problem-solving process be used in staff meetings, in the principal's office, in department meetings, in the faculty senate, in every place where problems are solved and important decisions are made.

Problem Solving Through Inquiry

The process of inquiry in its most sophisticated, most elegant form, is the scientific method—a combination of empiricism and deductive logic. In the simplest, most utilitarian form inquiry *is* problem solving. Inquiry is practiced by man alone and in groups. Inquiry is at times a means to an end, and at other times an end in itself.

The point could be made that the subject of problem solving is grounded in the philosophy of science or in epistomology, as problem solving is concerned with acquiring and processing knowledge. To use modern terms, problem solving is cybernetic in nature. Ideally, an individual processes information and filters this information through his or her personal value system. Since the individual knows the state of existing conditions, that individual decides whether or not personal values are being supported by these

9

conditions. If discrepancy exists, the person feels a need for change and processes more information which tells what to change and how to go about such a change.

The inquiring mind, then, is synonymous with human growth. The inquiring mind is open and rejects nothing out of hand. The inquiring mind sifts, it weighs, and it probes, looking for truth, for personal and social reality. While openness exists in this search, also a need is present for selectibility and for structure. Structure is provided by the set of values that are accepted, values which interact with the definition of the perceived situation and the definition of the problem at hand.

Educators have an important role to play in helping students develop structure. Too often however the idea that the teacher-professor is the expert is promoted. School is not so much a place for experts as it is a place where the search is ongoing. Whether teacher, counselor, or administrator, one should be an expert *first* on how to seek and acquire knowledge, and, second, on how to utilize findings. Situations should be planned and structured to give students the opportunity to solve individual and group problems. Perhaps, just as important, good examples should be set by being inquirers ourselves. Not only will this search for evidence present the appropriate role model for students, but this search potentially can guide decisions in the day to day activities of the school, lending more relevance to school programs.

THE SCHOOL AS A SYSTEM

A major obstacle to promoting problem solving in the school is the absence of a tradition for working together. The way schools have been organized from their very inception, with each teacher assigned a classroom, has offered little opportunity and encouragement to collaborate with other teachers. Thus, school staffs actually have limited experience in systematic and collaborative inquiry and with sharing the investigation of common concerns, issues, or problems in the school.

10

The School as a Biological System

An analogy to biological systems is an appropriate beginning for looking at a school system because characteristics of biological or living systems is the interrelatedness of the parts, a reliance among the elements such that a change in one element will cause changes in the other elements. The implication is that to understand the school as a system, one must consider all the elements and their interrelatedness. For example, the element of *communication among system members* will determine the use of *feedback in guiding school decisions* which, in turn, will affect the *internal climate* of the school.

The analogy to biological systems can be extended however beyond the interrelatedness of the elements. In both systems exist inputs, processes, and outputs. An input is either something to be processed (changed) by the system or something that has a major impact on the change of another input. Just as food is an input to the human body, an individual's need for recognition is input to the educational system.

The School as a Social System

While a school organization has the properties of biological systems, two important ways exist in which the school organization differs. *First,* the school organization is a social system; and *second,* the school, unlike mechanical or biological systems, has the capacity to change structure. If need be, the organization can develop "an extra arm: (a brand new department), a feat that animals cannot duplicate, at least by intention." Therefore, the system members in the organization, whether responding to demands from their environment or from their own members, can initiate basic changes in the system.

As a social system, the school's internal structure is built on relationships and values. The structure of a social system is determined by *norms* and by the distribution of *roles* and statuses of its members. At the same time, the expectations for role performance set the *boundaries* of the social system.

11

SOCIAL SYSTEM NORMS AND ROLE EXPECTATIONS

Values of a culture are made explicit through goals and objectives of its institutions. Goals are those things "worth striving for." Separate from these goals, but derived from them, are the institutional or system *norms*. According to Merton (1968), the norms of a social system regulate and control "acceptable modes of reaching out for these goals." Norms are expectations for the behavior of system members. Norms are not written, yet are known to all members. If one was to examine the norms of a particular school, these norms would tell much information about that school; one would know something of the working structure of that particular school. In addition, the degree to which norms vary over a period of time also will tell us the amount of change that is occurring.

For example, consider a high school where controls are strict on cigarette smoking within the school building with heavy penalties for breaking these controls. Teachers who observe a student smoking are "expected" by other teachers, as well as the principal, to report such an infraction of school rules. In another school, a teacher might ignore or pretend not to see the student smoking because this procedure is what usually is followed.

One's reactions to others, then, are guided by the existing norms of a school. Other system members are expected to act in accordance with the norms prescribed by their individual roles. Role types serve as a shortcut reference for individuals to call forth the set of relevant norms in a given situation. Norms for principals differ from norms for teachers, just as norms for students differ from norms for teachers. If a norm, for example, urges staff members to report students who are smoking on school grounds, a guilty student might fear being apprehended by a staff member but not by a fellow student.

One can say, then, that role incumbency or group membership is an easy reference for identifying expected behavior. Our perceptions of other's expectations for an individual as well as our expectations of oneself can be based on role and group membership. This internal structure of norms, roles, and boundaries are characteristic of all social systems.

12

EXISTING CONDITIONS IN SCHOOLS
A BUILT-IN RESISTANCE TO CHANGE

As previously stated, schools bear certain characteristics which are common to all organizations and social systems. Other characteristics are unique to schools alone. Schools operate with ambiguous goals and low staff-interdependency. Schools perform latent functions, such as child care, with a high degree of vulnerability. The schools' investments in technology are relatively small, i.e., salaries consume seventy to eighty percent of the total budget. Schools use staff training and development as their primary agent of change.

All of the previous characteristics necessarily will affect the effective operation of a school system. Some of these characteristics perpetuate a traditional resistance to change which ultimately hampers the achievement of educational goals. In part, an attempt is made to answer the question of why schools are protected from the forces of change that affect other organizations. Four of these forces are as follows: Low interdependence of staff, high vulnerability, goal ambiguity, and individual orientation.

Low Interdependence of Staff

In the last twenty-five years, schools in this country have undergone massive efforts at centralization. The number of small, one-school districts has practically disappeared. This move to centralization has led to new economy in education and has generally improved the number and quality of facilities available to the schools which had been in small districts. In all this movement toward centralization, though, the classroom has not been significantly affected. Teachers continue, to a great extent, to make curricular decisions as if the formal education of students began and ended in their classroom. Few, if any of the experiences, that occurred before the student came to the class are considered. The only item that is passed on is a grade—largely meaningless to anyone except the teacher giving that grade. Little opportunity is sought or afforded for teachers to get advice from their peers, to trade ideas, to plan programs cooperatively, or to collaborate to solve problems encountered by themselves or their students.

This lack of intercommunication has contributed to the feeling of insecurity that many teachers express about their own effectiveness. On the one hand, this isolation may allow much freedom to experiment in the classroom; but, on the other hand, this isolation also protects those who lack motivation or are incompetent. The majority of staff members, who do not fall in either of these categories, may be reluctant to surrender this freedom they have enjoyed behind their closed classroom door.

For schools that are still organized in the traditional way, with teachers and other role groups working alone, the first and most difficult task involves the change from a *separatist* norm to a *collaborative* norm. To bring about change, staff members will need non-threatening opportunities to collaborate with their peers as these teachers learn the skills necessary for collaboration.

High Vulnerability

The public school in America, probably more than any other public institution, is subject to criticism and a wide variety of demands from its immediate environment. This vulnerability of the schools is understandable because of the importance of the schools' "products." Schools are recognized as a major socializing agency for the young, the most significant one outside of the family unit. Schools, at least in the past, have performed the major allocative function in our society and have been, for many lower-middle class children, the route to climb the "success" ladder. "A good education for Johnny or Mary" has been the dream of many a parent who sought for a son or daughter more status and more money than the parent was able to achieve.

The more educated one became, the more egalitarian one became, creating a greater demand for more schools and equal education for all. This demand, of course, has made education a very expensive item in our local economy and created pressures for economy and efficiency. No other local governmental body makes decisions as important to the general public as does the school board. In this public situation, where decisions are being made which have an important effect on the quality of our children's lives, when children divide their time between home and school and relay school impressions to parents, where local decisions commit millions of dollars of taxpayers' money, a high degree of visability and vulnerability obviously exists.

14

Schools have developed an extremely sensitive position, or resistance, to conflict. Processing conflicts is psychologically stressful and disruptive to school operations. Several techniques have been developed to manage these potential conflicts, the most diffuse of which is gaining the support and encouragement of the Parent Teacher Association.

Goal Ambiguity

Another problem is goal ambiguity. Goal ambiguity is maintained in the schools because of the wide range of expectations that the public has placed on the schools. Schools, like other institutions in our democratic society, are pluralistic in nature and are expected to respond to a wide variety of publics. Schools, if pressed for goal clarity, have been in a position to say which one of these goals (all important and worthy) shall we ignore?

One way to work toward more goal clarity is for schools to provide clarity with respect to their programs and the achievements of students within these programs. This procedure provides the community with reference points from which goals can be inferred and through which the process of clarifying and priority establishment of goals can proceed. Schools for the most part have maintained as much program ambiguity by the use of informal decision making as has been goal ambiguity within the school-community. Lindblom and Braybrooke (1963, p. 63) have labeled this response by schools as "disjointed incrementalism." The elements of such strategy are

1. acceptance of the present situation with only marginal changes contemplated,

2. consideration of a restricted variety of alternatives excluding those which suggest radical change,

3. consideration of a restricted number of consequences for a given alternative,

4. adjustment of objectives as well as policies to objectives,

5. willingness to formulate the problem as data become available, and

6. serial analysis and piecemeal alterations rather than a single comprehensive attack.

Given this systematic kind of approach to solving the problems of schooling, neither alternatives nor outcomes are sharply evidenced and little change exists for significant change.

Individual Orientation

Another perspective is present from which one may view the current mode of problem solving in schools. Many schools approach problem solving from an "individual orientation." Neither systematic nor collaborative, this individual approach is psychologically based and seeks to solve school problems by changing the individuals within the system—teachers, students, and other staff members.

Consider, for example, the policies of staff development. The fact is assumed that if a teacher, counselor, or administrator takes additional coursework at a university in an area of his or her choice, that person will be more skillful, thus enhancing the school program. One understands an individual's right to make decisions about his/her own education. But what about the school as a whole organization? What about the specific skills needed to work with specific learners or the new skills required to meet changing needs? Under this individual orientation, little or no consultation occurs among staff members before making decisions about which skills will, in fact, benefit the learners as well as the staff.

When this individual approach is applied to student problems, the operating rationale professes that the school *presently* is organized for the benefit of all students. In practice this statement means that the student must, in every case, change until he or she "fits" with the school's rules and procedures, i.e., adjust the student to the system. Rules that were justified when they were adopted however become outmoded and then create new problems. With this "individual" approach to discrepancies, many identical cases must surface before someone discovers that perhaps the system, and not the student, should be adjusted.

16

THE SYSTEMATIC AND COLLABORATIVE APPROACH
(S-C)

Now the S-C Model, being socio-psychological in principle and inquiry based in practice, reflects the dual perspective of those labels. S-C Model rationale and objectives are directed toward both personal needs *and* organizational goals. When applied to the staff development problem, the S-C Model forces two questions simultaneously: What kinds of skills does a particular staff member personally need, and what is the priority for improving these skills in the school? When applied to student problems, the S-C Model urges consideration of each problem initially as feedback on the operation of the system—an alert to be watchful for similar problems that other students may be experiencing—thus allowing for systematic change when change is needed. When the student's problem is purely personal, the problem will more than likely surface as such.

The S-C Model is as humanistic as it is systematic and collaborative as the staff of an organization strives to make that organization more responsive to the clients it serves and to make school a more humane place to learn.

THE KEY TO CHANGE — HUMAN INTERACTION

Being human, of course, means being sensitive to human needs. The S-C Model *begins* with individuals in school and with their felt needs.

Needs that are unexpressed or unrecognized cannot serve as input to the system and thus may never receive the attention these needs require. In an environment where inquiry and interaction are encouraged, more individual needs are likely to surface. Then, existent norms may be re-examined, and discrepancies between norms and needs can be challenged openly. Norms do not change overnight because a few leaders deviate from them. Norms change when most of the system members decide that these norms should be changed and then are able to test the members' decision. The significance and degree of success of a change effort is directly related to the degree of personal involvement and commitment the change effort requires.

Calling for the adoption of systematic and collaborative problem solving, suggests profound changes for some school systems. This point is not to suggest that the changes cannot be effected; rather, this view is offered as a reminder of the nature and difficulty of the task. As with the example of low-interdependence, a change must occur in the norms; in this instance, a change from the norms of unsystematic or informal problem solving to the norms of systematic collaboration. In addition the complexity of schooling and the political context in which schools must operate place real constraints on the degree of formality of problem solving that can be attained. Systematic problem solving, in the ideal sense, is difficult to achieve in schools. Systematic problem solving, however, can be a goal for professionals to seek.

Just as disjointed incrementalism can be a strategy for protection and for managing conflict, systematic and collaborative problem solving can be a strategy whereby professioinals in American schools can begin to exert leadership by making clear to themselves and the public what alternatives they are choosing. The staffs of schools that are working together and have made decisions based on solid data will be in a position to place real alternatives before the public and push strongly for those alternatives which are educationally sound.

AN INTRODUCTION TO THE S-C MODEL

Up to this point in the Chapter, the words "inquiry" and S-C problem solving have been used as if they were synonymous; to a great extent, these terms are synonymous. The concepts which underlie each of these terms derive from a common principle, a common thrust. The principle of inquiry represents a basic need of intelligent people. The principle symbolizes the process of openly questioning, seeking answers, and testing solutions. Inquiry need not be restricted to individual problem solving however. When applied to group problem solving, the principle of inquiry can provide the input toward collaborative problem solving. The approach proposed is designed to develop the ability of system members to solve their *common problems* through *common inquiry*.

Let us turn now to an overview of systematic and collaborative problem solving. First, one might ask, what aspect of the model is systematic and what is collaborative?

Systematic Group Problem Solving

Being systematic means that decisions are "informed" decisions, that relevant information is available, and that the information is used before decisions are made. One way to enhance the probability that the information is being used is to follow a logical process. In the S-C Model six steps to this logical process are as follows:

1. Sensing the problem

2. Defining the problem

3. Selecting a strategy to solve the problem

4. Planning for the implementation of the chosen strategy

5. Implementing the plan and evaluating the process

6. Evaluating the outcome

To complete the systematic aspect of group problem solving, included must be four additional processes that should occur at each of the six previous steps which are the following:

1. Assessment— Gather together the relevant information

2. Analysis— Organize the information into separate elements (logical categories) and examine the relationships between the elements

3. Synthesis— Re-examine the total situation considering the relationships between elements

4. Decision Making— Make a choice, i.e., what is valued, or what step is next to take

Collaborative Group Problem Solving

The collaborative aspect of the S-C Model cannot be organized into steps that are independent of the six steps identified for systematic problem solving. Rather, collaborative problem solving is "laid on top of" the systematic process. Being collaborative implies that the previous steps are carried out by all staff members affected by a given problem. The collaborative process means sharing; the process means planning together, depending on another, and receiving feedback. Collaboration however does not imply that everything is smooth and free of conflict. Even though people are on the same team, share common interests, and work together, inevitably differences of opinion will arise. These differences will more than likely produce creative solutions if explored and resolved than if avoided. In all groups, situations may arise in which people are devious and manipulative, cloaking hidden agendas, and attempting to "manage" the outcome. Our point is that honest, systematic collaboration is a skill that must be learned, particularly within the school system where the opportunity for practice has been severely limited.

Whenever staff members detect a discrepancy between what exists and what is desired, the S-C Model invites inquiry and subsequent collaboration, in accordance with the following objectives:

1. To create an open, problem-solving climate throughout the school.

2. To supplement the authority associated with role or status with the authority of knowledge and competence.

3. To locate decision-making and problem-solving responsibilities as close to the information sources as possible.

4. To build trust among individuals and groups throughout the school.

5. To make competition more relevant to work goals and to maximize collaborative efforts.

6. To develop a reward system which recognizes both the achievement of the mission of the school and the school's development (growth of the school as an organization).

7. To increase the sense of "ownership" of school objectives and problems throughout the staff.

8. To help administrators manage according to relevant objectives rather than according to "past practice."

9. To increase self-control and self-direction for people within the school.

10. To share leadership.

IMPLEMENTING THE SYSTEMATIC AND COLLABORATIVE APPROACH

A GROUP PROBLEM-SOLVING MODEL

The group problem-solving model is intended to guide school staffs in both the *systematic* and the *collaborative* aspects of group problem solving. The steps in this Model and some suggestions on the ways in which the steps would be implemented will be discussed.

Sensing the Problem, Step 1

A common difficulty in group problem solving is that solutions to the perceived problem are suggested before the problem is defined adequately and agreed upon by persons involved. In the S-C Model, an attempt has been made to deal with this difficulty by making the problem-identification stage of problem solving more explicit by starting at the very beginning when problems are only "sensed." Thus, Step 1 in the S-C Model is *problem sensing*. At this stage, *individuals* sense that something isn't quite right. The individuals feel that some violation of an expectation or implicit standard is present. As one continues to experience this violation of an expectation or implicit standard, the question is asked, "What seems to be out-of-order?" One also may begin asking others to see if they, too, sense that something is wrong. As this process continues, a build-up occurs of assumed discrepancies between what is desired and what exists now, i.e., a problem, or an unmet need.

If one decides that a problem does exist and also decides that something needs to be done about the problem, then feelings, ideas, and concerns begin to be organized and one begins to ask, "Who else is affected by this problem?" Therefore, some of the first basic questions to ask oneself are the following:

1. Who else may be concerned or has verbalized the same or a similar problem?

2. Do objectives already exist which, if met, would solve the problem?

3. Is an office or person assigned to help solve problems similar to the problem(s) I am sensing?

4. Does a committee already exist to solve similar problems?

One issue to consider during this initial query process is the type of problem(s) being experienced. Some may be classified as simple problems for which a solution is reached relatively quickly. Some problems, however, are encountered on a regular basis which are more complex and require greater involvement and planning. The greater involvement is required because more people share, in some way, some part of the problem and its solution. Many of these complex problems remained unsolved because, as an individual, one tends to follow the same problem-solving process for more complex problems as one did for the simple problems; or one attempts to solve them individually rather than collaboratively.

Since the S-C Model is for group problem solving, let us assume that a problem is sensed which seems to be both important and complex and therefore requires group problem solving.

After the group is formed, the four basic questions should be examined so that each member's perception of the problem is heard by the other members. Usually the best process is to write each person's statement on a chalkboard or a piece of newsprint to assure that everyone's ideas and concerns are made known accurately.

Even though the members of the group agree that the problem sensed requires a group problem-solving approach, some members may surface individual or simple problems. Even though these problems seem inappropriate to be discussed at this time, individuals should withhold judgment and place the problems on a list of all the sensed problems. The next action in problem solving is to place the problems into categories from simple to complex. Following this process, the group should select the problems defined and place them in a priority list.

A Suggested Tool Skill to be Used for Step 2

Sometimes by providing technical assistance to problem solvers one is able to move more rapidly away from abstract conceptualizations of what is dysfunctional toward a more reality reality-oriented picture of what is desired. Perhaps the most universal tool utilized for this purpose is Force Field Analysis.

The second step in the Model is *defining the problem*. At this point, a list of problems has been developed and priorities assigned to them. This list gives a good idea of how this group views the problem. However, the problem(s) may not have been defined clearly enough to allow the group to proceed effectively.

How is the problem(s) defined? Up to this point, most of the information gathered has been self-reported, and most of the decisions made have been more individual decisions than group decisions. At this time, the group should begin looking more closely at what information is available and needed to assure that the problem is defined accurately. *Remember, the problem must be clearly defined and agreed on as the problem(s) to be solved by the group.*

Next, what must be done to get the clarity needed in defining this problem? Work through the four processes described previously. These processes are as follows:

1. Assessment,
2. Analysis,
3. Synthesis, and
4. Decision Making.

Let's look more closely at these four processes before proceeding.

Assessment. This process is the first systematic effort in group problem solving. In the assessment process the information necessary to describe the problem objectively is gathered. During problem sensing, many statements are subjective judgments—conclusions drawn after brief discussions with other staff members or informal observations which are screened through one's own value system. Very often these judgments are inadequate to use as a basis for making decisions and more objective information is needed. What is wanted is an accurate description of the situation that exists. The information needed to get this description can be obtained by such methods as the examination of records on file, interviews, survey questionnaires, or systematic observations of the people involved. When adequate information is gathered to define the problem, the group will then move to analyzing these data.

Analysis. This process involves reviewing the information gathered so as to understand the full meaning of the problem. Usually this involves dividing the information into parts so that the information can be inspected by different people and from different points of view. When the analysis process has been completed, the group should have a full understanding of the many aspects of the problem.

Synthesis. At this point in the total process the group would begin to put the parts back together, to present the findings and to search for the best understanding of the information so as to move closer to a complete and accurate definition of the problem. When synthesis is completed, the group is ready to make important decisions from the information.

Decision Making. This process entails choosing a desired course of action. The important issue now is *how* to make the decisions; e.g., voting, consensus, authorized leader, drifting, and so forth. An important concept is commitment by the group to abide by or, more importantly, to carry out a decision. Voting is an efficient means for determining the status of a group to answer the question, "Where does the group stand on this issue at this time?" If a large majority (eighty percent) exists on one side, this view might be considered the group's decision. However, if the group is divided evenly, pro and con, or if a large minority, say over thirty-five percent, is apparent then really no decision exists. Rather, a split exists in the group. The concerns of the minority need to be given further consideration.

Selecting a Strategy to Solve the Problem, Step 3

After a problem(s) is defined and agreed upon, our next task is to decide the best strategy, method or solution for solving a given problem. Two common strategies are followed in education. One is to assume that staff members lack knowledge and skill to become better problem solvers. As a consequence workshops, conferences and summer school has become the norm. The second strategy is to "tinker with the system" by making many small changes without looking at the larger picture. While these two strategies may be appropriate in many situations, it can be a limited sample of the potential alternatives for solving a given problem.

A useful typology for generating alternative strategies for solving problems identifies four elements which are common in all situations; the four elements are: 1) Goals, 2) structure, 3) Methodologies and 4) people. In other words, we can select a strategy for solving a problem by changing either the goals, structures, methods or actually changing the staff.

Each of these four elements is defined by Kurpius (1977) as follows:

GOALS: the purpose, mission, and expected outcomes for the organization resulting from the interdependent functioning of its units and departments

STRUCTURE: the reward system, communication patterns, role definitions, norms, programs, and hierarchy established by the institution to meet its goals

METHODOLOGIES: the methods and processes, such as committees, teaching techniques, computer assistance, problem-solving groups, and staff meetings, are examples of methodological approaches to meeting organizational goals

PEOPLE: the human attitudes, values, feelings and behaviors that are associated with meeting individual, group, and organizational goals

A second tool skill which has proven very useful for this step is called brainstorming. When using brainstorming with the above typology it is helpful to work each element separately and then choose the proper strategy(ies).

Force Field Analysis. One of the most useful methods which can be used for identifying the forces which both block and support problem solving and decision making is a process developed by Kurt Lewin and referred to as Force Field Analysis. Lewin felt that for every attempted change (decision) there existed two sets of forces. One set tended to support the desired change and the second set of forces acted as a barrier to reaching a desired goal. These forces are common in most working groups but usually are less of a barrier if they are identified and accepted as real factors to be considered when moving toward desired goals and objectives.

The outcomes of using this process then are the identification of the problems and the resources for moving toward the desired goal. This concept, when presented in diagram form, is presented in Figure 1.1.

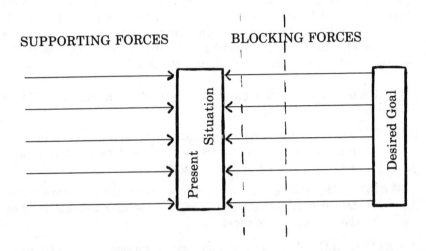

SUPPORTING FORCES   BLOCKING FORCES

Figure 1.1. Illustration of Forces Supporting and Blocking Change from Present Situation to Desired Goal.

The steps to follow when applying Force Field Analysis are as follows:

1. Define the *present* situation which needs to be changed, i.e., define the problem(s).

2. Define the *desired* situation, i.e., the goal toward which one is working.

3. List the forces which are supporting the desired change.

4. List the forces which are blocking the desired change.

   Note: If agreement cannot be reached on whether a given force is supporting or blocking, develop a third column called *Value Differences.*

5. Select blocking forces most easily modified.

6. Select supporting forces which are most easily implemented.

7. Choose the forces on which you intend to begin working.

    Note: Choose the combination of forces which will have the greatest influence, cause the least resistance, and promote the most desired and lasting change.

As one utilizes the information collected to develop objectives, strategies, and plans for problem solving and decision making, repeating the force field analysis process periodically may be important to determine the degree of accomplishment.

If no change is taking place, the conclusion is that the forces are balanced equally for and against so no movement is likely to occur unless blocking forces are removed or supporting forces are increased. Generally removing blocking forces is better than increasing supporting forces. A trend in education however has been to increase forces on the support side.

In Figure 1.2 is an example of one usage of force field analysis. The supporting and blocking forces respectively were identified from reviewing a committee.

The problems related to these findings could be as follows:

1. The organization recognizes but does not reward productive committees.

2. The organization recognizes and rewards only committee work upon which persons in authority positions agree.

3. Low trust exists among members.

4. Some members may lack required competencies to serve.

5. Some members want the problem to continue.

To summarize, force field analysis does not identify the strategies for problem solving and decision making but does pinpoint the forces which are supporting or blocking progress toward the desired objectives. This process usually is used in small groups but can be used in large groups if subgroups are set up.

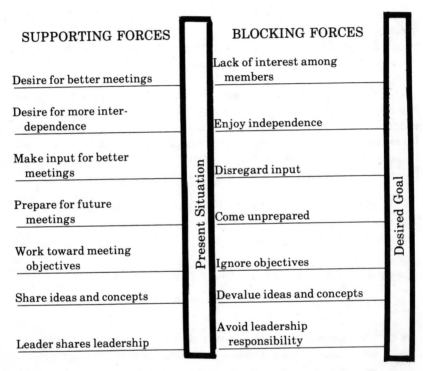

SUPPORTING FORCES

BLOCKING FORCES

Present Situation

Desired Goal

Desire for better meetings

Lack of interest among
members

Desire for more inter-
dependence

Enjoy independence

Make input for better
meetings

Disregard input

Prepare for future
meetings

Come unprepared

Work toward meeting
objectives

Ignore objectives

Share ideas and concepts

Devalue ideas and concepts

Leader shares leadership

Avoid leadership
responsibility

Figure 1.2. Supporting and Blocking Forces Identified When Force Field Analysis Was Applied to a Committee.

Brainstorming. Brainstorming is a group method of thinking up creative solutions to problems. In brainstorming, gathering quantity and obtaining diversity of ideas are major goals. The most important feature of brainstorming is its moratorium on criticism:

Nobody says, "That's not practical."
Nobody says, "That has already been mentioned."
Nobody says, "It will never work."

In brainstorming, every idea which is mentioned should be recorded, even if the idea is mentioned only in passing, or as a joke. Usual, wild, or apparently unrelated ideas are encouraged. Only after the group has listed as many ideas as the members can think of should they go back and consider the practicality or merit of the ideas which have been generated.

Through brainstorming, groups usually generate a surplus of good ideas—too many to follow through on every item. Ordinarily, the group will be forced to select only a few of the best ideas for further consideration. First in small brainstorming groups, and then as a whole group, group members would have to narrow the list of alternative strategies to a number which could be reasonably implemented.

Planning for the Implementation of the Chosen Strategy, Step 4

If a group worked through the previous three specific steps, the members would have systematically and collaboratively identified a problem, and the causes of this problem, and finally what actions need to be taken to solve the problem. These action steps, along with the identification of related resources, constitute the "plan of action," or the implementation plan.

A good implementation plan gives specific action details showing what action steps need to be taken, who needs to take them, when they should be taken, and what material resources (if any) are needed (Christie et al, 1972). An action team is needed to work out and record these details.

29

1. What action needs to be taken? A number of different tasks may need to be carried out in order to implement a general strategy that has been chosen. The actions should be recorded approximately in the order in which they must be performed. The more specific the outline is on what needs to be done, the easier will be the monitoring of the implementation of the plan and determining how close the actual process of implementation came to what was intended originally.

2. Who needs to take action? The point should be determined as to who will be involved in each of the actions on the list. Are specific kinds of expertise needed to carry out some actions? Is formal authority required for some actions? Should some interest groups (e.g., parents, students, district personnel) be consulted or represented to ensure that the actions taken will be acceptable? Are the persons who are needed to make the plan work willing to take the actions the group has defined?

3. When should the actions be taken? A realistic time schedule will be needed for implementing the actions in the plan. Enough time should be planned for all the little problems which are sure to come up and, at the same time, ensure that the job will get done before people lose interest in finishng the job. If the action outlined in the plan appear unusually different or time consuming, then probably the alternative strategy to be implemented is too broad or too vague. If this is the case, the team may decide to report to the group as a whole that the alternative strategy, as presently formulated, is too big for one action team to oversee the strategy's implementation.

4. What material resources (if any) are needed? Indicate in the plan what material resources (e.g., money, supplies, meeting rooms) are needed and the ways these resources will be obtained.

Implementing the Plan and Evaluating the Process, Step 5

At this point a dual function is initiated. The plan is put into action and, at the same time, the process of gathering information to monitor the implementation of the plan is begun. *This monitoring is process evaluation.* One also asks: Is the plan working? Is the plan being implemented as defined? Where are difficulties occurring if any? To answer these questions, once again *assess, analyze, synthesize,* and *make a decision* at the points where the problems are occurring. Some residual problems may be simple enough to be handled by one person. More complex problems may require that the task force be called for a special meeting or that specific people be consulted.

The importance of process evaluation is that the focus primarily is on the plan to determine if all is going well or if certain changes are needed. Needed changes should be inserted into the "plan" so that the revised plan will now become a *plan of action.*

Evaluating the Outcome, Step 6

The evaluation occurs at the end of the cycle to compare what exists now to what existed prior to the implementation of the plan. If measurable changes have been made as planned, a problem no longer exists. If the problem has not been solved satisfactorily, the group would *assess, analyze, synthesize* and *make a decision* about how to proceed. Usually, problems are not solved to complete satisfaction.

The fact is important to note that, while reviewing the outcomes of a plan, one often discovers some unexpected outcomes. Some of these outcomes may provide new insights, and others may provide new problems to be solved. In either case, to recognize these unexpected outcomes and include them in future problem-solving activities is significant.

As a way of review, a flow chart (Figure 1.3) illustrating the total group Problem-Solving Model as well as a few key process variables related to implementing the S-C Model is presented.

The Systematic and Collaborative
Group Problem-Solving Model

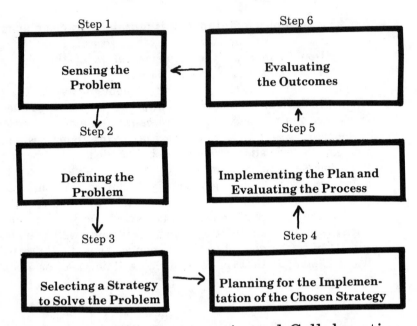

Figure 1.3. The Systematic and Collaborative
Group Problem-Solving Model.

Within each of these six steps in group problem solving are four
recurring elements:

Assessment:	Gathering together the relevant information.
Analysis:	Organizing the information into separate elements (logical categories), and examining the relationships between the elements.
Synthesis:	Re-examining the total situation, considering the relationships between the elements.
Decision Making:	Making a choice, i.e., what is valued or what step will be taken next.

OTHER CONSIDERATIONS IN PROBLEM SOLVING

A Model for group problem solving that we believe applies in any kind of organization has been presented. The S-C Model is based on the idea that the needs of individuals and the goals of the organization can be integrated sufficiently to allow for effective problem solving by a group.

The S-C Model is based on principles regarding the individual in his/her relationship to the group and on beliefs about the characteristics of groups that problem solve effectively.

The Individual in Relation to the Group

The individual characteristics promoting collaborative problem solving are as follows:

1. The more an individual participates in making a decision, the more he/she will see the decision as valid.

2. The more an individual sees a decision as valid, the more likely he/she will act on that decision.

3. The more an individual sees a decision as valid, the more likely he/she will support others who act on that decision.

Understanding and Utilizing Conflict

Conflict is a natural phenomenon which is both intrapersonal and interpersonal. Interpersonal conflict can occur only within a context of interdependence. Therefore, in interdependent organizations such as schools and universities, conflict is always present and varies greatly in amount, type, and definition. Generally, conflict should seldom be avoided, but if avoided, the avoidance should be because of a rational and objective decision.

Since conflict is a natural phenomenon, the treatment of conflict becomes an important concept. Can conflict be perceived as not 'bad' along with the movement toward its utilization?

Some common courses to the inducement and acceleration of conflict are as follows:

1. A lack of purpose for an individual or a group or an organization. Purpose is referred to usually as a mission, goals, or in some cases, a conceptual framework from which to develop the concepts and ideas into action plans.

2. A lack of precise and commonly defined objectives and/or statements which can be clearly understood by many and which may be judged as to progress and outcome.

3. Roles of members not clearly stated nor integrated. Who is responsible to do what? Schmuck and Runkel (1972) stated that disagreements or misunderstandings about one's role represents a major source of conflict in school organizations.

4. Varied commitment to objectives and criteria. If so, there is little choice but to return to the objectives section and identifying the objective which is causing the conflict. Value differences of individuals also should be explored, sometimes value differences occur when some members of a unit are working toward meeting organizational goals while other members are more committed to their personal goals or to members who control institutional rewards.

5. Self-interest priorities as when persons seek to use a group, or organizational unit to gain a desired reward without sharing this desire. This is a variation of the varied commitment of #4.

6. When the group or the committee assumes that its membership cannot change. Some members might be more capable in handling group early activities, i.e., brainstorming and conceptualizing, and not as useful in later activities, i.e., implementation of goals and activities. Recognition of this factor could lead to a later recomposition of the group.

7. Lack of contingencies. Many times a conflict is raised to an unnecessarily high level because of lack of a statement of expectations. Conflict can be managed through specifying objectives with stated criteria, time lines, and procedures,

34

for meeting that objective. Too often committees, teams, or departments do not have contingency statements which highly motivated and passive members can alike identify with to form mutually beneficial working relationships.

8. Power conflicts. These are difficult to pinpoint since power comes in many forms, i.e., status, position, or expertise. Generally, conflict arises by perceptions of misused power as in trying to gain personally (similar to #5), or in trying to increase one's own power over others. Often it is difficult to utilize this type of conflict without a form of outside assistance for group redirection. The person in power usually remains in power, but, of course, many power struggles can be worked out if the members have reached a stage of interdependence which will allow them to refocus on the purpose and objectives of the group and reach a decision on how to proceed. Conflict must be managed and directed in order for it to be utilized.

9. Authority conflicts. Authority is what is granted to a person by his or her position and power is acquired without necessarily a special organizational position. Conflict generally is related to authority when members of any group or organization are not allowed to disagree with those persons in positions of authority. Principals, department chairpersons, and others who do not allow all types of information to flow to them will soon discover that they are receiving selective information which is incomplete and often positive in nature. When this occurs, the conflict pool is building and if not attended to will either hinder the full functioning of the unit or will eventually develop into a crisis.

A crisis is usually a stage of conflict avoidance, and the utilization of this explosion is critical. Returning to the group purpose, objectives, criteria, values, etc., will usually provide the members with enough structure to rebuild relationships and move toward purposeful objectives.

Interdependence within units and organizations generally is stated as a necessary condition for people to understand each other and to work cooperatively. In some cases, maintaining interdependence may become too costly. When the cost becomes too high, a functional description of existing interdependent patterns should be revived and decisions made in regard to the need and priorities related to interdependence.

Giving and Receiving Feedback

Most of our internal self (attitudes, values, feelings and thinking) and our external selves (behavior) have been learned. This learning usually occurs in relation to the amount and types of information which is exchanged between people. This information can be of the cognitive-content form, or it can be of the affective-feeling form. Also it can be in either verbal or nonverbal form or both.

During the human relations movement in education, this interpersonal communication became known as *feedback*. As the term implies, *feedback is a communication process between two or more persons in which one person informs another person about how he/she is behaving*. In any given setting, feedback is present almost all of the time. Teacher to students, students to students, parent to child, and adult to adult are a few examples.

Have you ever assessed your feedback style and the consequences? Here are a few points to remember. Practice it yourself and, perhaps, teach the factors to others with whom you work.

Feedback, when given to another person, has three primary purposes (Kurpius, 1976):

1. *To identify discrepancies* between what that person assumes and what actually exists. Examples from teacher to student, "Jane, I was sure you were bored in school, but now I know that you are worried about your mother's health and think constantly about her."

2. *To openly support or reinforce* behavior which is appropriate and desired by another person. Example, student to teacher, "Mr. Jones, you really helped me when you explained to me how to give better feedback."

3. *To modify behavior* so actions and content are in line with the message intended. Example, student to student, "Next time when our committee is giving a report, it would be helpful if we balanced the amount of talk time for each committee member. During today's report, Carol tried to share her ideas but was blocked out by some of us who have stronger voices."

Given these three purposes, several criteria should be considered when giving feedback to another person or group of persons. These are as follows:

1. *Be descriptive* rather than evaluative. Describe your observations and/or reaction. Don't place a value on the feedback as 'good' or 'bad'.

2. *Be specific* rather than general. Using abbreviated forms of communication such as, "You are autocratic, friendly, or passive," are not as useful as feeding back specific statements related to a common experience.

3. Consider the *appropriateness* of the feedback. The person giving appropriate feedback should consider his/her need to give the feedback as well as the needs of the recipient of the feedback.

4. Is the feedback *usable* by the other person? Receiving feedback about behavior which appears to be difficult to change can only frustrate that person. Direct your feedback toward behaviors which the receiver can integrate into his/her change plan.

5. Who *desires* the feedback? Feedback is most useful if a person solicits feedback. Imposed feedback is less helpful.

6. *When* to give feedback. Generally, the best time to give feedback is when the receiver can associate the feedback with the behavior being described. The receiver's readiness is most important.

7. *Clarity* of feedback. Check to see if the receiver understands your message. Keep discussing the statement until the sender is satisifed that the message is clear.

8. *Accuracy* of the feedback. As a final check, review the statement for accuracy before you offer the feedback. Observations and perceptions can be faulty.

Hints to Establishing a Beginning Point for Group Problem Solving

A. What is a problem-solving group or team?

It is a subpart of a larger social system. By definition it is also a grouping of people formed together to cooperatively accomplish mutually beneficial objectives.

B. Why use group problem solving?

The following are common reasons. You may want to add others.

1. Multiple perceptions are helpful to reduce the potential to focus on the personalities of the people rather than to focus on the problem to be solved.

2. A greater range of knowledge, skill, attitudes, perception and role members can be introduced into the problem-solving team.

3. The forces for solving the problem can be increased.

4. The level of risk is shared and therefore reduced so progress is more assured.

5. Membership reinforcement to accomplish difficult tasks on time is more likely to occur.

6. Continuity is more likely maintained.

C. What entry variables should not be overlooked?

Schein (1972) has described a set of entry criteria for individual and group problem solvers (change agents) to consider. These criteria are access, linkage, suitability, leverage, and vulnerability. Two of these—access and linkage—are defined more clearly in the material that follows plus two others—acceptance and termination.

Access. Access to the people and structure of the system is the critical first step to any change thrust. Until access can be recognized, acquired and defined, it is clear that the first criterion has not been met and the change agent must seek out a new and different entry point.

One common entry point in a given change thrust is to begin at the top of the structure, i.e., the superintendent's office in schools or the Dean's or President's office in the university. While support from this level of the system is critical, the process is becoming less common to automatically "go to the top" as a first step. An alternative is for the people closest to the problem to define the problem situation as a first step and then decide the appropriate level of entry. Possibly the definition will call for going to the top or for the change team to sub-divide and enter at several levels of the system. With the change team model, the sub-units each have specified objectives to be met, i.e., collect data from the superintendent, interview fifty students, or analyze the utilization of resources. As the team becomes operational, several levels of the system are entered with information being returned to the total team for analysis and further decision making. Perhaps after recycling this process two or three times, more specific decisions can be made for the continued plan development.

Linkage. Linkage is that important element in any change plan which defines the relationship of the change agent/team events to the larger system. Is there a goodness of fit? Is the relationship likely to be adopted by other subsystems? Entry relates closely to linkage in that the change agent/team must understand the connection between position and informal power. Position power (principal) may be useless in a school building change thrust because the teachers are the controlling factor. For example, if curriculum renewal was the change agent/team thrust, the principal may have very little power with the faculty since the norms of that school are that the discipline areas/departments make those decisions and inform the principal.

A good case study of starting at the top of an organization and moving downward is that of introducing the innovation of modern math to schools during the 1950's and '60's. It was one of the first attempts at packaged materials prepared for classroom use, readily approved by top and middle management, accepted by teachers because it was new, potentially exciting, and supported from the top with adequate resources to implement the program. Even with this well organized and highly supported process, when one observed at the point of exchange between teacher and learner, the linkage was less easily observed.

Perhaps the university is the most difficult system to gain entry into due to its closed and protective tradition. Four clusters of decision makers are present—Board of Regents, top and middle administrators, student governments, and faculty including goverance and faculty individuals and groups who identify with academic freedom. In addition, often times a few high status, influential faculty members control most of the major decisions within a college or university. Given this situation, linkage is extremely difficult since no formal or observable pattern exist to which the change agent/team can link.

Acceptance. Here the important issue is gaining approval and support from the persons requesting the change. After gaining access and linkage, checking the system members to determine the degree of acceptance is vital. If acceptance is low, perhaps the change strategy could be redesigned or the first step could be repeated to determine if *people, procedures* or *issues* need to be reconstructed.

If the preceding steps have been worked through appropriately, possibly the change agent/team could begin to observe the effects of the work. Positive signs might include attitudes changing in favor of the change objectives, behaviors changing in the desired direction, and a larger group of people supporting the change strategy.

Influence on or acceptance of the strategy by the members may be observed by any or all of the following:

1. More people are inquiring about the change effort.

2. Others are wanting to join up.

3. More people are attending meetings.

4. People begin coming on time for meetings and remain until completed.

5. Leadership is shared at meetings.

6. Encouragement is required for continuing the change.

7. Problems related to the change strategy are talked about more openly.

8. Other needed changes are being discussed.

9. Help is offered by persons previously not involved.

10. Delicate issues are raised which previously were not discussed.

11. Special resources are made available by administration.

Termination. When is the change effort stopped? This is seldom discussed, but is an important issue. Change team members often feel that no end will come. The only way to guarantee an end point is by specifying objectives and criteria as a guide to determining when the desired change has been reached.

Since change is a process, one may say that the change thrust never ends. Once attitudes and behaviors have been changed, the effects are continuous. The prime point of stress here is that of self-directed change or self-renewing change. In this way, special change teams may terminate their efforts but the process continues.

Organizing and Conducting Better Meetings

Facts about organizing and conducting better meetings may sound like an over simplified heading however many small group meetings and committees fail primarily because of the lack of a set of procedures. The following list is prepared for the *group leader* or *committee chairperson* to review and share with the group as a set of guidelines to be followed by the group.

1. State or determine the overall task of the group, i.e., who the group is responsible to, the expected product (a recommendation, a new policy, a set of guidelines), who are

41

resource people to the group, if needed, and who receives the product.

2. State or determine the guidelines for the group. Examples are as follows:

   a. Length of meeting(s)
   b. Expected number of meetings
   c. Beginning and ending on time
   d. Effects of members coming late or leaving early
   e. Leader's role and responsibilities
   f. Members' roles and responsibilities
   g. Decision-making process followed, i.e., majority voting, consensus, criterion-referenced, etc.
   h. Need for recording and disseminating meeting minutes
   i. Physical needs

3. Develop and review agenda and set priorities.

4. Establish a climate of interdependence, objectivity, trust, and respect within group, i.e., conduct group business during the meeting, not in small groups following the meeting.

5. Allow all ideas to be heard.

6. Keep group on target (don't mix items) while recognizing the importance of interpersonal dimensions.

7. Clarify, test, summarize ideas, and issues.

8. Define and reach agreement on definition of problems to be solved.

9. Test for group ownership of issues/problems.

10. Select intervention for solving the problem.

11. State objectives which when met will solve the problems. If possible, determine who will be responsible for each objective.

12. Set up procedures for support and follow-up.

13. Summarize meeting and plan for subsequent meetings, if appropriate.

14. Terminate and disseminate findings appropriately.

The Delphi Technique for Future Planning. The Delphi technique is another method developed for helping groups and organizations plan for the future. When applied, the process tends to flatten out the decision-making process and creates a greater interdependence among the multiple levels of the members of an organization in regard to future planning. This process replaces the traditional committee approach, and since information and ideas are collected independently, all opinions have equal influence including opinions of persons in authority positions.

Weaver (1971) stated that the Delphi technique is most reliable as a tool to be used as
   (a) a method for studying the process of thinking about the future,
   (b) a pedagogical tool or teaching tool which forces people to think about the future in a more complex way than they ordinarily would, and
   (c) a planning tool which may aid in probing priorities held by members and constituencies of an organization.

The Delphi Technique Applied—The technique when applied can take several different forms. For example, members can be present in a room, or an instrument can be mailed to members. Either way, the intent is to share only the information collected from each person but not the person's name. The sequence is as follows:
   1. Identify group to be sampled.
   2. Prepare questions to guide the future thinking of these persons.
      Sample questions are as follows:
      a. What *priorities* do you think we should be considering during the next (month) (year) (five years), etc.?
      b. What *events* do you think will govern our future decisions?
      c. What *objectives* should we be preparing to meet in the future?
      d. What *time lines* should we consider?
   3. Mail or hand out question sheet which requests information desired. (This is an individual and not a group activity.)
   4. Collect and summarize all statements and return the summarizations to each respondent. Statistics such as median and interquartile range are common. This time ask each

43

respondent to explain their rationale for those responses that fall outside the interquartile range, or revise their own statements, if needed and rank each statement in priority order. Lastly, request that they list the probability of occurrence by placing a percentage mark (%) after each statement.

5. Collect and summarize this round of responses also to determine the degree of agreement among respondents. Next a third round of statements is prepared, and disseminated showing the range of agreements for the total group. Where respondent statements fall outside the interquartile range or differ greatly from the majority, request that these persons explain their reasons for their statements and whether or not they desire to make any changes toward the majority statements.

6. Collect and summarize this last round and you now have before you the feelings, ideas, hypotheses, and objectives of the members' samples with corresponding time lines and probability of occurrence statements.

Robinson (1977, p. 14) stated three characteristics to summarize the Delphi process,

1. Each participant responds to each sequential development of the questionnaire before seeing the inputs of the other participants for that same step.

2. Everyone knows his/her own responses but does not know who has made the other responses.

3. Input gained at one step of the process is shared in the results and feedback of the next step.

Utilization of the Delphi Technique Findings—Use of the findings varies depending upon the purpose for using the Delphi method. Generally speaking, a full range of uses can be considered from simply disseminating the findings, to building plans for future events, to assembling the members for discussion and debate of each of the future statements collected.

Note that the information gathered through the Delphi approach is (1) future-oriented and (2) may produce different information by an appointed committee, persuasion leaders, or other

44

more traditional approaches to setting goals and interventions for future plans and activities. The Delphi approach also supports collaboration, interdependence, membership, and ownership of problems and goals.

CONCLUSION

In this Chapter has been described the context in which problems occur, a range of variables and forces that interact in a learning and work environment, and a model for both conceptualizing and solving problems as they occur. Research findings and descriptive reports strongly support that people who function as effective problem solvers tend to be more productive people and more satisified with their work environment. The model and tool skills presented are intended to provide the reader with the concepts and skills necessary to become an effective problem solver, as well as to help others to become the same.

BIBLIOGRAPHY

Christie, S.C., Bank, A. Culver, C.M., McCann, G. and Rasmussen, R. *The problem solving school.* Dayton: Institute for Development of Educational Activities, 1972.

Kurpius, D.J. and Brubaker, J.C. *Psychoeducational consultation: Definition-functions-preparation.* Bloomington: Indiana University, 1976.

Kurpius, D.J. Implementing interpersonal communication in school environments. In J. Weigand (ed.) *Implementing teacher competencies.* Englewood Cliffs, New Jersey: Prentice-Hall, 1976.

Kurpius, D.S. A typology for gathering and utilizing consultation data. Miller, P. and Prince, J. (eds.) *The Future of Student Affairs.* Jossey-Bass, 1978.

Lindblom, C.E. and Braybrooke, D. *A Strategy of decision: Policy evaluation as a social process.* New York: Free Press of Glencoe, 1963.

Maslow, A.H. *The farther reaches of human nature.* New York: Viking Press, 1971.

Merton, R.K. *Social theory and social structure.* New York: The Free Press, 1960.

Robinson, S.E. Significant tool skills for the consultant. *National Society for Performance and Instruction,* 1977.

Rogers, E.M. *Diffusion of innovations.* New York: Free Press of Glencoe, 1970.

Schein, E.H. *Organizational psychology.* Englewood Cliffs, New Jersey: Prentice-Hall, Inc., 1972.

Schmidt, W.H. *Organizational frontiers and human values.* Belmont, California: Wadsworth Publishing Co., 1971.

Schmuck, R.A. and Miles, M.B. *Organizational development in schools.* Palo Alto, California: National Press Books, 1971.

Schmuck, R.A. et al. *Handbook of organizational development in schools.* Palo Alto, California: Mayfield Publishing, 1972.

Trist, E. *Towards social ecology: Contextual appreciations of the future in the present.* New York: Plenum Publishing Corporation, 1973.

Weaver, L. *Nonpartisan elections in local governments: Some key issues and guidelines in decision making.* Detroit: Citizens Research Council of Michigan, 1971.

2

ADULT AND CHILD
IMPROVING LEARNING ENVIRONMENTS
THROUGH BETTER COMMUNICATION

Charles J. Downing

The program described by Downing presents specific ways in which parents and teachers can work together to create the most productive learning environment for individual students. In addition to concentrating on the student individually, this approach may alter the network of social systems in schools by bringing parents into active problem solving through working with teachers in learning to communicate with students. With collaboration, parents and teachers can create a more optimal learning environment for an individual student. In the approach Downing advocates, statuses and roles of teachers and parents change: parents and teachers are considered a team, both being equally important in fashioning a student's particular environment. This approach differs from the more traditional in that home and school both share with understanding the concern for a child's behavior and achievement in school. When such a team approach operates effectively, the formal organizational structure of the school may vary from the usual because according to Downing's definition the primary purpose of the institution is to understand and provide the learning environment needed by individual students. From this perspective, the role and status of the student also change from the usual behavior patterns to which many adults are accustomed. Significant adults who made an effort to understand and to communicate accurately with a student place the student in a more responsible learning position than when the student's behavior and words are not taken seriously or are ignored totally. Ultimately, this approach to a learning team works toward creating an ideal learning environment for an individual student; and the feelings, values, behaviors and priorities change for those adults involved with the student's growth and development.

The premise of this program is involvement: parents, teachers, and other school personnel are all concerned with a school's learning environment. These people share the ideas of theoretical frameworks concerning communication with students, thereby collaborating to develop a common background that can eliminate many frustrations now common in student-learning. Descriptive examples help parents and teachers to learn how to understand a student's behavior, then communicate with the student as an individual. The content of this Chapter includes classifying behavior and interpreting its purposes; gathering needed information from students; encouraging open communication through attending behaviors such as reflection and paraphrasing; getting students to listen to parents and teachers; attempting to change a student's behavior; and resolving conflicts clear-cut illustrations are included with each content topic.

Throughout this Book the communication methods presented are valid examples for helping to bring about effective communication between individuals in general. An elemental consideration in Downing's program is contained in his reference to Shaw (1968) who

> found that a rigorous program of prevention focused upon significant adults, ultimately resulted in a decrease in need for treatment programs. Further, Shaw found evidence that child behavior could be more effectively influenced by changing the behavior of significant adults than by the direct intervention of guidance personnel working with children. (p. 3)

In summary, the open communication techniques presented by Downing are intended to help parents and teachers create environments in which individual students can learn effectively and, like Palomares, Downing places emphasis upon reducing the faulty messages communicated through "position power" held by so many adults over students. Downing's approach advocates that open communication among parents, students, teachers, and other concerned school personnel promotes substantial improvements in learning environments; a concept which should be understood and practiced by all involved in the educational process.

49

ABOUT

THE

AUTHOR

CHARLES J. DOWNING

Charles J. Downing is currently director of pupil personnel in the Lake Tahoe Unified School District, South Lake Tahoe, California. Downing's responsibilities include organization and supervision of the District's guidance program, psychological services, special education program, and health services. Downing has served as a visiting instructor in the Counseling and Psychological Services Department of the University of Nevada, Reno.

Downing's undergraduate training was completed at the University of California Santa Barbara, his masters degree was received from California State University, San Jose, and his doctorate was erned at Indiana University.

Dr. Downing brings to his present position twenty years of public school experience as a teacher, counselor and school administrator. Downing has worked directly with students of pre-school age and graduate students and all ages in between.

For the past twelve years Downing's primary focus has been upon the development of meaningful programs of parent education; this area of emphasis results from his own efforts as father to his daughter and two sons.

ADULT AND CHILD:

IMPROVING LEARNING ENVIRONMENTS

THROUGH BETTER COMMUNICATIONS

Charles J. Downing

The development of productive learning environments is largely dependent upon the effectiveness of the communication systems involved in the learning situation. Learning processes of children are extremely complicated activities. In order for learning to be accomplished effectively, efforts of a number of *significant persons* are required. The child should be functioning well, teachers need to behave in ways that contribute to the learning processes, and parents should provide optimal learning conditions for the child. For each person involved to behave in the most appropriate manner an effective communication system must be developed among these individuals. This Chapter describes methods by which parents and teachers can be trained in various skills that contribute to the learning processes and help develop effective learning environments.

The development of clear school/community communications will contribute to the building of learning teams of children, parents and teachers. To provide for the development of an effective learning team, school and home need considerable data about each other. A mutual understanding of objectives and expectations aids in providing consistent direction. When parents and teachers know how each conceptualizes the child, a greater understanding of behavior is possible. Such an educational team needs to be aware of

51

the particular data-gathering capacities of the other parties. The team needs good communication systems between the individuals on the team. Finally, the team must be aware of the behavioral change capabilities of both parent and teacher.

That a teacher is significant to a child's learning process has generally been conceded. A considerable body of research is available supporting the contention that teachers can be trained to effectively relate to children and manage their learning environment. In child development and educational literature much attention is given to the effects of parents' child-rearing practices. Human relationships within the home environments are considered to be among the critical factors influencing a child's total functioning. The emotional adjustment of a child is seen by Satir (1975) as closely tied to the parent-child relationship. The manner in which a child solves problems, interacts with others, and carries out everyday functions is largely determined by the learning that has occurred in the child's home environment. Clapp (1969) found that the degree of independence exhibited by the child is often a function of the teaching techniques of the parents.

Research studies point to the influence of child-rearing practices upon the learning performance of children. The emotional climate of the home is cited as contributing to some children's negative attitudes toward learning. The interdependence of parent attitude and student achievement was shown by Sze (1975) in a research study. Child-rearing practices are related to the manner in which children learn specific tasks. Children who feel they have personal control over the outcome of their own behavior tend to achieve better in academic work than do children who see their parents as the major control.

A close connection between growth-producing parent-child relationships and the nature of parental attitudes is apparent. Changes in relationships between the parent and the child are nearly always dependent upon a change of attitude by the parent. Wolff (1969) in a research study found that parents' attitudes are influenced by the level of understanding they possess concerning their child's behavior. Adults who are knowledgeable and understanding of the experiences of most children are more likely to be sensitive and helpful in handling children. The specific practices used in child care are of less importance than the spirit in which they are administered.

A child's learning is influenced by everything present in his or her home environment. People in the home are perhaps the most important part of that experience. Parents are teachers of their children. Parents may be unaware of what they are teaching or how the learning is occurring, but their impact is felt by the child. For example, Hess and Shipman (1968) found that the ways in which mothers interact with their children is the most predictable clue to the children's intellectual performance.

Parent-teacher training programs presented are designed to serve primarily as preventive measures. A major objective of such training is the reduction of learning difficulties with children whose parents and teachers have participated. Shaw (1967) has found that a rigorous program of prevention focused upon significant adults, ultimately results in a decrease in need for treatment programs. Further, Shaw has found evidence that child behavior is more effectively influenced by changing the behavior of significant adults than by the direct intervention of guidance personnel working with children.

THEORETICAL FRAMEWORK

The training program presented in this Chapter is drawn from a variety of theories of behavior change. The assumption is made that many intervention techniques are effective, given the appropriate circumstances. Alternative response patterns available to parent and teachers are examined during the program. An emphasis is placed upon the individuality of each encounter between parent and child. Thus, stereotyped responses and/or response patterns are not encouraged. Rather the adult is encouraged to be more aware of the stimulus prior to response. This specific program is designed to teach a *differential approach*. The participant is urged to ask: what child, when, under what circumstances, and what response is most appropriate? An important issue in the selection of a behavior change approach is the status of the individual in the learning process. For example, the significant adult who has more ready access to the management of consequences may choose a reinforcement strategy. If, in another case, a learner is struggling with a difficult decision, a very different procedure might be selected.

53

ENVIRONMENTAL CONDITIONS
OF OPTIMAL LEARNING

Regardless of the intervention strategy selected, the adult is urged to strive toward the provision of the following environmental conditions of optimal learning:

1. *The child experiences non-possessive warmth from one or more significant persons.* Such warmth is the unconditional caring of another which allows the learner to feel himself or herself a separate person with the inherent rights and responsibilities for self determination (Carkhuff & Berenson, 1967). Unconditional caring for a person means that a place will always exist for him or her in the relationship; this caring should not be taken to mean unconditional approval of behavior. Ideally, a child experiences such warmth from both parents; however, the warmth may be adequately provided by one parent or by other significant persons. This warmth serves as a reinforcer of learning.

2. *The child is encouraged to view himself or herself as a worthwhile person.* He or she is helped to see himself or herself as having physical and mental competencies sufficient to allow the individual to feel adequate as a person. The child is sufficiently free of fears that expectations allow for reasonable risk-taking behavior. The child is able to make self-evaluations of personal behavior in such a way that he or she is considered as self-managing. This view of self serves as a reinforcer of learning.

3. *The child experiences a climate of self-discovery.* The child is allowed freedom to decide for himself/herself what he or she learns, how he or she plays or works. The child is allowed to move away from the control of parents and teachers as he or she grows older. This condition includes the awareness within the learner that differences in people and behaviors are desirable. A climate of self-discovery includes the rights of individuals to make mistakes. This condition provides the opportunity for the child to be self directing.

4. *The child is able to see other people as worthwhile.* He or she is encouraged to develop a sense of valuing and caring for others. Such caring may be expressed in behaviors of social

54

reject, add or delete objectives from the list. Parent-teacher groups frequently accept the entire package at first presentation. As participants become more comfortable, they usually share needs which dictate the reformulation of objectives.

The concepts and techniques presented in this Chapter comprise a total training program for parents and teachers. The reader is urged to utilize those ideas, techniques and sequences which best fit the objectives of the group served.

WAYS OF LOOKING AT CHILDREN AND THEIR BEHAVIORS

Before considering specific behavior change systems, often a helpful approach is to examine the manner in which some adults conceptualize children. That is, how does the adult classify the child's behavior? Such classification usually relates to some sort of good-bad spectrum. Further, what are the seemingly causal factors of the behavior as viewed by the adult? Although determining causality may not be essential to behavior change, the adult's view of causality often influences one's behavior.

This influence is illustrated by the case example of a primary grade boy who severely beat a girl classmate. The beating was of such extent that the boy was excluded from school until family counseling was initiated. Faculty members were appalled by the nature and severity of the incident. Some staff members felt the child must be psychotic and should not be allowed to return to school. A counselor pointed out that the family history included a regular pattern of physical beatings in the home. The father had beaten mother, mother had beaten the boy, and father had beaten the boy. The suggestion was made that perhaps the child had merely learned an inappropriate behavior as a part of a normal learning pattern. From this perspective the faculty members could relate to the child in a different manner. Appropriate controls were put into action to avoid a repetition of the original incident, but this action did not prevent school personnel from teaching this boy productive behavior. If a parent or teacher views a child's behavior as resulting from reasonably understandable factors, the adult probably will behave in a facilitative manner.

One way of looking at children and their behavior involves classifying that behavior along an evaluative continuum. People observe the actions of other persons and in some way evaluate those actions.

The diagram in Figure 2.2 represents one system for classifying human behavior along an evaluative continuum. The diagram offers four options for the person classifying behavior. Some observable behavior may be seen as desirable or highly positive. Other behavior may be evaluated as tolerable, meaning the behavior can be accepted but is not necessarily highly thought of by the observer. Both of these classifications are for behavior which is positive. On the negative side of the diagram, some behavior is considered undesirable. These actions are of a negative nature but fall short of provoking intervention. Intolerable behaviors are so negative as to cause the observer to act in some way to stop the offending behavior.

A system of classifying behavior has great utility for teachers and parents when used as an observation guide. The observer may wish to focus on a particular child for a specific time period and classify all observed behavior. Yet another use of the system involves the observer noting those behaviors he or she was *aware of* during a time period. Such observation records provide considerable diagnostic data for improving learning environments.

Desirable Behavior	Tolerable Behavior	Undesirable Behavior	Intolerable Behavior

Example: Child at bedtime

Desirable Behavior	Tolerable Behavior	Undesirable Behavior	Intolerable Behavior
Prepares for bed, before being asked!	Prepares for bed when asked.	Dawdles in getting to bed.	Refuses to go to bed.

Figure 2.2.   Classification of Behavior System.

The classification of behavior system illustrated in Figure 2.2 has helped to surface many important concepts in parent-teacher discussion groups. One exercise used with this system, involved asking the participants to think about one of their children or students. Participants were asked to identify a few examples of that child's behavior that fit each behavior category of Figure 2.2. In discussion of the exercise, the following major points are usually forthcoming:

1. Most behavior of children is desirable or at the very least is tolerable.

2. Adults often spend more time reinforcing undesirable behavior than in rewarding desirable behavior.

3. The process of classifying behavior and carefully observing may help adults to appreciate the behavior of children.

4. Adults may find the behavior they seek is already present. If the adult *expects* to see children behaving in desirable ways, that behavior will probably follow.

A system for classifying behavior based upon subjective judgment raises many questions of consistency. Behaving consistently with children is probably a never-to-be-realized goal. Adults have good days and not-so-good days. The difference between tolerable behavior and undesirable behavior may be determined largely by what kind of day the teachers or parents are having.

McIntire (1970) suggested that the main task of parents and teachers is choosing the behaviors to reinforce positively. For this selection process, an individual should have a classification/observation system in mind. Adults who work with children are urged to examine carefully the way they look at children and their behaviors.

THE GOALS OF CHILDREN'S BEHAVIORS

Dinkmeyer and McKay (1973) suggested that parents and teachers would profit from considering the goals or purposes behind the behavior of children. Like most people, children want to belong—to feel part of a group. To belong to a group the child must find others who want *him* or *her*. The child may behave in rather strange ways to insure that people show something that says they want that child. Although children usually have a purpose behind their actions, they often cannot tell the observer why they behave as they do. The child's "I don't know why" should not prevent the parent or teacher from seeking an understanding of the goals of behavior.

When an adult views a child's behavior as undesirable the adult has difficulty considering the goals of that child's behavior. Satir (1972) suggested that parents or teachers might consider that children usually have honorable goals behind their behavior—even misbehavior. Honorable goals refers here to goals of behavior which have a positive nature. The following exercise has proven useful in workshops for parents and teachers to illustrate this concept.

> The leader role plays the following situation. Bill, a thirteen-year-old boy, shouts at his mother, "Leave me alone! I can't stand you! You're always telling me what to do!"

The group leader asks participants to respond to questions, such as the following:

How would you interpret Bill's message?

What assumptions would you make about his feelings?

How might you check out those assumptions?

What does Bill want to happen between him and his mother?

The discussion following such consideration often touches many areas. One might interpret Bill's message as representing a dishonorable goal or negative motive. The mother might see his behavior as being very disrespectful to her because of her own anger. The mother might assume that Bill is trying to "get to" her and cause her to be angry. If the mother makes the above interpretations and/or assumptions, she will probably behave in ways appropriate to those mental images. For example, she might say, "Don't talk to your mother like that" or "You're just trying to

60

get me mad—get the hell out of here!" or "Go to your room until you can speak to me in a civilized manner." She might become even more upset and punish Bill for his disrespect. The mother might strike him or shout at him. If Bill really "gets to her" she is more likely to behave in punishing ways. In one sense the mother has exhausted the alternatives she sees for herself and resorts to punishment.

The leader now asks the group to consider Bill's original message. The following questions usually assist participants to examine their own attitudes. Could you try to interpret that message as having *honorable goals?* What *honorable* things might Bill want to occur between him and his mother? Response examples of honorable goals might include the following: desire for attention, desire for independence, or unrest with invasion of his life space.

Assuming that participants have been able to develop some *honorable* goals for Bill's behavior, they are then asked to determine ways to check out their assumptions.

A sample conversation representing one system might go something like the following:

Bill: "You're always telling me what to do!"

Mother: "Seems to you like I'm running your life!"

Bill: "Yeah, for crying out loud, Mom, I can take care of myself."

Mother: "If I'd leave you alone, you'd be able to handle things for yourself?"

Bill: "Sure. I don't need you to tell me everything to do."

Another exercise which has proven helpful involves asking parents or teachers to think about one of their children and some *misbehavior* of the previous week. The adults are then asked to identify possible goals of behavior and the consequences. The discussion following such consideration usually emphasizes several key points.

61

1. Children often seek the attention of others with their behavior.

2. Attention seeking is an honorable goal—everyone wants and seeks attention.

3. The method of seeking attention is usually the problem and not a dishonorable goal.

4. Many adults behave as if children were *out to get them.*

5. If adults consider the goals of children, they can often avoid being personally threatened by the misbehavior.

6. A consideration of the consequences of the behavior often explains why a child behaves as he or she does.

Another way of considering children, then, is to consider their motives from a positive view. If an adult can seek explanations for behavior, that adult can be more effective in teaching appropriate means for attaining the child's goals.

A good rule for working with children is "always seek more information!"

Some information-gathering activities which have proven helpful to parents or teachers are the following:

1. Have parents select one of their children. Parents are then asked to observe this child carefully for one half hour or longer. Parents are to make a log of the *tolerable* behaviors they observe. Parents usually are surprised at the amount of such behavior observed.

2. Parents or teachers are asked to observe their home (classroom) for a week. Parents then are asked to describe the atmosphere ... feeling tones ... of the home or teachers of the classroom.

3. Parents are asked to involve the entire family in an exercise—they are to look for behaviors of each other to reinforce, i.e., things they like and want to see more often.

Figure 2.3. represents a summary of ways to look at children and their behaviors.

I wonder what this child wants?		What does this child get out of that?	
Desirable Behavior	Tolerable Behavior	Undesirable Behavior	Intolerable Behavior
I want more of this kind of behavior!		I don't like this and it can best be changed by ignoring the behavior.	This behavior must be stopped or changed immediately.

Figure 2.3. Ways of Looking at Children and Their Behaviors.

LEARNING ABOUT CHILDREN AND THEIR BEHAVIORS

In this part of the training program the concern is with ways parents and teachers learn about children and their behaviors. The methods utilized to gather data are important because of their effect upon children. Adult behaviors are prevalent which will serve to enhance communication with children and improve the nature of learning conditions (Weigand, 1971). These adult behaviors will be discussed in this section.

Perhaps the most significant parent-teacher behavior affecting the learning process is the exhibition of non-possessive *warmth*. Such warmth has earlier been defined as caring for another person which allows the person the rights and responsibilities of self-determination. The parent is behaving in such a way as to say to the child, "I love you—so much that I allow you to make mistakes!" Such parent behavior might be described as acceptance of the child. Acceptance in this context refers to a willingness to receive another person in a relationship with *no strings attached*. The need or desire to change or control the other person probably will exist, but in this caring concept the other person has a place in the relationship, even if he or she does not change or submit to control.

For most parents and teachers displays of warmth for their children are easy and spontaneous; some adults, however, must learn ways to express affection for children. Parents and teachers of teenagers often require assistance in converting affection systems which were effective when the children were younger. Adults whose own history was essentially affect-deprived usually require training in how to express warmth to children. Parent-teacher discussion groups may provide a variety of practical experiences in *loving* kids. High school teachers often are surprised to hear that parents *want* teachers to be affectionate with their children. Once teachers have received *permission* to show children affection, these teachers tend to be very creative in displaying appropriate affection.

Perhaps the most effective means of adults exhibiting non-possessive warmth to children is to hear what they are saying. For many adults no reason exists for listening to children. Such parents and/or teachers must be convinced first that some value lies in listening to children. Vargas (1977) has suggested that "father knows best" for children—if what father knows comes primarily from the child. Adults frequently do not have enough information about children to allow these adults to be accepting. Parents and teachers often must be reminded of the honorable goals of children's behavior.

The value of information available from the child is illustrated by the following case. James was referred to the school psychologist by his teacher. The teacher was greatly concerned by the drawings which James repeatedly brought to school from home; all were drawn completely in red crayon, *blood red.* After much testing and interviewing, the psychologist finally asked James why all of his pictures were in red. James replied, "That is the only color crayon I have!"

In this program, adults are reminded of the information available from the child. The child often is the only source of data concerning the individual's feelings or internal stimuli. These feelings greatly affect the child's behavior. For example, the high school freshman may feel he or she can *never* live up to the academic record of an older brother or sister. This youngster may choose to try for success in another area such as athletics or by doing little or nothing. Parents and teachers need to know how children are interpreting their world.

64

The parent-teacher group is asked then to focus upon more effective methods of communication with children. One suggestion is for the adult to attempt to become more aware of person-response pattern. Helpful techniques in this regard include asking one's spouse or fellow teachers for feedback, tape recording exchanges with others, and keeping records of types of communication techniques used in specific time periods.

Another suggestion for better communication with children involves a review of the first part of the training program. That is, if adults focus upon what is desired in the relationship by them and the children, the adults will be reminded that more information usually is needed.

Attending behaviors are presented as a specific procedure by which adults can improve chances for communication with children. The following list of suggestions for helpful attending behaviors is given to the training group:

1. Relax physically.

2. Let your posture be comfortable and your movements natural: for example, if you usually move and gesture a good deal, feel free to do so at this time also.

3. Use eye contact by looking at the person with whom you are talking. Vary your gaze rather than staring fixedly.

4. Follow what the other person is saying by taking your cues from the individual. Stay with the topic that is introduced, rather than jumping from subject to subject.

5. Let your responses indicate to the other person that you are with the individual as he/she talks. Try to get inside his/her shoes and let him/her know that you understand what he/she is experiencing and feeling.

6. Try to reduce the child's defensiveness by communicating consistently that you are not in a contest. This behavior can be done by reducing the use of comments as, "On the other hand," "Yes, but," "Have you considered . . .," or "That may be true, but . . ."

7. Acknowledge and appreciate those elements of communication which represent your estimate of appropriate human behavior.

8. Carefully observe the body movements and functions of the child. Posture, tone of voice, eye expression, rate of speech and breathing can give clues to the child's feelings and ideas.

The group may next be asked to add to the list of attending behaviors. Usual additions include the avoidance of interruptions. Parents and teachers often point out that they cannot always listen to a child. As a result, the list is expanded to include the need to be open and honest with a child when you cannot listen to him or her. Participants often point out the usefulness of short phrases to encourage further talk, such as, "O.K.," "Yes," and "I see."

The training group is encouraged to accept the value of effective communications with children. Attending to a child while the child talks communicates to that child that you think he or she is a competent person. A willingness on the part of significant adults to listen to children goes a long way toward building their self-esteem. For the child to develop confidence in his or her ideas and capacity to communicate, the child needs opportunities to practice with people who are significant and who care.

LISTENER INVOLVEMENT

Certain risks are inherent when adults simply listen attentively to a child. One risk is that the listener may not clearly understand the meaning of the child's conversation. Unfortunately, the hardworking listener often will assume he or she understands the communication perfectly. A second risk involves the child's assumption that the listener agrees with him. Yet another risk may take the form of a child bored by a one-way conversation. The training group is therefore introduced to some techniques for adult involvement in the conversation.

The point is assumed that the listener is interested in two objectives: (1) in obtaining greater verbalization from the other person and (2) in greater understanding of the messages transmitted. The training group is asked to examine five types of listener behaviors designed to reach one or both of these objectives. The five types of listener behaviors are paraphrasing, checking out a perception, admission of confusion, questioning, and summarizing.

Paraphrasing

This behavior is aimed at making certain the listener understands the ideas, information and feelings of others. Paraphrasing involves stating the other's idea in your own words or giving an example that illustrates your understanding of other's statement. A good paraphrase is usually more specific than the original statement.

Example

Parent: "Mrs. Smith is an inadequate teacher!"

General
Paraphrase: "You think she's not right for education.

(If the parent agrees with this, you will not know what he means by "inadequate." You think you understand his meaning.)

Specific
Paraphrase: "You mean that Mrs. Smith is incompetent?"

(The parent might answer "No. She is competent but she doesn't plan properly." This paraphrase leads to clarification of parent's idea.)

When you paraphrase, you show what your level of understanding is and then enable the other person to present their clarification of your specific misunderstanding.

Before you accept your understanding of an input you should make certain that the remark to which you are responding is really the message the other person intends to send. Paraphrasing is one way of checking this process.

Checking Out a Perception

This behavior is aimed at making certain you understand the feelings of another person. This process involves stating what you perceive the other person to be feeling. A good perception check says: "I want to understand your feelings; is this the way you are feeling?"

Examples

> "Did you feel disappointed that nobody responded to your suggestions?"

> "I get the feeling that you are angry with me."

A perception check specifies the other's feelings in some way, such as, "disappointed", "pushed out of shape", and so forth, and does not express an intended judgment of the feelings. This checking comment merely conveys, "This is how I understand your feelings. Am I correct?" A slight variation of the previous techniques involves a direct reflection of feeling or content.

An example of a reflection of feeling

Child: "We didn't go on the hike today because it rained, even after we had been planning it for over a week."

Adult: "You sound pretty disappointed."

Teenager: "I don't think the school should tell kids not to smoke pot."

Teacher: "You think your use of marijuana is of no concern to the school."

Admission of Confusion

When the listener is confused as to the content, feeling tone, or direction of the conversation, the listener may try a simple admission of this confusion.

Examples

Parent: "Jim, I'm confused as to how you want me to help you."

Counselor: "There seem to be several feelings connected with this decision. I'm confused as to which is more important to you."

Teacher: "Class—I'm not getting this concept across. Help me out, where are we missing connections?"

Being willing to admit one's confusion and to attempt to eliminate this confusion is a trust-building behavior. In such a case the person with the problem has evidence that the listener is not pretending to understand and that the listener is really trying to get the message.

Questioning

An important skill in increasing verbalization and in acquiring more information is *questioning*—the ability to frame open-ended questions.

Such questions ask how, why or what and appear to say to the other person "Tell me about . . ."

Examples

"How did that happen?"

"Can you describe how you felt?"

"Why did you leave your last job?"

"Can you tell me any more . . .?

"How will you react to him in the future?"

Summarizing

Summarizing in a conversation is a type of pause—restatement of the situation—for mutual checking to determine if both parties are together. Either party can initiate the summary. The summary need not only occur at the end of a transaction. The purpose of summarizing is to seek understanding. A summary may be initiated by one of several phrases such as:

"Could you sort of summarize where you see us going?"

or

"I've heard a bunch of things—let me see if we're together."

or

"This is where I think we are . . ."

Exercises for Increasing Listener Involvement. Several training exercises have been used to assist adults in determining effective ways to involve themselves in conversation with children. The following are examples of such exercises. An excellent source of other activities is the six-volume series, *Handbook of Structured Experiences for Human Relations Training* by Pfeiffer and Jones (1969-1976).

1. A written list of statements is presented to the adults. All of the statements contain a reasonably clear statement of feeling. The adults are asked to write a reflection of feeling to each statement. The group then discusses the nature of the written expressions.

Examples

"The teacher chewed me out in front of the class today for fooling around."

"We didn't go skiing today because of the wind, even after we had been planning it for over a week."

"You always make me clean up our room even if John was the one who messed it up."

"I just can't seem to keep up in all of my classes at the same time."

"I'll bet I know why John doesn't like me; it's 'cause I do better in school than he does."

"I think when a girl is twelve years old she should be able to pick out most of her clothes!"

2. An interaction tape recording is developed to provide a sample of adult-child conversation. This tape may be taken from a recording of a counseling interview, a taped role play or participants may make their own stimulus tape. The tape then may be used in a variety of ways, as a stimulus for discussion of effects of responses, as a sample of verbal behavior to which to respond, or as material for rating the nature of the response.

Example
Adult: "Joe, please take out the trash!"

Child:	"O.K. Mom, just as soon as this program is over!"
Adult:	"I can't wait until the program is over. do it Now!"
Child:	"Aw, heck. You're going to ruin the whole show for me!"
Adult:	"Don't talk to your Mother like that!"
Child:	"You keep telling me to tell you how I feel . . ."

3. The group is divided into dyads. A list of children's statements is provided to each pair. The pairs are asked to quiz each other for reflection of feeling statements. When the list is exhausted, one member of the pair is asked to discuss his or her concerns about a child with his or her partner. The partner is asked to practice reflecting feeling messages at appropriate times.

Sample List of Children's Statements

"Oh, boy, I can't wait until spring vacation!"

"I really get tired of all the homework Miss Bowman gives us!"

"I don't think Miss Bowman likes me."

"Mom, what can I do? I don't have anything to do!"

"I sure blew it today—all of the guys are mad at me."

"Wow, I got an 'A' today in spelling!"

The group then is encouraged to discuss the effects of listener behavior upon the relationship. The discussion usually will reflect similar observations among members. These observations improve the understanding of each point of view, each person is provided an opportunity to correct or clarify his or her position, each can examine his or her own feelings, the participants may begin to see a basis for each other's behavior, and may recognize that both parties are able to observe that feelings are acceptable. More global outcomes of the use of such techniques may involve the determination by the participants that some behaviors may be more appropriate than others, as well as a continuing of the conversation.

4. Another data gathering suggestion which may be introduced to the group involves *combining observation skills and reflection of feeling*. For example, if Jane is moping around the house, the parent might say: "Jane, you look kind of upset—something bothering you?" Or if John seems deliberately to break a piece of school equipment, the teacher might say, "John, you are not allowed to tear up other people's properties. You must be pretty mad to act that way."

Jane and John may tell the adult what is bugging them (more data), they may get the message that adults accept sad or angry feelings, or they may even come up with an appropriate alternative behavior. The children may continue to act out their feelings in ways the adults have trouble accepting. In this case the parents or teachers will want to look for other responses which may prove more effective. In whatever way the adults respond to children the goal is to try to say, "We are interested in you and we care enough to try to understand you."

The important point stressed in the exercises is that effective listener involvement is active in nature. The listener is working hard to read all of the messages, both verbal and non-verbal. The listener is attempting to be aware of his or her own level of emotional involvement and of the nature of cognitive assumptions. Because the inferences made by the listener about other people often are inaccurate, to confirm these assumptions is important.

HOW TO GET CHILDREN TO LISTEN TO PARENTS AND TEACHERS

The training program to this point has placed an emphasis on the idea that children have data that are valuable for adults. Now the focus changes to the adult data which are of value to children. In both cases the major problem is how one can communicate this significant information to the other.

72

That parents and teachers possess information desirable to children is evident. As a result of their experience, adults possess data critically needed by children; but how do they communicate this fact to children? A first basic contention of this program is that *adults can best teach listening skills by modeling* the desired behavior. To the extent that parents and teachers listen to children—show they respect them and their ideas—children will listen to adults.

A second basic contention of this program is that *children deserve straight forward answers* to their questions. Usually when a child asks a parent or teacher a question, the child is ready to listen. Usually the child wants only limited information at the time of asking, not the accumulated knowledge of the world. An example of this need is a child's typical reaction after receiving a lengthy response to a question, "Gee, what a long answer to such a little question!"

In the discussion of data-gathering procedures, the acceptance of feeling was examined briefly. Children often express some rather strong feelings to adults, only to have them disregarded or debated. Joe, a ten-year-old, tells his mother, "Mrs. Smith is a terrible teacher!" Mother may respond by defending Mrs. Smith and denying Joe's right to feel as he does. The result is that Joe is very unlikely to hear Mother's arguments.

The entire issue of feelings in interpersonal relationships is often confusing. A model for viewing interpersonal relationships, which has been helpful to people in their attempts to conceptualize the process of such relations and what happens between a given stimulus and the related behavior, follows. This model suggests that for each person in the relationship a series of happenings occurs within that person during each encounter. Figure 2.4 illustrates a sequence of internal processes as they might occur with an individual. Figure 2.5 illustrates sequences of internal processing during an interpersonal encounter.

The model suggests that a strong relationship exists among feelings or ideas, objectives, and behaviors. People do not always behave with an awareness of this connection. Further, people do not always appear to have in mind an objective that logically relates feelings to behavior. Sometimes people are angry and strike out, behaving in a manner that is totally unrelated to what they want to

```
┌─────────────────────────────────────────────────────────────┐
│                  INTERNAL PROCESSES                           │
│                                                               │
│  Stimulus                                                     │
│  (or recognition thereof)      — "I see a candy bar!"         │
│                                                               │
│  Feelings or ideas             — "I feel hungry."             │
│                                                               │
│  Determination of objectives   — "I want to eat the candy bar."│
│                                                               │
│  Behavior                      — "I buy and eat the candy bar."│
│                                                               │
└─────────────────────────────────────────────────────────────┘
```

Figure 2.4. Sequence of Individual Internal Processes.

```
┌─────────────────────────────────────────────────────────────┐
│              INTERNAL PROCESSING DURING                       │
│              AN INTERPERSONAL ENCOUNTER                        │
│                                                               │
│                  Person 1                    Person 2         │
│                                                               │
│  Stimulus:   Meets John on    Stimulus:  Meets Mary on campus.│
│              campus.                                          │
│                                                               │
│  Idea:       Thinks John can  Feelings:  Feels strongly attracted│
│              help her with her           to Mary.            │
│              history.                                         │
│                                                               │
│  Objective:  Wants to get John Objective: Wants date with Mary│
│              to help her with                                 │
│              history.                                         │
│                                                               │
│  Behavior:   Talks about trou- Behavior:  Talks about a forthcom-│
│              ble she is having            ing social event.   │
│              in history.                                      │
│                                                               │
└─────────────────────────────────────────────────────────────┘
```

Figure 2.5. Sequence of Internal Processing During an Interpersonal Encounter.

happen. For example, a football player turns the wrong way and causes a fumble. The angry coach may call the player out of the game and refuse to let him play again. The coach might say that what he wants to happen—his objective—is to stop the player from fumbling the football. One cannot quarrel with the outcome of the coach's behavior, to fumble on the bench is difficult! However, one might question if the coach's behavior is appropriate for teaching the player not to fumble. If the objective were to teach the player to hold on to the ball, a more effective behavior might involve whether or not the player knows why the fumble occurred and what he can do to avoid the same mistake being made again.

This example indicates that at times behaving in effective ways is very difficult, especially when strong feelings are involved; yet, some football coaches calmly provide useful information to players in the heat of a close contest. Possibly such people have learned an awareness of their emotions and thought processes and consequently are able to maintain a clear view of their objectives.

In summary, a person's affective/cognitive state influences a person's behavior. Between feelings/ideas and behavior occurs a development of objectives process, influenced by feelings/ideas and often determining the subsequent behavior. Therefore, awareness of affective state and thought processes, in self and others, is important in interpersonal relationships. This awareness may assist people in being more explicit within their own minds as to what they are wanting to happen in the relationship.

Exercises for Clarifying Objectives

The following exercise has proven helpful in assisting parents and teachers to clarify their objectives.

1. *Role Playing the Parent.* The participants are asked to respond to the child in these situations as if he or she were their own child.

   a. This incident takes place in a fourth grade classroom. The children have been given an assignment which calls for individual or small group seatwork. The teacher indicates that when the work is completed the class will go outside for physical education. The teacher further tells the class that he must talk at the doorway with the principal for an extended period of time. When the principal leaves, the teacher discovers very little work has been accomplished.

b. Your family is hiking in the woods, far from civilization. Your seven-year-old boy is leading on a clearly marked trail. After a break for a drink of water, you realize the seven-year-old has gone ahead. After a frantic half-hour search, you get a call from a member of the party assigned to wait at a crossing trail and are told that the seven-year-old is with him.

The group is asked to share first how they would have *responded*. Secondly, the group is asked to share how they would have *felt*. The participants also may want to examine the effects of feelings upon the responses. Perhaps evidence will be given of the feelings coming through non-verbally. The discussion usually progresses naturally to some better ways of responding. Such methods probably will include more clear identification of personal feelings, concrete owning of those feelings, being open with responses from those feelings, and experimenting together as to more appropriate behavior.

The following exercises are designed to help participants move from the conceptual level toward effective behavior in dealing with children.

2. *Dyad Exercise.* Parents are asked to identify behaviors of their children that are of concern to the parents. Parents then take turns in stating their feelings about these behaviors to their partner. Partners should try to respond with their perception of the resulting feelings within the child. The dyad's topic may then be their reaction to their skill level in identifying feelings and establishing the relationship to behavior. The dyad's topic can then become to problem solve more effective awareness techniques for themselves.

3. *A Family Conference Exercise.* This exercise is done as a group role play. Participants are assigned each of the following roles and asked to role play a family sequence.

Mom:	Concerned with lack of cooperation from family since she has returned to a job outside the home.
Dad:	Concerned with poor state of housekeeping recently.
Laura (16):	Concerned with additional demands placed on her.
Greg (14):	Feels things are fine; lets everyone do his own thing.
John (11):	Concerned because bedroom is always messed up by older brother.

(Mom is working for the goal of adding on the house — bath, bedroom, and family room. All of the family have been involved in planning for the new expansion.)

Rules for the role play family conference: Inputs must be owned (I feel . . . , I think . . .). All inputs must be responded to before continuing the role play. That is, someone must show the speaker that the previous statement was heard. Dad will initiate the conferences.

In the processing of any or all of the exercises the participants usually identify some similar reactions. First, participants often protest about the difficulty in consistently identifying their own feelings. Second, participants often experience difficulty in consistently behaving in a fashion congruent with their feelings. Adults can be encouraged in their efforts by the knowledge that awareness is often the first step in cognitive behavior change.

SOURCES OF INFORMATION

Often parents and teachers are not content with an examination of their own skills in communication. They frequently want more sources of data about children.

Again, the participants are referred to the observation process as a valuable source of information. Observing total behavior may be very helpful in placing specific behavior in perspective. A careful baseline tally procedure also may place the frequency of a particular type of behavior in perspective.

The bibliography contains a variety of readings which are a source of information about children. Other expert opinion usually is more close at hand. Participants in this program are encouraged to consult with experts—teachers, counselors and others who work with numbers of children. Often a child's behavior may appear inappropriate to parents when the child is observed in isolation. The same behavior among a group of similar-aged children may be quite normative.

SOME IDEAS ABOUT CHANGING
CHILDREN'S BEHAVIOR

The first assumption of this training program is that all human behavior is purposeful and goal directed. The second assumption is that nearly all human behavior is learned. These two assumptions allow for developing human potential, of eliminating undesirable behaviors and increasing desirable behaviors through the learning process.

This training program also is based on the concept that learning is composed of at least two major factors—*the respondent,* as well as *the operant.* With this concept in mind, intervention strategies should be based on the position of the person with regard to the learning cycle. As a result, this training program encourages parents and teachers to develop a variety of behavior change techniques.

These persons may not be aware of their goals or of the processes by which they have acquired their present behavior, however, this very lack of awareness provides an intervention point for behavior change. An example of such lack of awareness is presented by Patterson (1968), who demonstrates that in all aspects of life, people constantly are learning ways to respond to both people and situations around them. Even if people do not realize the fact, people are teaching each other and learning from one another all the time. Think about how you have been taught to talk about certain topics with certain people. When people listen, one talks; when people stop listening, one stops talking or at least changes the subject. Ways in which people teach or change each other are often referred to as *social learning.*

Parents learn to behave in certain ways with their children, which may range from scolding and spanking to kissing and hugging. Social learning of parents comes from their associations with other people. The manner in which parents behave toward their children appears to be learned from observing other parents, particularly their own parents. People *tend* to rear their children as they were reared.

Social learning theory suggests that children *learn* how to behave. Children can be taught both misbehavior and desirable behavior (Vockell, 1977). By the same token, parents learn child-rearing behaviors; they can be taught both ineffective and effective ways to relate to their children and to manage the behavior of children.

Planning for Behavior Change

Management of behavior, to which we previously referred, occurs every day of our lives, but most of this management happens by chance without planning. In this part of the program, participants examine ways to provide optimal learning conditions through behavior management. By helping children become more competent personally and socially, parents in turn can be helped to build these optimal learning conditions.

If children are really worth having around, they should be worth spending a few minutes a week with which is necessary for planning so that improved relationships may develop. Such planning would focus upon efforts to approximate consistent behavior by parents and/or teachers. Identification of those behaviors classified as desirable and undesirable requires some planning time. Further, significant adults need to differentiate carefully between important and trivial behaviors. At the same time adults should plan time to remind themselves of the important parent-teacher behaviors. Vargas (1977) has suggested that the most important tasks for parents are the identification of desirable behavior and its positive reinforcement.

This training program suggests that several effective behavior change systems are available. An overview of several of these systems is included.

Environmental Change

The easiest accomplished procedure for bringing about behavior change involves *environmental change*. If such a change is feasible, the change represents the most economical system available. A parent-teacher judgment is called for in this procedure. By changing the environment, one may deny a child a valuable learning experience. The child's developmental level is the best guide in this situation. Is this child ready for this particular learning?

Environmental procedures include the following:

1. *Reorientation of significant adults.* Reorientation may include the training of parents and teachers in more effective relationship skills as attempted by this training program. In some cases reorientation may require an actual change of significant adults. Such drastic change occurs more often in school where the child may be moved from one classroom to another. Occasionally a change of parents becomes necessary.

2. *Provision of opportunities aimed at producing the desired behavior change.* Providing such opportunities may take the form of substitution of acceptable alternatives to behavior that is undesirable. This process may involve providing learning situations in which success is likely. For example. the teacher who provides considerable structure for an experience new to a group of children.

3. *Restriction of a child's opportunities aimed at reducing the chance of error or misbehavior.* Parents often limit the play areas of small children to reduce hazards. Factories utilize safety lines to reduce hazards. Parents and teachers often can control behavior by restriction of a child's play area or of potentially dangerous play things.

4. *The reduction of stimulus material as an effective behavior change technique.* Some children require an environment with a limited number of distractions in order to function well. Times occur when all children can benefit from a limited excitement level.

5. *Behavior management by gearing the child's circumstances to his capacity.* School work which is too demanding often results in behavior problems. When the closet clothes rod is too high, the child's coat must be hung up by an adult, when the rod is arranged at a lower level the child can be expected to hang his clothes.

Exercise for Environmental Change. Training group participants are asked to complete and prepare to discuss a worksheet on which are listed Items 2 through 5 of the environmental change procedures. This worksheet is shown as Figure 2.6. The task involves devising a use for each of these ideas in the participant's classroom or home.

When this exercise is discussed, adults often share many strategies for easy behavior changes. Adults tend to reduce the use of environmental change as children grow older, yet industry has found the approach to be a potent influence of behavior.

Cognitive Change as a Behavior Change Strategy

Participants were asked to examine several methods for bringing about behavior change by helping children make cognitive changes. These methods included 1) *goal orientation,* 2) *bolstering the child's esteem,* 3) *improving the child's desicion-making skills,* and 4) *providing access to alternative behavior by direct teaching.*

Goal Orientation. The Adlerian psychologists have long encouraged people to work with the goals of behavior when developing strategies for change (Dinkmeyer & McKay, 1973). This training program already has explored the manner is which the adult's perception of the child's goals influences the relationship between adult and child. In this phase of the program, participants are asked to examine ways to change behavior through consideration of the child's goals. The Adlerian system of goals of behavior places emphasis upon the following:

1. Attention getting

2. Power

3. Revenge

4. Display of inadequacy

81

CHANGING THE ENVIRONMENT

People respond to cues and stimuli in their social and physical environment. Their response or behavior gets some kind of reinforcing results. Following this principle, if we change the cues in the environment, we often get change in a child's behavior.

1. Provide opportunities *(Give me a chance, Mom!)*

2. Reduce the excitement level *(Sure quiet around here since Mom left!)*

3. Restrict the child's chance for mistakes *(Hey, Mom! This playpen is sure slowing me down!)*

4. Gear things down to the child's size *(It takes me fifteen minutes to climb up high enough to hang my coat!)*

5. Plans and reminders *(Hey, Mom! Look at that! Those astronauts spend five years getting ready to fly, and they still use check lists!)*

Figure 2.6. Environmental Change Worksheet.

Parents and teachers are encouraged to broaden their prospective of children's goals in order to include more detailed purposes for behavior.

The suggested *format for examination* of goals as a behavior change technique includes:

1. Assisting the child in identification of what he or she wants to happen.

2. Reaching agreement concerning the acceptability of some goals, which may involve some compromise on the part of both adults and child.

3. An examination of implementation procedures. How do we get what we want to happen?

4. A follow-up procedure, including, reinforcement of efforts toward goals and possible adjustment of goals.

Exercise for Goal Orientation. Participants are asked to describe briefly a child's behavior which concerns them. The group is asked to use the previously suggested format to discuss the case. Next, adults are asked to try the format with one of their children and later report their results to the group.

Bolstering the Child's Esteem. The Adlerian's concern with goals of behavior can be closely related to the position that self-esteem is important to behavior change. This approach holds that a person's sense of self-worth is based on how he or she is seen by significant others around the individual. *A child in contact with parents and teachers who regard that child as a person of worth, capable of effective living, and moving toward reasonable goals, will develop a favorable sense of self-esteem.*

Thus, a strategy for behavior change might be to establish certain premises about a child so that the child will behave according to those expectations. Among these premises are the following:

1. That the child is a person of worth.

2. That he/she is entitled to be viewed with favor.

3. That he/she possesses a capacity for favorable growth.

The parent or teacher must behave in a manner that provides high levels of the conditions for optimal learning described previously. This approach assumes that such conditions encourage stronger self-esteem and more effective behavior on the part of the child.

Another strategy for the use of self-concept as a behavior change technique involves how a child describes himself or herself. If parents and teachers can obtain a picture of the child as that child talks about himself or herself, then the parents are in a position to strengthen or change that picture. If the child's statements about self are essentially positive, the adult can reinforce this view by pointing out behavior which gives evidence of such a picture. For example, "John, you seem to feel fairly confident about your academic ability. I would have to agree, especially when we look at your work in my class!" On the other hand, the child may present negative descriptions of himself, and the adult may help build a more positive picture. Again, the verbal picture needs to be reinforced by evidence of competency.

Exercise for Bolstering the Child's Esteem. Parents and teachers are asked to keep a week-long record of statements made by their children which imply the nature of their self-esteem. In each example the adult is asked to draw together behavioral evidence to support a positive view of that child. The assumption is maintained that such positive evidence is available for *every* child.

Improving the Child's Decision-Making Skills. Another cognitive approach to behavior change involves assisting children with effective decision-making/problem-solving skills. People learn their methods for decision making and can be taught to use these skills to bring about more appropriate behavior. If children are repeatedly assisted in an effective process and rewarded by effective outcomes, the process soon becomes a tool for determining reasonable behavior. The role of the adult appears to be to help the child become aware of the following:

1. The goals involved in the decision.

2. The conditions of self and circumstances.

3. The available alternatives.

4. The consequences to be expected from the various alternatives.

5. The values related to the decision.

Further, the adult can help the child establish criteria for choosing among alternatives. The anticipated result is that the child develops a procedure for decision making/problem solving to be used in future situations. For a more detailed discussion of problem-solving technique please refer to the Chapter of this book written by Kurpius and Christie.

Providing Access to Alternative Behavior by Direct Instruction. Perhaps the most obvious cognitive behavior change techniques involves the use of direct instruction. A major basis for maladaptive behavior is lack of knowledge, information, or experience. When people are provided with new and pertinent information, they are usually capable of applying the new information to their situation and of making appropriate behavior changes.

Such instruction may take several forms. Among the most potent teaching tools is *modeling,* which involves performing the desired behavior in a way that the child can observe and imitate. A friend went shopping with her nine-year-old daughter recently. At the grocery store check-out stand, the Mother asked a man with only one item to go ahead of her rather than wait while her full cart was checked out. In the parking lot the Mother collected her cart and another empty cart and returned them to the store front. As they were driving home, the daughter said, "Mom, I was just thinking, you sure made a lot of friends today!"

Other forms of direct instruction include the *giving of directions, providing needed knowledge of information, clarifying or making understandable complex concepts,* and *helping children with the meaning of a particular occurrence.*

Reinforcement Model

The reinforcement model, which is consistent with the other behavior change techniques suggested, is in daily use by all parents and teachers. Such a model follows a pattern: when the child does what the adult expects the child to do, the adult will do something the child wants the adult to do, and the adult then can expect the child to react in that manner more often.

The following represents a reinforcement model used in this training, and some descriptive terms used are defined as follows:

1. *Cue or Stimulus*—Provide an organism with information about what behavior to perform to get rewards.

   Kinds of cues:

   (1) Physical environment—people, places, and things.

   (2) Social environment—talk, praise, feelings, and non-verbal messages.

2. *Behavior*—A *behavior* is something a person does.

   Examples: hits a sister or brother

   does one's arithmetic problems

   smiles at me

   a. A behavior is observable. That is, a behavior can be seen by people. When behavior is counted in reference to a time period we have a BASELINE which is expressed as:

   occurrence of a behavior

   time

   as example: six times per day

   b. The steps in specifying a behavior are as follows:

   (1) To name the behavior.

   (2) To describe the conditions under which the behavior is to occur.

   (3) To indicate limitations.

   (4) To describe the success level.

3. *Rewards or Reinforcements*—Rewards (reinforcements) are events or activities which immediately follow behaviors and maintain or modify (increase or decrease) these behaviors.

   Example: *events*

   social praise—"You are a good boy"

   physical—ice cream

activity

playing with friends

doing what one wants to do

a. Kinds of Reinforcements

   (1) *Positive reinforcement*—anything (social or physical) that is needed by the organism and which strengthens a behavior so the behavior is more likely to recur; behavior tells one what he or she *should* do.

   (2) *Negative reinforcement*—unpleasant events or activities which the organism wishes to avoid and which make the behaviors these events precede less likely to recur; negative reinforcement tells one *what to do to avoid* something.

   (3) *No reinforcement*—unlearning of behavior because the behavior is not rewarded, ("we don't do something that doesn't work") called extinction of behavior.

   (4) *Punishment*—an aversive or unpleasant event which occurs after a specific behavior; punishment does tell the organism what behavior one should not do; too much punishment does not tell one what he or she should do; too much punishment suppresses behavior but does not help to unlearn a behavior.

b. Reinforcement schedules

   (1) *Regular schedule*—reinforcing a response every time the response occurs, which brings about rapid learning.

   (2) *Intermittent schedule*—reinforce some, but not all, occurrences of the desired behavior. This intermittent approach makes behavior persistent and resistant to change. Uneven intermittent schedules are generally preferred (Vockell, 1977).

Reinforcements can be used in changing behavior in a variety of ways. Two procedures are outlined here for the use of reinforcement theory—the use of successive approximation and contingency contracting.

Successive Approximations. If a behavior occurs in some small amount, the rate of that behavior can be increased by regular positive reinforcement of the behavior according to the following outline:

1. Identify behavior and decide how often you would like it to occur.

   > Example: Johnny can only study at home for five minutes. I wish he would study for one-half hour per day.

2. Positively reinforce the five minutes of study with special praise or activities until five minutes of study occurs every day.

3. The intermittently reinforce five minutes of study a day and regularly reinforce ten-minute periods on those days when it occurs.

4. When ten-minute periods are established, follow the same procedure on up to one-half hour of study a day.

5. When the expected length of study does not occur, do not negatively reinforce or punish, simply ignore it.

Contingency Contracting. When a desirable behavior does not occur and you want that behavior to occur, you can utilize *contingency contracting.* More simply, contingency contracting means *"arranging the conditions (rewards) so that the child gets to do something he or she wants to do following something you want the child to do."*

If a child has an *undesirable behavior* you would like to change, start here:

Step 1: a. Identify (first for yourself) the behavior(s) to be changed and develop a baseline of the occurrence of the behavior.

b. Specify the rewards that maintain the undesirable behavior.

c. Decide what you would do if the child performed the behavior you think desirable.

88

If you only want the child to start performing a *new behavior* start here:

> **Step 2:** Decide with the child what the new behavior will be. (If you need proof of a problem, show the child the baseline.)
>
> Specify the behavior together by naming the behavior, the conditions for the behavior occurrence, the limitations of the behavior, and the level of success.

Decide with the child what rewarding events you can provide or in what rewarding activities the child can engage if he or she performs the behavior. The statement should be similar to, "If you carry out this behavior, you can do this or will get this."

> **Step 3:** Decide whether the old behavior is so strong you need to suppress it by negative reinforcement and whether or not lack of reinforcement will extinguish the old behavior. If you decide to use negative reinforcement, determine what the negative reinforcement will be. Remember, the child's behavior that removes your negative reinforcer is being strengthened; make sure that that behavior is your desired behavior.
>
> **Step 4:** Develop a strategy to get the child to *practice* the new behavior and positively reinforce that behavior on a regular schedule every time the behavior is performed.
>
> **Step 5:** As soon as the child has practiced the new behavior enough so that the new behavior is more likely to occur than the old behavior, remove any negative reinforcement so that the old behavior can occur with no reinforcement and be extinguished.
>
> **Step 6:** Change to an intermittent schedule of reinforcing the new behavior (make the intervals between reinforcements longer) so that the new behavior will be resistant to change.

Step 7: Be aware that occasionally the child will slip back into his or her old behavior, and as an adult you may need to repeat the steps to achieve the new behavior.

Exercise on Contingency Contracting. Participants in the training program are asked to perform the following exercise as homework. They are asked to select a child from their home or classroom as a target population. Then they are asked to proceed with these steps on contingency contracting. They are expected to report their progress at the next group meeting.

1. Working with behavior

    a. Name the undesirable behavior.

    b. How often does undesirable behavior occur?

    c. Under what *conditions* does undesirable behavior occur?

    d. What reward (reinforcement) maintains that behavior (a parent's response or someone else's response)?

    e. What would happen if the child did the desirable behavior?

2. Contracting

    a. Describe new, desired behavior to be learned: (Name that behavior, conditions under which the behavior is to occur, limitation of behavior and criterion for success.)

    b. If the new behavior is perfomed, what will the adult do?

    c. State the contract upon which the adult and the child might agree.

    d. How will you get the new behavior to occur?

RESOLUTION OF CONFLICT

When conflicts occur in the home or classroom adults often forget about the primary condition of learning, that is, *nonpossessive warmth.* In such circumstances, parents and teachers tend to think in terms of their own hurt, anger, and disappointment. Some adults see conflict as a failure in the relationship.

During a conflictful situation, the parent or the teacher may experience increasing difficulty in listening to children, considering the honorable goals of their behavior, looking for desirable behavior to reward, or even considering appropriate directions for adult behavior. Under such stress the adult often resorts to punishment. Experts have suggested that parents and teachers should learn to maintain their composure. Such demands are unrealistic and serve only to add to the guilt feelings of the adult who explodes on occasion.

An alternative strategy suggests that an adult simply withdraw from the conflict for a time. This temporary withdrawing technique provides an opportunity to regain one's composure, develop strategies, and adjust the focus on the problem. Of course, such retreat is not always possible; removing the child from the conflict for a cooling off period may be necessary. In either case, the child needs special attention at a later time to ensure that he or she understands that the withdrawal is from the conflict situation and not from the child as an individual.

The previous suggestion of withdrawal will not always work. The most careful plans of adults will sometimes fail and composure may be lost. Children need to see such explosions. The world is not made up of calm, objective counselors!

Often during conflict, adults resort to the use of punishment. While this program does not suggest that the use of punishment is wrong or should always be avoided, the program does suggest punishment must be used with care and understanding of its possible effects (Vockell, 1977). One reason that punishment is used is that punishment does have an immediate effect. Usually, some behavior is controlled as a result of punishment. Because adults see immediate results, the reaction is positively reinforcing to the adults. Punishment has worked before so it will be tried again. The fact may be that the adults are uncertain as to what behavior really was changed. The child may still be doing the same things but has now learned not to let parents or teachers see him/her behaving in that way.

Yet another reason for the use of punishment is that punishment serves as a tension release for parents. The circumstances of conflict leading to punishment are often emotionally loaded, resulting in an explosion of feeling on the part of the adult. One way of exploding is to punish the other person.

Under some circumstances punishment is an appropriate teaching device, but punishment must be used carefully to be effective. The punishment must be rather absolute to be totally effective. For example, society can control anti-social behavior by locking a person in a cell. If the person is allowed to associate with other prisoners or to rejoin society, the punishment is less absolute and less effective. This example might be distasteful to many people for various philosophical reasons, but the example does serve to point out the relative control effects of punishment. Punishment as an effective teaching device is difficult to use and requires careful planning.

Punishment is usually resorted to when adults run out of alternatives. The adults simply do not know what else to do. The fact may be that the child and the parent do not know what to do. If the expected behavior has not been clearly defined for the child, he or she may not know what to do to avoid conflict.

Problems in Using Punishment

Punishment tends to be more connected to the emotions of parents than to the behavior of children. A given behavior by a child may be tolerable, and therefore ignored, when a parent is in a happy mood. The same behavior may be seen as intolerable after the parent has had a difficult day. Frequent use of punishment may result in the child paying more attention to the emotions of parents than to personal judgment of appropriate behavior. The child may be thinking, "This is bad only if I get caught!" or, "This is okay as long as Dad is in a good mood!" In one sense parents may be teaching the child to tend more to *external controls* of behavior than to one's *own value system*. Problem behavior may continue as long as punishment is related to the emotions of parents. Such connection also controls adult behavior. If the child is taught that he or she must do what adults want only when adults look serious, adults may have to practice looking serious!

Another problem in using punishment is that punishment tends to reduce the total behavior of the child *observable* by the parent and therefore reduces the effectiveness of the parent. The use of illegal drugs by teenagers leads to an example of this kind of interaction. The youngster who tries to discuss the relative value of drug use and tells his or her parents of a friend's experience, may find that friend outlawed. One wonders if the teenager learns to leave the friend alone or not to discuss delicate subjects with one's parents. Some people go out of their way to find behavior to support. As a result, they tend to have access to more total behavior of the child and are more influential in the child's learning. When frequent punishment is used, both parent and child are inclined to avoid each other, again reducing the importance of the parent. Punishment does not provide much information about desirable behavior. Punishment tells the child what he or she did wrong, but very little about how to do something right. Finally, if punishment is applied often it becomes more difficult to use positive reinforcement. Parents are so busy looking for undesirable behaviors that they overlook the desirable behaviors children perform.

The net result of the punishment cycle seems to be confusion. The objective of punishment usually is to stop some undesirable behavior and replace it with a desirable behavior. But the result of frequent and harsh punishment is often the reverse.

Alternative to Punishment

To point out the weakness of punishment as a teaching device is all very well but what parents and teachers need are some workable alternatives. The *first* suggestion offered involves *learning more* about the child, the behavior in question, and children in general. Before deciding upon a procedure for dealing with a child in a given situation gathering all the relevant data possible is wise. What actually happened, how often, what was the pay off for the child, and whether or not the behavior was unusual for a child of a particular age. To gather the important data, parents need to use their skills in observing their child, listening carefully to what he or she shares with them, and learning about the development of children.

A *second* alternative to punishment is *helping a child to solve his or her own problems* before the problems develop into major events and become problems for parents. When adults observe children carefully, they notice occasions when children accept their own problems. "Dad, I've got a problem with my homework!" or, "I sure don't like Mark, he's mean!" These declarations are important events, for these events give the adult the opportunity to help the child solve his or her own problems.

a. Perhaps the most appropriate behavior for the parent at such a time is to listen carefully and to let the child know the parent is attending.

b. The next important adult behavior on these occasions is for one to withhold advice until one is certain the problem has been identified and the child has not been able to develop a satisfactory answer on his/her own. A good rule of thumb is to wait for the *second* request for advice.

Parents who help their children solve their own problems find themselves in much less conflict with their children, a state which results in reduced use of punishment.

A *third* alternative to punishment is to *ignore specific undesirable behavior*. At least three classes of behavior lend themselves to this procedure.

a. *Trivial and unimportant things children do constitute a type of behavior to be ignored.* The more carefully adults observe children, the more adults are able to distinguish trivial behavior from activities which are important to the relationship. Such behavior can be irritating to parents and requires careful planning if this trivial behavior is to be ignored.

b. Another type of behavior that *can be improved by withdrawal of attention is the kind of action that usually goes away as the child grows older.* These actions often are little habits such as nose-picking, thumb-sucking, and many so-called nervous habits. Often the less attention paid to these behaviors the quicker they disappear. Eventually, the developmental revision of habit takes care of the problem. Parents need access to some references regarding normative behavior to use as rough guidelines. A variety of good child growth and development books are available. As suggested earlier, the parent also can observe his or her child in the classroom and judge for oneself what is normal behavior.

c. The third type of behavior that adults might try ignoring *is a specific undesirable behavior which has been observed to be supported by continued attention.* In such a case an attempt will be made to extinguish the behavior by removing the reinforcement or reward. Again adults must plan carefully for this extinguishing procedure to work. Adults must be

94

patient, for they can expect more of the undesirable behavior as they begin to ignore, later when the fact is apparent that the pay off is no longer available adults can expect the behavior to be reduced in frequency. Identifying a somewhat related *desirable* behavior to reinforce while ignoring the undesirable activity, is probably a good idea.

The *fourth* alternative to punishment is to somehow *change the undesirable behavior without use of punishment.* A brief review of some techniques which help children to change their behaviors follows:

a. Explain to the child what he or she is doing and why the behavior is undesirable to you. If necessary, teach a behavior that would be desirable.

b. Provide an example or plan with the child an acceptable alternative to the behavior which upsets adults.

c. Identify those behaviors which a child does right and positively reinforce them. This approach particularly is helpful if the problem area involves limited performance of a specific behavior. For example, if parents are upset with a teenaged son or daughter because he or she does not help around the house as much as the parents would like, they might try identifying those things the child does which are helpful and reinforce those activities. Gradually, parents can expect to see more helpful behavior if the reward system is accurate.

d. Change the circumstances around the behavior. When a baby begins to walk, parents remove dangerous and breakable items from the child's play area to avoid the undesirable behavior of falling or injuries.

e. Contract with a child to change his or her undesirable behavior. The contract might be summarized, "If you do this, then I'll do this."

The fifth alternative to punishment is to consider the irrational nature of the punishment cycle. Parents and teachers often find themselves caught up in a continued cycle in which parent punishes child, child punishes parent in return, and parent punishes child for punishing parent. Somewhere the cycle has to stop. This point is usually marked by the parent and child withdrawing from each other. The following steps are suggested as a way to avoid this cycle:

1. Provide opportunities for desirable behavior.

2. Reward the desirable behavior with very positive consequences.

3. Limit the use of punishment only to those most completely *intolerable* behaviors.

EVALUATION SYSTEMS

Evaluation of a training program is the most difficult part of the program. Current literature strongly suggests the use of performance objectives (See Chapter 5 by Froehle) which specify outcome behaviors for parents and teachers which can be measured. For example, an objective test of samples of desired knowledge responded to at a given level of accuracy by participants often is used as an appropriate outcome measure. Such a system leaves some interesting questions unanswered. What is the relationship between knowledge and subsequent behavior? How long will the response knowledge be retained?

The basic technique suggested for evaluation in this program is to couple a service population approach with an objective-related approach. This type of evaluation means that the training participants (service population) are asked to be primary evaluators of the program and that the criteria for evaluation should be the objectives previously determined.

If the participants have taken part in determining objectives, participants are usually well prepared for assisting the evaluation. An objective-related evaluation procedure becomes a reinforcer of parent efforts as personal behavior changes. Adult participants in such a training program are in the best position to determine the degree to which they have acquired what they expected from the program. Such adults are able to evaluate their own degree of success in terms of implementing effective ideas. In such a system, repeated reference to objectives encourages evaluation based on individual behavior change, since the objectives will have been adopted individually.

96

Some researchers have utilized assessment instruments to measure outcomes of parent-teacher training programs. Schaefer and Bell (1958) developed the *Parent Attitude Research Instrument* for the study of parent attitudes. This instrument has some weaknesses but remains among the strongest devices for measuring parent attitudes. Shaw (1967) revised the *Parent Attitude Research Instrument* with some success, resulting in the *Family Life Attitude Inventory*. The latter instrument is a somewhat streamlined model of its ancestor and is more easily administered. The *Semantic Differential* as devised by Osgood (1957) is widely utilized for evaluating outcomes of training programs in which attitude change appears important.

Perhaps the most desirable evaluation procedures would involve the determination of long-range outcomes. For example, does participation in a parent-teacher education program affect children's learning? The suggestion is that the variables are so vast, in number and effect, that any such study would be meaningless.

The critical questions in evaluation of such a program can best be answered by the service population. The critical evaluation questions are as follows:

1. Did the participant obtain what he or she wanted from the program?

2. Was a change evident in the participant as a result of the program?

3. Was the change positive or negative?

REFERENCES

Carkhuff, R.R. and Berenson, B.G. *Beyond counseling and therapy.* New York: Holt, Rinehart and Winston, 1967.

Clapp, W. F. *Dependence and competence in four-year-old boys as related to parental treatment of the child.* Washington, D.C.: ERIC Document Reproduction Service, 1969

Dinkmeyer, D. and McKay, G. D. *Raising a responsible child.* New York: Simon and Schuster, 1973.

Hess, R. and Shipman, V. *"Maternal attitude toward the school and role of the pupil, some social class comparisons."* Paper presented to the 5th Conference on Curriculum and Teaching in the Depressed Urban Areas, Columbia University, New York, 1966.

Le Shan, E. J. On *"How do your children grow?"* New York: David McKay, 1972.

Krumboltz, J. D. and Krumboltz, H. B. *Changing children's behavior.* Englewood Cliffs, N.J.: Prentice-Hall, 1972.

McIntire, R.W. *For love of children.* Del Mar, Calif.: C.R.M. Books, 1970.

Osgood, C. E., Suci, G. and Tannenbaum, P. H. *The measurement of meaning.* Urbana: University of Illinois Press, 1957.

Patterson, G. R. *Living with children.* Champaign, Illinois: Research Press, 1968.

Pfieffer, J. W. and Jones, J. E. *A Handbook of structured experiences for human relations training.* Volumes I - V, La Jolla, CA: University Associates, 1969-76.

Rose, S. D. *Treating children in groups.* San Francisco: Jossey-Bass, 1973.

Satir, V. *Peoplemaking.* Palo Alto, CA: Science and Behavior Books, 1972.

Satir, V., Stachowiak, J. and Taschman, H. A. *Helping families to change.* New York: Jason Aronson, 1975.

Schaefer, E. S. and Bell, R. Q. *"Development of a parental attitude research instrument."* Child Development, 29, 1958, pp. 339-361.

Schmuck, R. A. and Schmuck, P. A. *A humanistic psychology of education.* Palo Alto: National Press Books, 1974.

Shaw, C. R. *When your child needs help.* New York: William Morrow, 1972.

Shaw, M. C. and Rector, W. *Parent and counselor perceptions of their participation in group counseling.* Monograph #3, Chico, CA: Interprofessional Commission on Pupil Personnel Services, 1967.

Sze, W. D., *Human life cycle.* New York: Jason Aronson, 1975.

Vargas, J. S. *Behavorial psychology for teachers.* New York: Harper and Row, 1977.

Vockell, E. *Whatever happened to punishment?* Muncie, IN: Accelerated Development, 1977.

Weigand, J. E. *Developing teacher competencies.* Englewood Cliffs, N.J.: Prentice-Hall, 1971.

Wolff, S. *Children under stress.* London: The Penguin Press, 1969.

3

THE HUMAN DEVELOPMENT
APPROACH
A PREVENTIVE MENTAL
HEALTH CURRICULUM

Geraldine Ball
Uvaldo H. Palomares

The Human Development Approach designed by Palomares, Ball and others, contains a strategy for providing a learning environment in which students have the opportunity to express feelings and to listen to and interpret the expressions of others by participating in Magic Circle sessions. Simply defined, the Human Development Approach is an effective educational program in the area of developing positive mental health, concentrating on emotional and social development. Suggested topics and techniques for session leaders are provided in the Activity Guides.

In any classroom some students do more talking than others. Those students who contribute little or nothing at all in class participation, or who offer no constructive behaviors, have learned that desultory behavior is as rewarding as participation. Certainly, motivating students to contribute through class participation is a problem, particularly a problem of inexperienced teachers. The program suggested by Palomares and Ball builds a teacher-student structure that helps each student to make a contribution to self as well as to the class; also this program helps each student learn how to listen carefully to self and other participants.

Theoretically, this Human Development Approach assumes the fact that each student has certain human needs such as receiving attention and approval, being listened to and appreciated, and giving and receiving affection. The session concept is based on needs people have to "understand their own emotions and the emotions of others and to improve their ability to relate to their social milieu." The program helps a teacher to create the environment in which students can develop and experience how to relate to these needs in the areas of "(1) Awareness, (2) Mastery—or self confidence, and (3) social interaction."

Interestingly, the techniques and practices employed in adult organizational development activities frequently are directed toward the same human needs. If adults need to learn emotional communication behaviors in order to perform daily work activities effectively and if adults need to participate in problem solving and decision making related to their own needs, Palomares and Ball suggest schools need to use the Human Development Approach as part of the regular instructional program. Too, the program developers emphasize the developmental intent of the program because students learn how to use the interpersonal skills increasingly needed by adults in organizational settings other than classrooms.

The affective environment developed by use of the Human Development Approach is, of course, a conscious attempt to influence the values of students who have not learned how to associate values with human needs; not only feelings may need change, but also priorities. For example, a student who has talked incessantly previously may need to learn how to listen carefully to what others have to say. Although designed primarily for students, the Human Development Approach may be used in any group session which gives attention to emotional needs considered important in communication behavior. The Approach may be used with different age groups because it concentrates on "a series of sequentially developed topics relating to issues everyone faces in living in contemporary western culture."

The Human Development Approach can change the social structure of a school by changing norms, roles or statuses. In this Chapter is an example to point out how a session structure can provide students with an opportunity to take leadership positions while simultaneously learning supportive behavior from a leader because all participants in a Magic Circle session listen to the contributions of all other members. During a session leadership responsibility may be shifted temporarily to a student in the same way that shared leadership is expected in adult meetings. Such a role change creates a temporary reaction by students until they recognize the impact of shared responsibility for learning over the traditional model which is primarily teacher directed.

Palomares and Ball consider students as consumers. This fact places teachers, administrators, and other school personnel in a role different from the traditional role. If school activities are considered as services for student consumers, changes in the social system and formal organizational structure of the school may produce an environment in which students can more effectively and more completely develop both affectively and cognitively. The Human Development Approach paves a way to serve the individual and group needs of maturing students who, as informed adults, will influence the society of

104

tomorrow to become more responsive in shaping the norms which dem-onstrate that people in positions of responsibility, influence, and leadership must model those behaviors which will influence and main-tain a truly positive mental health existence for all members of society.

ABOUT

THE

AUTHORS

GERALDINE BALL   UVALDO H. PALOMARES

Geraldine Ball, M.S., a former classroom teacher, is Director of Curriculum Development at the Human Development Training Institute. She is the co-developer of the Magic Circle and the author of Innerchange. Ms. Ball holds a Master of Science degree in Education from the University of Southern California, and is completing her doctoral work in Humanistic Psychology through the Humanistic Psychology Institute.

Uvaldo H. Palomares, Ed.D., a former classroom teacher and university professor, is President of the Human Development Training Institute. He is a well known public speaker, is co-developer of the Magic Circle, and a contributor to the Innerchange program. Dr. Palomares earned his doctoral degree in Education from the University of Southern California.

The Human Development Training Institute (HDTI) is a people oriented organization which has been publishing educational materials and conducting educator workshops since 1967 and is located in La Mesa, California.

106

THE HUMAN DEVELOPMENT APPROACH

A PREVENTIVE MENTAL HEALTH CURRICULUM

Uvaldo Hill Palomares and Geraldine Ball

If educators could be brainwashed overnight to think of themselves as business people and students as consumers, their relationships with students would probably be radically changed! Producers know that the very existence of any business depends upon its ability to provide a product or service which the consumer personally experiences as needed, desirable, and worth purchasing. Further, that business thrives if it is able to stay in tune with the consumer, refining its product or service in accordance with the consumer's fluctuating tastes and changing needs.

In contrast, many individuals within the educational system seem to forget that the very existence of their employment is dependent upon students, who are the ultimate receivers of *their* products and services. Compared to market production, very little effort is expended by the educational system to ascertain student preferences and needs. Educators, in contrast to producers, spend their energy arbitrarily doling out products and services which are often lacking in relevance, but which students rarely have the opportunity to evaluate. The fact is that the students themselves are evaluated. Though receivers, students do not enjoy the status of consumers because, rather than having a choice, students are viewed as captives within the system. Treatment of students is often impersonal, negative, coercive, and even harsh, and the same legal and social factors which result in educators failing to view students as consumers also contribute to their viewing students as less than complete persons, ignoring students' rights as human beings. The condition of not viewing students as complete persons frequently deteriorates even further to one of not viewing them as persons at all, but rather as objects. As such, students have traditionally been perceived as lacking in the knowledge, ideas, and resources with which to contribute to their own learning process. The responsibility has fallen to educators to impart to students (in a one-way process) the missing knowledge, while students have been traditionally expected to listen, obey, learn, and behave.

THE "MAGIC CIRCLE" AND "INNERCHANGE" PROGRAMS ALTERNATIVES IN EDUCATION

Within the existing educational system, the Human Development Program, created by Uvaldo H. Palomares, Ed.D., Geraldine Ball, M.A., and Harold Bessell, Ph.D., provides an alternative which has the potential of radically changing the learning environment by providing circumstances in which students are listened to and treated as respected consumers for at least a short period of each school day. The Human Development Program systematically takes away the conditions wherein an adult is inclined to overlook the personhood of students and treat students as objects. The Human Development Program has two major subcomponents: The "Magic Circle" for students from preschool through grade six, and "Innerchange" for junior and senior high school students. Both programs are curricular in design and convert a number of educational and psychological theories to multi-faceted processes in which teacher and student (and student and student) daily practice different ways of relating. The curriculum and the process act as avenues by which to enter the individual and shared experience of students and deliberately join that experience with the teaching/learning process, and, in the case of secondary school students, with specific subject areas as well.

Generally stated, the Human Development Program is an affective/confluent educational program in the area of preventive mental health, concentrating on emotional and social development. The Program is designed to give students the opportunity to become involved constructively in developing their own personal effectiveness, self-confidence, and understanding of the dynamics of interpersonal relations.

The Human Development Program systematically incorporates what master teachers do every day to instill responsibility and self-confidence in students. Curriculum is developmental and sequential for each grade level through grade six. The secondary curriculum also is developmental with a suggested sequence which is presented in separate packages for junior high school and senior high school students. In both programs, the scope and sequence of the activities provide experiences for the development of knowledge and skills needed for effective personal adjustment, ability to communicate with others, success in academic endeavors, and other life challenges. In the Innerchange curriculum these activities are focused on contemporary issues such as career education, drug abuse, crime prevention, values exploration, human relations and multi-cultural understanding.

The Human Development Program is based on the concept that (1) positive human interaction can be a very powerful force in making life meaningful for all persons and that (2) a certain amount of structure, or types of structures, can be utilized to guide and enhance the quality of the interactions that take place. For this reason, Magic Circle and Innerchange both follow a very definite structure with respect to overall application.

The vehicle for that structure and the nucleus of the Program is the circle session, often referred to as the "Magic Circle," in the elementary grades. (The name "Magic Circle" was coined by an exuberant child at the end of a particularly heart-warming session when he declared that the circle was just "like magic.")

The circle session consists of a small group of students (usually seven to twelve) who gather with the teacher or student leader to consider and discuss a particular topic or question for a prescribed period of time each day. Each circle session follows a structured format, or process model, which consists of the suggested presentation of content plus a relatively simple but specific set of ground rules governing the behavior of participants. The specific, safe, and accepting format of the Human Development Program circle session allows for spontaneous expression and encourages human beings to relate to one another in such a way that they learn to value one another.

In the Human Development Program circle session students and their teacher daily share thoughts and feelings and discuss behavior through activities directly related to social and emotional development. Communication in the circle session is never coercive or confrontive. An atmosphere of acceptance prevails throughout the twenty- to thirty-minute session and students are encouraged to share genuinely their feelings and to learn to listen and give attention to one another.

Theoretical Bases and Objectives

The Human Development Program circle session *process* is based on certain theoretical assumptions, such as the need for human beings to receive attention, to be listened to, and to understand the reason for doing what they are asked to do. The first of these needs is met during the participation phase of each session, the second is met during the review in which the participants listen reflectively to each other, and the third is met during the cognitive summary phase of each for his or her positive behavior session. These phases will be described in more complete detail later. Each child is reinforced consistently and positively throughout the session for his or her positive behavior by the teacher and by the other children.

Human beings need to be appreciated, to receive approval, and to give and receive affection. These higher needs also are generally met by the circle session process after the group members become comfortable with each other and with the format of the session. At this point, discussions become more meaningful and students visibly begin to "tune in" to, and like themselves and each other, thereby increasing each child's self-esteem and appreciation of others. As the process continues, these human needs continue to be met.

When the *content* of the Human Development Program was being developed, we again turned to theory. We attempted to isolate the qualities or characteristics that individuals possess which we consider to be personally and socially effective. We found that these qualities related to needs all persons seem to have in common, such as the need to understand personal emotions and the emotions of others, and to improve their ability as individuals to relate to

110

their social millieu. At length we refined these needs to three somewhat overlapping categories which we call: 1) Awareness, 2) Mastery—or self-confidence, and 3) Social Interaction. As we developed the Magic Circle materials (an ongoing process) our task was to create and field test topics for circle sessions which directly related to those basic theoretical areas. The results were "jumping off places," "cues," or topics for circle session discussions which relate to important issues that everyone faces in living.

Later, when the content of the Innerchange program was being developed, we found that the same three categories could be seen as equally relevant in the lives of secondary students. Because the secondary school student is involved in the developmental task of establishing personal identity, he or she often asks such questions as "Who am I?" and "What can I do?" We saw these questions (and others like them) as directly related to the growth areas of Awareness and Mastery respectively. We also saw the secondary school student's deep concern for his or her relative success in peer relations as directly related to the category of Social Interaction.

The goals of the Human Development Program are to promote the following in students:

1. improved self-concept
2. a keener awareness and respect for self and others
3. improved skills in interpersonal relationships
4. easy, more effective communication
5. understanding and awareness of one's own emotions and the emotions of other people
6. the understanding that everyone experiences all of the emotions, but each in his or her own way
7. greater skill in the areas of decision making and problem solving
8. increased ability to assert themselves rationally and manage conflicts creatively
9. a conscious willingness and ability to be in charge of their own behavior and lives

Specifically stated with respect to behavior, the Human Development Program attempts to increase a student's ability to

1. articulate thoughts and feelings verbally and feel natural while doing this.
2. listen attentively to others as a positive habit.

3. reflect back to another person what he or she said as a natural part of conversation.
4. increase his or her ability to verbalize an understanding of how thoughts, feelings and behaviors operate in people.

WHO CAN BENEFIT?

The Innerchange program is new. After three years of research, development and field testing by Author Geraldine Ball, the program was first made available in April, 1977. Innerchange is directed primarily toward junior and senior high school students and its field testing has been restricted to that target population. However, because Innerchange addresses a broad range of relevant *human* issues, such as racial and sexual equality, assertiveness, justice, and system change, Innerchange is appropriate to use with any person over the age of eleven, and the program is already being implemented with groups of youth and adults in settings other than the secondary schools.

The Magic Circle program, which was written for elementary school students and has been widely used for over ten years, has been shown through a number of research studies to be effective for a broad range of individuals and groups. The Magic Circle program has been successfully implemented with groups ranging in intelligence from "gifted" to mentally retarded, and has been used very successfully with disturbed and educationally handicapped children, although it was not designed primarily as a treatment program.

School districts which have integrated their students racially have used the Magic Circle as a means of bringing about communication and understanding among the students (Palomares, 1969). Educators who work in bilingual education programs have found the Magic Circle to be helpful in providing students with an opportunity to improve their ability to communicate with others through spontaneous verbal interaction (Saavedra, 1970; Palomares, 1973). Families have adopted the circle session as one way of making optional use of the time individual members can be together. A number of churches have incorporated the program

112

into their own religious education courses (LaChapelle, 1969). Since the Human Development Program relates to the elements of life that human beings have in common, namely feelings, thoughts, behaviors, and living with other humans, the Program's usefulness and appeal are very broad.

As curriculum, the Human Development Program presents a series of sequentially developed topics relating to issues everyone faces who lives in contemporary western culture. The Program capitalizes on the natural desire in people to speak and seek attention, to gain approval and to learn to understand better themselves and their world. Thus, the Human Development Program combines content of interest with a vehicle which affords the participant the opportunity to learn a number of positive social interaction skills in a "here and now" situation. Enough structure is provided to asssure that significant concepts are systematically dealt with in an atmosphere where the ground rules are understood. Yet, unlike many classroom learning situations, spontaneity is a key ingredient. Only the participant who is speaking knows how he or she feels, or what he or she thinks, relative to the topic. Participants are encouraged to speak from their own experience and the comments they make are accepted. No one is probed, criticized or confronted in any way and no one moralizes to anyone else. In this manner, all participants, even those who elect to say nothing, are valued for speaking and/or listening in the session. An atmosphere of cooperation and respect for each individual begins to develop and increases as the group meets each day. Helfat (1973), in describing a Magic Circle in a public school classroom, stated:

> Through such daily experiences in the "Magic Circle"
> . . . children, at a young age, develop social skills and
> sensitivities. They learn to empathize with each other
> and they gain tolerance of each other's foibles. A
> classroom becomes a place to learn about one's self and
> others. (p. 31)

Prevention—Not Therapy

We believe no ceiling exists on mental health. Our society has long been concerned with such matters as pathology, dysfunction, treatments, cures, and crisis intervention. Health has been viewed as the state people are in when they are not visibly sick. Seemingly, we rarely consider the idea that health, like illness, can exist in degrees. The basic purpose of the Human Development Program is to enhance health. The Program does not focus on illness. The Program is neither therapy nor sensitivity training. Rather, the aim of the Human Development Program is to capitalize on each individual's life force to create an environment in which people can become instrumental in their own growth and development.

In 1964, when we began developing the format and writing the materials for the Human Development Magic Circle Program, we started with preschoolers. We decided at the outset that we were interested in creating an approach that would develop positive personal and social skills in human beings when they could learn the skills most easily—in early childhood. We believe that behaviors and attitudes are learned, and that students who feel good about themselves, believe that they can achieve, and show that they want to get involved in the educational program *LEARNED* that attitude. *Somewhere, someone* convinced them that they were okay as persons and that they could learn. A positive educational direction has been set for those young individuals for the rest of their lives.

In his private practice, Harold Bessell reported that many of his adult clients came in with such common problems as feelings of having failed, lack of motivation or sense of direction, confusion, guilt, lack of identity, a sense of alienation, social ineptness, and an inability to get along with other people—whether spouses, bosses, colleagues, or friends. Dr. Bessell generalized that every troubled individual seemed to be (1) unaware of him or herself as a feeling, thinking, behaving individual (and unaware of this triad of functioning in others), (2) lacking in self-confidence and self-respect, or (3) unable to interact effectively with other people. Very often clients had problems in more than one of these areas.

Bessell (1972) stated:

> For most patients, therapy is a painful, expensive, protracted experience that often comes too late ... The damage has been done; pain and guilt have twisted a human life into their own grotesque image. And the therapist must somehow piece this fragile, pain-filled human being back together. Little wonder that therapy is rarely wholly successful. Our skills and

knowledge abound in palliatives, but lasting cures are still rare. Moreover, for every patient we treat, it is an unhappy fact that there are hundreds, even thousands more who desperately need therapy but cannot afford it or, would not be able to find a qualified, let alone effective therapist available to help them.

These are disturbing truths that must perplex and trouble every therapist as he struggles with his responsibilities. They raise vital, nagging questions for all of us. It was in answer to these questions—and the frustration we all feel at the issues they imply— that the Human Development Program was born. (p. 350)

Not all people by the time they are adults have such serious psychological difficulties that they need therapy, but we have found that everyone, no matter how "normal" or even psychologically healthy he or she might be, can always become happier and healthier through participating in activities like a Human Development Program circle session. Everyone needs attention, a chance to speak, to be listened to and to deal verbally with important life issues. As we designed the Program, we were convinced that if people had a different set of experiences as young people, they would grow to be more effective as adults. Negative feelings and attitudes in people are not created by single events, but rather by whole series of small experiences which shape the ways in which people relate to themselves and to the world. Conversely, positive attitudes are formed incrementally by a series of positive experiences. For this reason the Human Development Program was developed sequentially and developmentally and teachers are urged to use the Program daily, or to plan experiences as close to the ideal as possible.

In our schools today many students communicate attitudes such as, "I hate school," "I don't believe in myself," "I can't," and "I won't." But often, only after more serious acting-out behavior begins does the teacher refer these children for psychological services. We, among others today, are saying, "Instead of waiting for problems to occur, train the teachers, or train the counselors to train the teachers, to start with all of the students, systematically providing experiences in which they will learn to feel: "I'm OK," "I'll try," "I think I can!" Counselors who develop in-service training programs for teachers which encourage positive personal interaction in the classroom can reduce the amount of energy spent in remediation later (Palomares and Rubini, 1973).

In Castan's (1973) article, "Alternatives to Corporal Punishment," she described how Stephanie Judson, a young Quaker teacher from Pennsylvania uses the Magic Circle as an antidote for aggression. She stated that:

> Although Quakers are ideologically committed to nonviolence in the external, physical sense, Ms. Judson explains that they often have difficulty dealing with anger and frustration inside themselves. These, she says, are often released in violent language. Not in such threatening language as "I'm going to kill you," but in put-down language.

> Using the "Magic Circle", she has the kids sit around in groups to share experiences that made them feel angry or sad. She doesn't comment on or evaluate these feelings; she simply listens . . . This technique of non-judgmental listening teaches that it's safe to explore feelings. (p. 22)

TOPICS RELATING TO AWARENESS, MASTERY, AND SOCIAL INTERACTION

As was mentioned previously, specific content has been developed for the Human Development Program and field tested with groups of students in the three basic, somewhat overlapping, theoretical categories, or growth areas, of Awareness, Mastery, and Social Interaction. In the elementary school curriculum, each available Activity Guide for use by the classroom teachers or other group leaders provides units or sequentially presented sets of topics, each relating to one of the three areas. The curriculum at the junior high school and senior high school levels contains units, each with specific circle session topics and individual activities, designed to focus students' attention on at least one of the same growth areas. Awareness, Mastery, and Social Interaction, and units and topics relating to them, are further described.

116

Awareness

Awareness is critical to mental health. Aware people do not hide things from themselves. Aware individuals are capable of discriminating between the features and events (feelings, thoughts, dreams, values) that exist in the exterior world and the ones that they experience within themselves. Aware people understand that others feel, think, and behave in ways very similar to their own, but also realize that because individuals process information from the exterior world through unique sets of experiences, their reactions may be quite different. Aware people are in touch with the value of the past and the possibility of the future from a pivotal point anchored firmly in the certainty of the present. Such people order their lives flexibly and effectively on a moment to moment basis. Aware people know who they are and how they function.

Therefore, Awareness is a significant element in the Human Development Program. Activities relating to the three growth areas in the Program—Awareness, Mastery and Social Interaction—have been planned and are presented, in such a way that the objective of increasing awareness in students will result. However, specific units on Awareness are warranted. These specific units, in a direct manner, focus the attention of students on their feelings, thoughts and behaviors—the three cornerstones of human experience.

Often people are aware that they think, although they often underestimate their cognitive capabilities, and they know at varying levels of understanding that people are behaving creatures, but in the area of feelings many individuals lack awareness. For some people, some feelings seem unacceptable if those feelings are negative (anger, jealousy, fear) and undeserved if they are positive (for example, when a person receives a compliment and refuses to accept it). What we hope to demonstrate experientially to students through their daily involvement in the Human Development Program in general, and in the Awareness units in particular, is the fact that all people experience all of the emotions that can be experienced and that emotions cannot be judged right or wrong, good or bad, in a moral sense. Unfortunately, many people do attempt to judge their own and other people's feelings. Sometimes individuals do not acknowledge emotions that do not hold with the image they would like to have of themselves, and some persons will criticize and try to "take away" emotions from others ("Now, don't feel that way. Cut it out right now!").

We believe that behavior may be evaluated, both by oneself and by other people, but feelings simply exist. To try to negate one's own feelings, or to attempt to take away a feeling held by someone else, only compounds the situation, as neuroses, insomnia, ulcers and miscommunication between persons will testify. For this very reason, the feelings of each student, more than the content of his or her remarks, are a focal point and are accepted in every circle session. Rogers stated in *On Becoming a Person* (1961):

> . . . when I can accept another person, which means specifically accepting the feelings and attitudes and beliefs that he has as a real and vital part of him, then I am assisting him to become a person: and there seems to me great value in this. (p. 21)

Thought can be the blueprint for humanity's noblest actions. The works of Socrates, Michelangelo, Shakespeare, Dorothea Dix, Beethoven, and Dr. Ralph Bunche, to name a few, were conceived first in their minds. Conversely, the most destructive actions of human beings were thoughts first. Causes and ideals give meaning to our lives. We can remember things, use logic, make decisions, solve problems, and fantasize to name a few functions of our gift of intellect. This gift separates us from all other life on this planet. Yet we see that many humans use this gift without corresponding responsibility. If we are to progress (or even survive) as a specie, we must begin to realize that our capabilities must be used with consideration for all life.

The Human Development Program, in a unique way, attempts to increase students' awareness that the ability to think is a great power that all people to a greater or lesser extent possess, and that this ability may be used constructively in a multitude of ways. By participating in circle sessions, students will have the opportunity to be more aware of how often they use personally their thought processes to make life meaningful and productive.

By sharing their experiences, students also become exposed to another dimension of awareness. Students begin to realize that other people think, feel, and behave too, not because this fact is pointed out to them, but because they actually experience the thinking, feeling and behaving functions of others in the circle sessions. A sense of the uniqueness of self and others is in this way gradually raised to conscious awareness. If students are going to develop a sense of personal responsibility, they must first be aware of and understand the individuality and the integrity of others, since only such understanding will lead to concern and caring for others. Students will then be more likely to realize that they can never assume that everyone is just exactly like them. The needs, problems, values and preferences of others, whether the individuals involved be one's relatives, neighbors, fellow citizens, fellow inhabitants of the world, or fellow living creatures, must be considered before action is taken.

In the Magic Circle program, a number of units, each including various topics aimed at increasing the awareness of participants in the circle, have been researched and developed at each grade level from preschool through the sixth grade. Awareness units, each with specific circle session topics and supporting activities, are also available in the Innerchange program for junior and senior high school students.

Sample Magic Circle Awareness Topics
An initial topic—preschool and kindergarten:
"I Can Show You Something I Feel Good About"
A topic presented in the 4th week—Level I (first grade):
"Having Mixed Feelings About Something"
A topic presented in the 19th week—Level II
(second grade):
"My Wild Imagination"
A topic presented in the 27th week—Level III
(third grade):
"I Did Something That I Did Not Feel Like Doing"
A topic presented in the 23rd week—Level IV
(fourth grade):
"If I Could Do Anything I Wanted To Do"
A topic presented in the first unit—Level V (fifth grade):
"Something That I Think Is Beautiful"
A topic presented in the fifth unit—Level VI
(sixth grade):
"Who Am I Culturally?"

"Warm Fuzzy" Awareness Topics (Magic Circle)

"On A Warm Summer Day I Feel . . ."
"My Pet" or "If I Had a Pet It Would Be"
"In the Rain I Feel . . ."
"At S set I Feel . . ."
"Little Puppies Make Me Feel . . ."
"A Time I Was Laughing and Couldn't Stop"
"If I Were on the Beach (or Lake, River, etc.) Right Now"
"My Favorite Song Is . . ."
"The Smell of Fresh Baked Bread Makes Me Feel . . ."
"A Gift I Enjoyed Giving"
"The Funniest Movie I've Ever Seen"
"A Nice Experience That I Want to Share"
"When I Look at Trees I Feel . . ."
"Warm Sun on My Body Feels . . ."
"A Friendly Arm on My Shoulder Feels . . ."
"Kittens Make Me Feel . . ."
"A Time When I Felt Happy"
"A Pleasant Surprise"
"A Gift I Liked the Most (That I Received)"
"A Time When I Was Alone and It Felt Good"
"A Dream I Had That Was Nice"

Sample Innerchange Awareness Units

Feelings, Thoughts, and Behavior (junior & senior high)
Dreaming (junior & senior high)
Values (junior & senior high)
Perception (junior & senior high)
Being a Teenager (junior high)
Going Through Those Changes (senior high)
Looking at My Many Selves (junior & senior high)
Heroes, Models, and Villains (junior high)
I Gotta Be Me, You Gotta Be You (junior high)
Feelings Are Facts (junior & senior high)
Misconceptions (senior high)
Authenticity and Facades (senior high)
My Real Self and My Masks (junior high)
Prejudice (senior high)
Reality and Other Realities (senior high)

As the group members discuss the specific topic for the daily session, students begin to realize that everyone can relate to the common ground of the topic, but that each person's response is uniquely his or her own. Since the group process, ensured by adherence to the ground rules, is one of acceptance, not confrontation, each student's response is drawn from his or her own experience. When a student shares what he or she thinks and feels, no one judges the response as a "right" or "wrong" answer.

Mastery

Effective people perceive themselves as being "okay," i.e., they have a healthy degree of self-esteem, self-confidence, and a sense of personal agency. In trying new challenges, effective people do not strongly fear failure. Effective people most likely have experienced success more than failure and probably when these individuals were successful a significant person noted their success and commented on that success to them.

We believe that individuals are more likely to achieve mastery in their endeavors when they have a feeling of mastery about themselves, than when they lack self-confidence. Generally, people who believe in themselves are the ones who continue to succeed and the more these individuals succeed, the more they believe in themselves. Thus, a beneficial cycle is created, giving meaning and joy to the lives of self-confident people and providing them with strength and momentum for meeting the difficult times that are inevitable for all persons.

As noted previously, other people and their responses to what we do play a critical role in whether or not we see ourselves as masterful. If others make us aware that they are taking note of our efforts and comment positively to us when we try, or try and succeed, our awareness increases that we do have energy and capabilities. Conversely, without favorable comment, we are less aware of our capabilities even if we do try things and experience success. This explains why so many brilliant, capable people do not regard themselves as such. Rather, they are painfully aware of their limitations and shortcomings. Our culture has many ways of causing individuals to focus on weaknesses rather than assets and abilities.

In the Human Development Program we call belief in oneself a feeling of "I canness" and our goal in the Mastery sessions is to incrementally imbue each student with this feeling in a systematic fashion. For this reason, the Mastery sessions in the preschool, kindergarten and first grade are unique from those sessions dealing with Awareness and Social Interaction in that the sessions involve the performance of a task. The major purpose for these sessions is to give each child a success experience. *The task itself is not the focus.* Rather, the task is a vehicle set up for the purpose of giving the students *deserved, positive feedback* immediately after their successful performance, at an important time—when their peers are present. When children perform the task, which has been geared to their performance level in order to assure success, the leader comments on the action using the words, *"You can* (carry a tray) all by yourself!"* or *"Can you ever* do things like that!"* The leader also may ask the child's peers to comment on his or her successful performances of the task. The key words are *you can,* and we believe these words are probably the two most important words a child ever hears. (For that matter, they are important for all of us to hear—no matter how old we are.)

Sample Magic Circle Mastery Tasks (for preschool, kindergarten, and first grade)
"I Can Wash My Hands"
"I Can Hop"
"I Know Which Has the Most and Which Has the Least"
"I Can Fit Things in a Box"
"I Can Count"
"I Can Use Colors"

The Mastery sessions at grade levels beyond first grade do not involve the performance of tasks. Nevertheless, older students can profit from hearing the same positive responses from teachers and other significant people as they are observed performing the many social and academic functions which involve them in the classroom and on the playground or campus each day. We intend that as a result of hearing positive commentary about their efforts and receiving the benefits of the circle sessions dealing with Mastery, students who participate in circle sessions and related activities will become more aware of their strengths and less debilitated by knowledge of their weaknesses. For these reasons, the Mastery sessions are planned and presented in such a way that students may become more aware of their competencies and other positive qualities.

We are attempting to help students "get in touch" with their effectiveness. Students are given the opportunity to tell each other about things they have seen each other do that they admired and appreciated, and they are urged to tell the group their accomplishments and successes. They also are given a chance to deal with some of their feelings of frustration and failure, and in so doing they discover that everyone has these feelings to some degree.

Sample Magic Circle Mastery Topics (ages seven to twelve)

Presented in the 5th week—Level II (second grade):
"I Was Able To Get What I Needed"
Presented in the 13th week—Level III (third grade):
"Something I Just Learned How To Do"
Presented in the 27th week—Level IV (fourth grade):
"I Made A Promise and Kept It"
Presented in the third unit—Level V (fifth grade):
"Something I Learned Easily"
Presented in the sixth unit—Level VI (sixth grade):
"I Did It Because It Needed to be Done"

Sample Innerchange Mastery Units (junior & senior high school)

Learning
Creativity
Leading and Following (junior high only)
Authority (senior high only)
Winning and Losing
Succeeding and Falling Short (junior high only)
Success and Failure (senior high only)
Risk-Taking
Handicaps and Limitations
Money, Money, Money
Problem Solving
Decision Making
Accomplishments and Goals
Taking Charge
Bodymind
Careers

The achievement of success, through a feeling of mastery, or "I Canness" is not the only concern of the Human Development Program. History speaks to us of many individuals who were effective and capable and who found great success in their endeavors, however, some of these people achieved success for themselves at the expense of others. Such individuals exercised their abilities and their powers selfishly and irresponsibly. As in our discussions on Awareness and Social Interaction, this vital factor of accepting responsibility is again stressed. By focusing on their positive behaviors and accomplishments, attention is directed toward the internal and external rewards that can be gained from responsible behavior in terms of human enhancement and appreciation.

The structure of the Program, as equitably as possible, attempts to meet the needs of all of the students in the group. Everyone who wants one, gets a turn. Everyone is heard. Everyone's feelings are accepted. Comparisons and judgments are not made. The circle is *not* another competitive arena, but is guided by a *spirit of cooperation.* As Bessell (1972) stated: "The day's fringe lesson—there need be no losers in order to have winners in a group." (p. 361)

Therefore, an important component of the Human Development Program is that cooperative wheels are set in motion. We believe that when students practice fair, respectful, non-competitive interaction with each other, they will benefit greatly from the experience and will be likely to employ naturally these responsible behaviors in other life situations. The aim of the Human Development Program is not to participate in producing a masterful, but limited, person; rather we hope to help students become responsibly competent.

Social Interaction

Relating effectively with other people is a challenge we all face, and that challenge presents itself continuously throughout our lives. Most of us experience varying degrees of anxiety and frustration in at least a portion of our relationships with others. Accurate, meaningful communication between people is complex and difficult to achieve. Yet some individuals appear to be consistently effective in their personal and social interaction. These people seem to be capable of perceiving the moods of others. They are sensitive to more than one level of communication, and are able to process non-verbal as well as verbal messages. Effective communicators express their own thoughts and feelings clearly, and they also say and do things which seem to facilitate the communication of others. Such people are aware not only of how others affect them, but also of the effects their own words and behaviors have on others and they accept responsibility for their choices.

According to Harvey Jackins, in his book *The Human Side of Human Beings* (1972), every person is inherently intelligent, zestful and capable of loving, cooperative relationships with others. With respect to this third characteristic, Jackins stated:

> This relationship seems to consist precisely of enjoying *affection to* another person, enjoying *affection from* another person, enjoying *communication* with another person, and enjoying *cooperation* with another person. (p. 27)

> These (behaviors) seem to constitute the essential human nature. All the rest of human behavior and feeling except these three inate characteristics and their results, is acquired, is *not* inherent, is the result of something having gone wrong. (p. 28)

Jackins continued to explain that what goes wrong is that we get hurt and these hurts affect our intelligence, our zest for living and our relationships with others. We find it difficult to accept, or listen to, or cooperate with each other because all of us have been hurt many times and in many ways. We then have great difficulty liking, trusting and sometimes even respecting others and they have the same difficulties with us. Our social interactions thereby suffer and we do not enjoy each other as we could potentially. Logically, the next question is, "What can we do about this situation?"

Students with whom we work deal with other people every day—their peers and significant adults. These students need positive interpersonal experiences and information in the social realm in order to offset prior difficulties and to build healthy relationships with other people. Yet, as Carl Rogers (1973) pointed out in his book, *Becoming Partners,* the educational system has largely failed, in any systematic way, to meet the need of students to understand and get along with other people.

Students who are surrounded by people who will give them attention in the form of positive interpersonal experiences are fortunate. A highly desirable situation is for teachers and other adults to be models of healthy, responsible interpersonal behavior in their relationships with students. Students who are listened to frequently, and whose feelings are accepted, are likely to learn, over a period of time, how to listen to and accept others.

In a deliberate way, the Human Development Program has been designed so that these basic experiences in effective communication will occur for at least twenty or thirty minutes each day in the lives of the students who participate in circle sessions. The Program attempts to promote the positive qualities that are *inherent,* as Jackins claimed, in all of us. Through the Program's format, process, and content, students are allowed to practice positive modes of communication which we have later seen them transfer to other situations.

The units on Social Interaction attempt to bring the fundamental issues in interpersonal transactions and communications to the student's awareness. Students are given the opportunity to discuss what goes into a relationship that makes it a friendly, caring, trusting one, and they also examine some of the problems that commonly occur in relationships. The focus in circle sessions is on *how* particular behaviors affect the emotions of other people, on the need for flexibility in complex interactions such as problem solving, and on the value of open communication.

Frances Castan (1973) has quoted Norman Newberg, Director of the Affective Education Program in the School District of Philadelphia, as stating: "We've a Sunday School idea of how people should ultimately behave, but no one defines or describes the intermediate steps (p. 27)." The Social Interaction topics which concern "nitty gritty" aspects of human involvement are presented in sequence in order to develop and nurture an understanding of those intermediate steps.

Sample Magic Circle Social Interaction Topics

Presented in the 15th week in preschool and kindergarten, and stressing cooperation:
"I Can Pick Up Blocks With You"

126

Presented in the 13th week—Level I (first grade):
"Somebody Did Something That I Liked"
Presented in the 16th week—Level II (second grade):
"I Did Something That Somebody Liked"
Presented in the 8th week—Level III (third grade):
"Somebody Did Something That I Did Not Like"
Presented in the 16th week—Level IV (fourth grade):
"I Made Somebody Do Something He/She Did Not
Want To Do"
Presented in the second unit—Level V (fifth grade):
"How I Show Someone That They Can Trust Me"
Presented in the seventh unit—Level VI (sixth grade):
"I Got Some Help I Didn't Want"

Sample Innerchange Social Interaction Units (junior &
senior high school)

Communication
Trust
Helping (junior high only)
The Helping Relationship (senior high only)
Friendship
Culture
Influence
Assertiveness
Responsibility
Being In and Being Out (junior high only)
Inclusion and Exclusion (senior high only)
Conflict Management
Sex Roles
Pairing
Parenthood (senior high only)
Justice
Changing the System
Love (senior high only)
Reaching Out

THE TEACHER'S ROLE BROUGHT INTO FOCUS

The importance of the role of the teacher in the educational
process cannot be underestimated. In evolving the Human
Development Program, we wanted to develop and include a number
of valuable features, and one of the first of these was a study of the

127

characteristics of a group of teachers referred to as "teacher-artists." Almost everyone can remember the one teacher who stands out as having been different from all the others. You may remember one from your own schooling, or you may have heard about one from a friend who remarked, "I had this one teacher I really liked! Oh, she made us work, but all the kids liked her. Boy! We learned more from her than all the others put together!" These relatively rare teachers had an art, a different way of relating to students. In studying this select group, we extracted from their natural behaviors some common elements that might be taught systematically to all teachers. Some of these were as follows:

1. Showing a desire to encourage students to speak about their feelings and ideas as a valid part of the learning process.

2. Giving careful attention to the feelings and thoughts students express and acceptance of them.

3. Having an ability to set a cooperative, rather than a competitive atmosphere, in the classroom.

4. Concentrating their energy in reinforcing positive behavior.

5. Having patience.

6. Showing a characteristic of *expecting* students to learn, based on high esteem for each individual and on a realistic knowledge of each student's growing capabilities.

These behaviors are some which teachers must practice in order to conduct a "bona-fide" Human Development Program circle session. Most teachers incorporate a portion of these behaviors in their daily classroom teaching, but our ulterior motive" was to have teachers begin using positive behavior patterns in which they would practice all these behaviors. We hoped that a "rub off" effect would occur and that these behaviors would gradually become more and more natural to teachers and be common operating procedures for them throughout other activities involving students. Reports from a number of school districts using the program indicate that this has indeed been happening (Elbert, 1970).

Leading the Circle Session

The Magic Circle Activity Guides in a detailed fashion outline the exact procedures to be used in leading the circle session. Similarly, the Innerchange Leader's Manual gives specific suggestions for initiating circle sessions in the classroom, as well as information regarding leadership of the circle session. Procedures are described in detail, and include such specifics as suggestions for questions to ask in each session, and suggestions for how to deal with certain behaviors and incidents that might occur. A statement relating to the general responsibilities involved in leading the session is presented.

The leader's first responsibility is to set a warm, personal tone in each session. An attitude of seriousness blended with enthusiasm conveys the idea to students that this is a potentially interesting and meaningful activity. In the initial session, and at appropriate intervals, the leader goes over the ground rules for the circle sessions with the students. These rules are as follows:

1. Each person may have a turn to speak if he or she wishes, taking only his or her fair share of the time.

2. Everyone will listen to the person who is speaking, without any interruptions, and will accept the speaker's feelings by not confronting him or her in any way.

3. Each person will stay in his or her own space.

4. Destructive behavior such as coercing someone to speak, probing, interpreting or making "put-down" remarks will not be accepted or allowed. (Put-downs make any group experience unsafe. No matter who is put down, any put-down means we are all vulnerable. If someone laughs, all must be able to share the fun or the atmosphere is unsafe. When silence feels comfortable, it is safe.)

To begin each activity, the leader reminds the students of the topic for the session and clarifies this topic if needed, in order to help the students think of something that they could share that is relevant to that topic. As each student has his or her turn to participate verbally in the session, the leader models good listening.

129

When the student finishes his or her statement, the leader first asks open-ended questions of the student in order to elicit more self-expression if the student has not said much. If the student has not told about the feelings he or she had with respect to his or her statement, the leader asks the student what feelings were experienced. Appreciation is expressed to students after they participate.

The students may ask each other questions during this phase of the session, but the leader has the job of allowing no probing, interpretation, or confrontation. The leader tactfully brings the group back to the focus if digressions occur.

Whatever ideas or feelings a student expresses in the session are accepted, with the exception of destructive or derogatory remarks. Students also are urged not to name names of family members or other people in the session. We are interested in each other's personal feelings and ideas, not information about each other's homes or families that "are none of our business." If a student strays somewhat from the topic, this is accepted. Again, this behavior is modeled by the leader of the session who demonstrates that differences in the feelings group members have are natural and are to be expected. The group leader never moralizes or coerces a student to speak in the session if he or she does not want to do so.

As students become more comfortable with the circle session format, the leader allows them to take increased responsibility in the session. When the group is ready, student leadership training is initiated. Beginning with grade five, groups of students may reach the point where they are meeting independently each day with student leaders who alternate with the teacher in taking full leadership responsibility of ongoing sessions, thus allowing the adult leader to work with other groups of students as well. (The rationale for student leadership will be presented subsequently in this Chapter.)

Once or twice during the activity or at the end, when every student who wishes to participate has had a chance to do so, the leader conducts a review of what has been shared by each person who spoke. The leader names a student who participated and calls on a volunteer to tell that student what he or she related, being sure to repeat the feelings as well as the content. In this way motivation for developing effective listening skills becomes a strong force in each student. As the sessions progress, students become increasingly proficient listeners.

By way of a summary or culmination for each session, the leader asks one or more questions of the students requiring them to think in a cognitive manner of the possible lessons and insights that they may have gained from this affective experience. Often, meaningful discussions result from the presentation of the summary questions, but the main purpose is to give the students something to think about. The leader is careful to allow the students to answer the questions themselves, and not to supply the answers for them. The leader's objective is to present experiences for them, and questions to them, that will help them to become inner directed, rather than outer directed, having a sense of commitment to the conclusions and courses of action that they decide upon in their own minds.

Everyone who leads circle sessions has his or her own personal style. There is no perfect way to do it. Leaders develop their own styles as they work with the Program. The new leader should think of him/herself as a novice for the first year. Human Development circle sessions are challenging. The sessions require energy and practice but, like almost everything that takes hard work, they bring great rewards.

Transcript of a Minimally Edited Tape Recording of an Actual Circle Session with Fifth and Sixth Graders Led by Their Teacher

Preliminary and Closing Remarks by Geraldine Ball

(From Magic Circle Activity Guide)
Level VI

The topic for this session is "How I Would Solve Someone Else's Problem," which is presented in the final Mastery unit of the Level VI Activity Guide, entitled, "Disappointments, Problems and Decision-Making." Briefly stated, the objectives of this session were to provide opportunities for the children (1) to tell about how they were able to see solutions for the problems other people had, (2) to discuss the feelings of the people involved in each situation, including their own, and (3) to discuss why it is easy so often for us to solve someone else's problem and hard to solve our own.

The group of twelve children who took part in this session consisted of five fifth graders and seven sixth graders. The students were led by their teacher, who had been conducting circle sessions with each of her classes on a regular basis for five years.

Ms. Blakemore:	Yesterday in our circle we talked about problems that we had that we were able to find solutions to. Today we're going to be talking about "How I Would Solve Someone Else's Problem." I'm sure that all of you have known somebody at one time or another who had a problem; somebody here at school, somebody at church, at home . . . any place where you get together with people. And they may have told you about their problem and maybe you said to yourself . . . "Gee! Why is there a problem? There's a very easy solution to that problem." Possibly you tried to tell them how to solve their problem. If this has ever happened to you, would you like to tell the rest of the group about it?
Larry:	I remember one day somebody in my family couldn't find her cigarettes and I told her I knew where she put them. I told her to look in the basement or something like that and then she looked and they wasn't there, and I finally told her where they was. I told her to look under her dresser.
Ms. Blakemore:	And did she find them?
Larry:	Yeah.
Ms. Blakemore:	Can you remember the feelings that she seemed to have when she couldn't find what she wanted?
Larry:	She thought I had them.
Mr. Blakemore:	She was blaming you.
Larry:	'Cause I'm always hiding something on her.
Ms. Blakemore:	Did she have some feelings that you could get a hold of?

132

Larry:	Yeah.
Ms. Blakemore:	What were they?
Larry:	Kind of . . . funny feelings.
Ms. Blakemore:	They were funny?
Larry:	Once she'd be half playing, then she'd be serious . . .
Ms. Blakemore:	Oh . . . first of all she was going to play about it, and when it got to be too long, she got angry? How did you feel when you finally told her where they were?
Larry:	I felt mad. I wanted her to kick the habit.
Ms. Blakemore:	You were trying to help her, and she wasn't going to kick the habit. Okay . . . that's good.
Gary:	I have a question. Did she ever quit smoking?
Larry:	No.
Henry:	Was you trying to make her stop smoking?
Larry:	Yeah.
Gary:	Oh . . . the time me and someone else was shopping and she couldn't find what she wanted because she wanted to buy some new tennis shoes and she went in the wrong department. The tennis shoes were way in the back of the store and she was looking all over the front and she couldn't find them and I asked her, "Why don't you look . . .uh . . .why don't you go . . ." and she says, "Shut up Gary" and "Be quiet" . . . and then she just said "I wonder where them shoes are?" So I said,"Why don't you look in the back?" And she says, "Shut up" and then we was almost towards the back and she saw the tennis shoes and I told her, but she says "Shut up" or I was going to get in trouble.

133

Ms. Blakemore:	How did she seem to be feeling about the problem?
Gary:	She felt angry.
Ms. Blakemore:	She was angry?
Gary:	Uh, huh.
Ms. Blakemore:	What feelings did you have then?
Gary:	When she told me to shut up?
Ms. Blakemore:	Uh, huh.
Gary:	I felt upset because she really wouldn't let me tell her.
Ms. Blakemore:	It's not always so easy to help somebody solve their problem.
Larry:	Like my grandmother; she was looking for the sewing machine and it was right under her nose . . . you know . . . the towels and my pajama bottoms were on top of it, and she couldn't see it. And then know what I did? I just said, "Why don't you look under my pants, they may be under there."
Ms. Blakemore:	Okay. How did grandma feel?
Larry:	She felt mad.
Ms. Blakemore:	She was mad. How did you feel when she was angry?
Larry:	I felt like I was going to get my head cut off.
Ms. Blakemore: Gary:	Uh, huh. Gary? Well, when my great grandmother didn't want to go the hospital . . . and me and my mother . . . we got upset. We had a talk about it and then I talked to her and asked her, "How do you think it makes us feel about . . . about . . ." And the next day when I came home from school she was at the hospital . . .
Ms. Blakemore:	Okay. So what you're saying is: your great grandmother was sick and she wouldn't do anything about it.

Gary:	Uh, huh.
Ms. Blakemore:	And you wanted her to.
Gary:	Yep.
Ms. Blakemore:	And you actually talked to her about it yourself?
Gary:	Yeah, while mother was at work.
Ms. Blakemore:	Do you remember, kind of, what you said to your great grandmother?
Gary:	Yeah, I said, "It's making me unhappy about you being sick out here and you won't go to the hospital so the doctors can do something about it."
Ms. Blakemore:	Uh, huh. How did you feel when she finally went?
Gary:	I felt happy.
Ms. Blakemore:	And she is okay?
Gary:	(Nods.) I have another one. When me and my friend . . .we went to the pool hall to play some pool and he didn't have no money. All he had was a dollar. To play pool it costs a dollar and I had some money in my . . . in my . . . piggy bank . . . and we went back home and got it and then he wanted to buy something and he didn't have enough money and then I said, "Do you want some of my money?" "Do you want some money?" He said "No", and he ran out of money. And then I asked him, "Do you want some money?" and he say "No." And so we was almost about . . . about twelve blocks from home and the car ran out of gas . . . and I said, "You want some money?" He said "No." "We'll just walk home." And we started walking and he said, "Let me have the money now," because he got tired of walking *(Laughs)*.
Ms. Blakemore:	How far away were you from home then?
Gary:	About five blocks.

135

Ms. Blakemore:	What kind of feelings was your friend having? He really had several problems, not just one. How was he feeling about them?
Gary:	Angry. He didn't want anybody telling him nothing.
Ms. Blakemore:	Probably felt a little foolish then . . . All those things happening to him.
Gary:	Yeah.
Ms. Blakemore:	Allen?
Allen:	Yeah. One day my father . . . he was looking for his belt. He couldn't find it. And I helped him. It was hanging on his hook.
Ms. Blakemore:	What was your father's feeling when he was looking for his belt?
Allen:	He was mad.
Ms. Blakemore:	How did you feel when you were able to supply the belt?
Allen:	Happy.
Ms. Blakemore:	Any other questions for Allen? Henry?
Henry:	Somebody in my family lost his keys to the car and he had locked the car and the keys was in the ignition . . . and then my mother had a pair of keys to the car and she couldn't find them because she had left them in the door. Then I went out there and got them.
Ms. Blakemore:	What door did your mother leave those in?
Henry:	Front door. Then I went and got the keys . . . opened the car door and got those keys . . . then I locked the door again and brought the keys in. I put my mother's keys back in the door and I put the other keys on the dresser so she would see them. Then she went there and she said, "There the key is. I wonder where they've been?" I said, "They was in the car." She said, "How did you get them?" I said, "I got the keys off the front door" and she went to the front door and there they was.

Ms. Blakemore:	How did you suppose . . . just try to pretend that you own that car and you just got out and you slammed the door and you looked and there are the keys still hanging inside.
Henry:	But we got a thing . . . you know like you open the door and the key is down there and it makes a sound and she didn't hear it. She shut the door.
Ms. Blakemore:	How do you suppose she felt when she did that? How would you feel if it happened to you?
Henry:	Feel like kicking the car.
Ms. Blakemore:	. . . like kicking the car. Would anybody else have a different feeling than that?
Tony:	I'd be mad at myself.
Gary:	I'd say to myself, "You're stupid."
Ms. Blakemore:	Yeah! I . . . think I'd be with you. I'd think, "Boy, did I do a stupid thing." Especially if it makes that noise so that it warns you that the keys are still in there.
Henry:	She left all the keys in there.
Ms. Blakemore:	How'd you feel when you were the one that could help?
Henry:	I felt all right.
Mr. Blakemore:	Yes. It's an all right feeling to be helpful. Kenneth?
Kenneth:	My father lost his cufflinks and I knew where they were. And then . . . my father said, "You don't know where they are . . ." I said, "Yes, I do." He had been looking everywhere for them. And I said, "Dad, I know where they are." He said, "No you don't" and he kept looking for them and I said, "Dad, let me find them." He said, "No." Then, he kept on looking for them and he finally said, "Okay, you can go look for them." They was in his dresser drawer.

137

Ms. Blakemore:	Did you have any feelings inside when he kept telling you, "No, don't look for them?" . . . and yet you knew where they were and he was jumping all around the house trying to find them?
Kenneth:	He was mad.
Ms. Blakemore:	Where do you feel that kind of anger when it . . . when somebody is just really stopping you from doing something? Where do you feel the anger?
Kenneth:	Right here *(points to throat)*.
Ms. Blakemore:	In your throat? Anybody ever feel it in their stomach? Allen does.
Allen:	Your stomach twitters.
Ms. Blakemore:	It seems to get tight or something . . . I don't know. It does funny things . . . Kenneth?
Kenneth:	Well, my mother lost her twenty dollar bill and I gave her mine and she got happy.
Ms. Blakemore:	Okay. She lost it?
Kenneth:	Yeah. And I gave her mine from out of my piggy bank.
Ms. Blakemore:	And how do you think she felt when you were willing to give up your twenty dollars to . . .
Kenneth:	Happy.
Ms. Blakemore:	Gary?
Gary:	Well, my mother had a flat tire on her car and she needed ten dollars to get a new tire and she had the money saved for the rent and she didn't want to use it so I had fifty dollars in my bank account and I told my mother she could use it.
Ms. Blakemore:	Gee. Fifty dollars.
Gary:	Yeah. My father gave it to me to put in the bank.
Ms. Blakemore:	You got more than I thought . . . And how did your Mom feel when you helped her out?

Gary:	Felt happy . . . And now I got eighty dollars in the bank.
Ms. Blakemore:	How would you like to make some nice old lady happy?
	(Uproarious laughter)
Ms. Blakemore:	Steve?
Steve:	Once me and my friend went to the store and he didn't have any money to buy a soda so I said, "Are you going to buy the soda?" And he said, "I don't have enough money." So I gave him the money so he could buy a soda.
Ms. Blakemore:	Looking at you right now I'd say you still feel good about it . . . Yeah . . . That's a real neat thing to do and you're still grinning over it. How'd your friend feel?
Steve:	Happy.
Ms. Blakemore:	How'd you know?
Steve:	He thanked me.
Ms. Blakemore:	Gary . . .
Gary:	Me and Allen and my mother and my father went to Disneyland. It was about . . . about 11:30 and me and Allen went into the haunted house and I told Allen that . . . that as soon as we get down to almost at the end . . . they're going to have this big old mirror and you're going to look in the mirror and maybe there's going to be a ghost sitting beside us. Then I said, "Move over" and we was going down the hill and Allen says "I don't see no big mirror . . . I don't see no ghost in here" . . . I say, "You can't see it when you're looking in the seat. You've got to look at the mirror." He says, "I don't see no mirror" and then when we got right down the ramp, I said, "Look Allen," and he said "I don't see nothing," and then the ghost got in the car with us and then Allen says, "Get out of the way. Get out of here." And I said to Allen, "It isn't real."
	(laughter)

139

Kenneth:	He thought the ghost was real?
Gary:	Yeah, and I told him, "It's not real," and he said, "Yes it is . . . Get out of here! Get out of here!" and I showed him that it wasn't real and Allen said, "Oh, it's not real" and then we came to another mirror and we looked in and the ghost was gone.
	(laughter)
Ms. Blakemore:	It was Allen's problem?
Gary:	Yeah . . . it was in the haunted house. Before that we started rolling and some ghost stood up and we seen this candle lighter . . . this big thing like the old candles with all those candles on it . . . four candles . . . We seen it moving in there. That's what you guys gonna see when you go over there.
Kenneth:	A chandelier?
Gary:	No. You know them things that they hold like they got candles on it . . . but it got candles on it.
Kenneth:	I know, That's a chandelier . . . like a chandelier.
Gary:	No. You know, like they have in "Dark Shadows." We seen the thing moving by itself — moving back and forth . . . and we seen this coffin and there was somebody with green hair trying to get out, saying, "Let me out of here! Let me out of here!" They was nailed to the coffin.
Kenneth:	It was a piece of wood or something . . .
Ms. Blakemore:	This problem sounded like it was fun. It was kind of a fun problem.
Gary:	It was! Allen said, "Get me out of here! Get me out of here!"
	(laughter)

140

Henry:	Allen, was you scared?
Allen:	Yeah. And then we were going like this (makes hand motions) . . .
Gary:	And then we seen this thing when we went into the Pirate's Cruise. We seen these skeleton bones and we saw this coffee pot and the lid opened up and the skeleton came out and said, "Ooooooooooooh" and Allen say . . . "Ahhhhhh."
	(laughter)
Ms. Blakemore:	Larry . . .
Larry:	One time somebody I know couldn't find her keys and I didn't want her to go. She was going to go to Los Angeles — to Santa Maria — around there. I didn't want her to go because everybody was supposed to go to my friend's house to spend the night. But I didn't want to because I wanted to watch the "Six Million Dollar Man," but he didn't have a TV. So I hided the keys. Then she said, "Where are the keys?" She asked everybody, "Where are the keys?" and I just kept going like that, "Ummm, ooh, umm" (humming). And then she found them in my back pocket.
Ms. Blakemore:	In your back pocket? This is a problem that you created for her, right?
Larry:	That's true.
Ms. Blakemore:	Okay. When she found those keys, what did she do?
Larry:	She say, "Come on, come on." *(Yanks own hair to demonstrate).*
Ms. Blakemore:	Uh, huh. She pulled you by your hair? Henry?
Henry:	How did she feel when she felt them in your back pocket?
Larry:	She felt kind of happy and kind of mad. She was mad because I hided them and happy that she found them.

Ms. Blakemore:	Yeah. She had the two feelings.
Henry:	Did you get to go?
Larry:	No.
Henry:	Stayed home?
Larry:	Everybody did.
Ms. Blakemore:	Do you mean that it worked and everybody stayed home?
Larry:	All she went was to Penney's to buy my sister some shoes and came back.
Gary:	How did she know they was in your back pocket or how did she find them in your back pocket?
Larry:	She saw them . . . you know that blue thing? She found one of them.
Henry:	Was it jingling in your pocket?
Larry:	No. It was just sticking out.
Ms. Blakemore:	Okay. Earl?
Earl:	One day I parked my bike in the driveway and my father ran over it with his truck. And I talked to him that night in the den about fixing my bicycle and he said I'd have to raise up half of the money. *(Laughs.)* So I sold some scrap iron.
Larry:	Some what?
Earl:	Scrap iron.
Ms. Blakemore:	Did you get the new bike?
Earl:	Yeah.
Ms. Blakemore:	So this was *your* problem. You had a scrunched bike and you needed to get half the money to get a new one. Okay, so when your Dad said to you, "Okay Earl, now you're going to have to save up half the money for that bike," how did you feel?
Earl:	I didn't think I could.

142

Ms. Blakemore:	You felt kind of hopeless . . . like it was a hopeless task for you to try to do?
Earl:	Yeah.
Ms. Blakemore:	Where did you get the idea for the scrap iron?
Earl:	My father had it. He gave it to me a long time ago and I never put it to use.
Ms. Blakemore:	Hmmm. Okay. Is there anybody who thinks that they can go around and remember what the different people have said? Okay, Henry?
Henry:	First, Larry said about the cigarettes . . . when he hid them under the chest . . . I forgot . . . under the dresser. And she asked him where they was and he told her that he forgot. But he told her he didn't know where they was. And then . . . *(long pause)* . . .
Ms. Blakemore:	Do you remember why he was doing that?
Henry:	Yeah, trying to help her kick the habit.
Ms. Blakemore:	Okay what about somebody else? Do you remember what they said?
Henry:	Oh, yeah. Gary. When he said about someone and him. They went to the . . . went shopping to get some tennis shoes and she wouldn't let him tell her where they was — they was in the back and he told us he had mixed . . . bad feelings about it.
Ms. Blakemore:	Can you remember anybody else? . . . *(pause)* . . . Do you want to pass it on to somebody else?
Henry:	Yeah.
Gary:	When Henry said about how someone left his car keys in the car and about Larry. He wanted to go with somebody and he had to stay. And Larry said about his sister . . . getting tennis shoes.
Ms. Blakemore:	Allen, do you remember what Steve told us?
Henry:	Oh. I know!

143

Ms. Blakemore:	Okay, Henry.
Henry:	Yeah. When his friend didn't have enough money for a soda and he give it to him. And Gary helped his great grandmother and his mother to buy a new tire and Kenneth gave his Mom his twenty dollar bill.
Ms. Blakemore:	Tony?
Tony:	When Allen went to Disneyland he was scared of the ghost. And Kenneth . . . when his father lost his cufflinks and he helped him find them. And Earl helped himself with his own problem by selling scrap iron to raise half the money he needed to get a new bike.
Ms. Blakemore:	That's right. You all did very well on that. Okay, now I'm going to ask you two questions. The first one. Think about it before you answer. Think about it for just a couple of seconds: *Why do you think it's so easy for us when we don't have a problem to know how to solve somebody else's problem? Why is that always so easy?* Henry?
Henry:	'Cause sometimes they have easy problems.
Ms. Blakemore:	Okay. Sometimes the problem is easy.
Larry:	'Cause you know where they are.
Henry:	You know what they're talking about.
Ms. Blakemore:	You understand their problem. Gary?
Gary:	It's easier when it's not *your* problem. You can find an easier solution for it, but when it is your problem it gets kind of hard. You have to find somebody to solve your problem.
Ms. Blakemore:	You just answered my second question. I was going to ask you, *why is it sometimes very hard to figure out a solution for your own problem?*
Gary:	You have to find somebody to settle all your problems 'cause it's very hard.

144

Ms. Blakemore:	How come then Larry and you, Gary, could have the very exact same problem and you *(looks at Gary)* can tell him exactly what to do . . . you know how to take care of his . . .
Gary:	Yeah, but I couldn't do it myself.
Ms. Blakemore:	Why is this?
Gary:	I don't know . . .
Ms. Blakemore:	What happens?
Larry:	You get lost—minded.
Steve:	You lose something.
Ms. Blakemore:	You what, Steve?
Steve:	You lose something. You forget where it is. Then they might know where it's at.
Ms. Blakemore:	Yeah, but what happens to us when we really have a problem? What happens inside?
Gary:	You lose your mind. Your conscience. You forget about it.
Larry:	You get . . . You get . . .
Tony:	You're just trying to help.
Ms. Blakemore:	Okay. What was that, Larry?
Larry:	You get anxious.
Ms. Blakemore:	Right. You get more anxious about your own problems—the other guy . . .
Henry:	When it's your own problem—*forget it.*
Gary:	You tell them about their problems but when you want to settle your own problems you don't remember how you settled the other person's problem.
Ms. Blakemore:	Does your anger ever interfere?
Gary:	Yes, sometimes.

Ms. Blakemore:	Dan, how about you? Do you find it difficult to solve your own problems?
Dan:	Yeah.
Ms. Blakemore:	How many have you had lately?
Dan:	Four.
Ms. Blakemore:	You had four? Could you tell us about one?
Dan:	When I couldn't find my ball. We was at the park, me and Steve yesterday and then Allen and me started to play catch. I threw my ball on the ground and I went all over everywhere looking for it, and I asked a friend if she see somebody get it. And she said, "Yes, it's in my purse."
Ms. Blakemore:	She had it in her purse?
Dan:	Uh, huh . . . my little sister went and got it.
Ms. Blakemore:	Okay. While you were looking for it, what kind of feelings were you having?
Dan:	I was mad 'cause I couldn't find it.
Ms. Blakemore:	Okay. Your anger, then, was interfering with solving the problem and I think really that's what happens; we get so frustrated and we get . . . What was your word? *(Looks at Larry.)*
Larry:	Anxious.
Ms. Blakemore:	We get anxious. We're upset.
Gary:	We get disappointed. It seems impossible.
Ms. Blakemore:	Yeah. It just seems impossible. It makes it much harder for us to think of good solutions to help ourselves, it's always easier to help the other guy.
Gary:	Yeah, to help the other guy.
Ms. Blakemore:	Well, our time is up. I sure enjoyed this circle. Thanks for doing such a good job of talking and listening.

146

Critique of the Session by Ms. Blakemore

Participating in a Human Development Program circle session is extremely enjoyable. The program helps all of us to understand each other better and our shared experiences during a school year become much more significant.

While I led this session I kept in mind the following specific objectives:

1. to give the children the experience of identifying the problems that others face,

2. to allow the children to recognize that they can help in solving the problems of others,

3. to give the children the opportunity to become aware of how others may feel when they have a problem,

4. to help the children to recognize how they feel when they can assist someone else with a problem, and

5. to help the children to realize that when it's not their problem they are not as emotionally affected as the one who has the problem.

I feel that the children stayed with the topic quite well and enjoyed discussing it. There was a lot of humor going on that was not picked up in the transcript. Unfortunately, the non-verbal techniques that I used in leading the session, which are very important, weren't picked up either. For example, I will often put my hand on the knee of a child who appears to be distracted. Or I will place my arm around the child who rarely speaks or perhaps has just shared for the first time.

I don't usually ask a child to share after I have asked the children to review what was said in the session, however, Dan rarely shares during a session and he was ready to do so. Since I really wanted him to have a turn, I called on him at the end of this session when he looked ready, despite the unusual timing.

To critique myself as the leader, I believe that I paraphrased and responded fairly well in most instances. I feel that I repeated

147

what the children said a little too often perhaps, but I was doing it for the benefit of the tape in case the children's words did not come over well. I tried to give positive reinforcement, but was sometimes judgmental in my responses. I do try to avoid this, but sometimes evaluative remarks just slip out.

In general, I believe that the objectives for this session were attained. The transcript shows the wide variety of responses that the children produce. The transcript also shows that the children are enthusiastic about, and enjoy participating in, the program very much.

Critique by Geraldine Ball of the Session

This Magic Circle session came across to me as a very dynamic, heartwarming and enjoyable activity that was meaningful for everyone involved. I was impressed by the responses that the children made and with the skill with which the session was led. The responses of the children were particularly significant when one considers that a number of these children were extremely reluctant to speak at all about anything when they entered the class at the beginning of the school year. In this session they were very involved, sharing their experiences and feelings, listening attentively and asking questions of one another about their feelings. The children told about a variety of experiences that related to the topic. In many cases children related incidences in which they successfully helped the person who had the problem, and in others children stated openly that they were instrumental in *causing* some of the problems they talked about. These children demonstrated awareness of their own behavior and a lack of reticence to speak openly and honestly in the group.

Some of the skills demonstrated by the leader of the circle session were as follows:

1. Stating the topic in such a way that continuity of meaning from prior sessions was explicit and expectancies for the present session were clear.

2. Reflecting verbally ("mirroring" and paraphrasing) to the children what she heard them say.

148

3. Asking relevant questions, focusing mainly on feelings and eliciting full expression.

4. Demonstrating the ability to identify and laugh with the children.

5. Keeping the session moving in a tactful but efficient manner.

6. Skillfully culminating the activity by asking the questions that sparked the children to discuss energetically the intellectual component of their session and to come up with insightful statements and new vocabulary relating to its meaning.

Suggestions which I would make are as follows:

1. Encourage the children in the review phase of the session to address the feelings that were reported during the participation phase, rather than just the experience.

2. Abolish all evaluative remarks ("okay," "that's good," "right") as responses to the experiences and feelings reported.

Evaluation

Evaluating the session. No matter what happens in a circle session, without the following two elements, it is really not a Human Development circle session:

1. Everyone gets a turn who wants one.

2. Everyone who takes a turn gets heard.

What do we mean by "get a turn?" Imagine a pie divided into as many pieces as there are people in the circle. Telling the students that everyone will get a turn, whether they want to use it or not, is like telling them that each one will get a piece of pie. Some students may not want their piece today, but they know the piece is for them to take, if and when they want it. As the leader, you are present to protect this right. Thus, getting a turn not only means a chance to talk, but also an assurance to the student that he or she has "space" that no one else will violate.

When the students take their turns, the other members of the group will be listening. No attempt will be made by anyone to manipulate what a participant is offering. That is, the person speaking will not be probed, interrupted, interpreted, analyzed, put-down, joked at, advised, preached to, or made to feel uncomfortable. The process of "listening to" in the Human Development Program is defined as the respectful focus of the listener's attention on the speaker for the purpose of letting him/her know that the listener heard what the speaker said. This process is confirmed in the review phase of each circle session. For this reason, a session is not complete without a review of what each person who spoke to the topic said.

The lowest risk method for conveying to persons the feeling that you have heard what they said seems to be to "feedback," "reflect," "parrot," or "mirror" the speakers' own words. By repeating certain words that a speaker used that appear to have special significance, the listener in a sense assures the speaker that he or she has been heard. An alternative to reflecting is the use of paraphrasing, in which the listener uses his or her own words to convey to the speaker what the listener thinks the speaker was saying. As leaders model these skills in the circle sessions, students will learn them through imitation.

In summation: The only way that a circle session can be evaluated is by these two criteria. Did everyone who wished to, speak? and was each person who spoke, heard? Thus, if only one or two students chose to speak, and, if the fact that they were listened to was confirmed in a review, even if they didn't say very "deep" or "meaningful" things, the circle can be considered a success.

Analyzing the session. For a deeper analysis of each session, particularly with respect to leadership, a series of questions exists which the leader may wish to answer. Merle Cummings, Human Development Program consultant, has developed the following guide as a self-assessment procedure for the circle session leader.

A Leader's Guide for Analyzing the Session

Sometimes to evaluate just what has happened in a session is very difficult. How well did it go? Were the needs of the group met? If I am to be open and honest with others, I must first be open and honest with myself. Developing this attitude and behavior is a slow, never-ending process; that process takes courage and patience but the rewards of knowing are worth the effort.

The first place to search for answers is within myself. At the end of a session a careful analysis of my feelings, aided by answering the following questions, may reveal why some things work and why some other things are not as successful.

1. Did everyone have a turn?
2. Was someone especially pleased?
3. Were moments of silence comfortable?
4. Were some members excited about the next meeting?
5. Is the pressure on my body inward, or outward, as I think about the session?
6. Did I really want to be with the group?
7. Did I put someone down today?
8. Was I put down today? What did I do?
9. Did I blame someone today?
10. Which person do I like best?
    a. Describe the person to yourself.
    b. What do I like best about him/her? Why?
    c. Who else do I know like him/her?
    d. Who was the first person I ever knew like that?
    e. What do I want this person to do?
    f. What is this person afraid of?
    g. What would I do if I had those fears?
11. What am I afraid of?
12. Who is the first to criticize me?
13. With whom in the group am I the most pleased?
14. If I show anger, who would like my behavior?
15. Who would be the target of my angry behavior?
16. If I were giving out love, who would get the first share?
17. Where would I run out of love?
18. With whom would I like to share a good session?
19. What needs of mine are met in the group?
20. Are the needs met by the group the same needs as mine?
21. Do I hold back anger? Why?
22. If I had become angry, what would have happened?
23. Who would criticize me for getting angry?
24. Do I sometimes hold back a good feeling?

25. Does someone get embarrassed if I share good feelings? Who?
26. Something nice that I could say to each member of the group is . . .
27. Something nice that I could say to myself is . . .
28. A way that I could take what I don't like about someone and change it into a positive statement is . . .
    a. Someone who talks too much: "James, you express yourself very freely."
    b. Someone who is always negative: "Carol, you often see things differently."
29. If someone asked me to sit in a group so that they could know me better, would I like that?
30. When someone accepts me and is interested in me, how do I feel?
31. When someone listens to what I am saying and asks questions, how does that make me feel?
32. If someone tries to make a safe place for me to be myself, how do I feel toward him or her?
33. Which members of the group are most different from me?
34. Do I want them to be like me?
35. What about them do I like?

Evaluating the Human Development Program

In order to evaluate the outcome and the overall effects of the program, *The Developmental Profile,* patterned closely after the Fel's Rating Scale, was designed. The Developmental Profile provides a means by which the student's personal progress in the areas of Awareness, Mastery and Social Interaction may be rated as objectively as possible. The Profiles have been effectively used in a number of research studies and by teachers who simply wish to measure the social and emotional development of the students in their classrooms.

The Developmental Profile also has been used by researchers who were not necessarily evaluating the results of the Human Development Program, but other variables effecting the social and emotional growth of students. The uses of the Developmental Profile range from informal, isolated utilization by school personnel

METHODS
IN HUMAN
DEVELOPMENT

NAME: _____
(Last)   (First)   (Middle)

GRADE: _____ SCHOOL: _____

TEACHER: _____ YEAR: _____

Developmental Profile

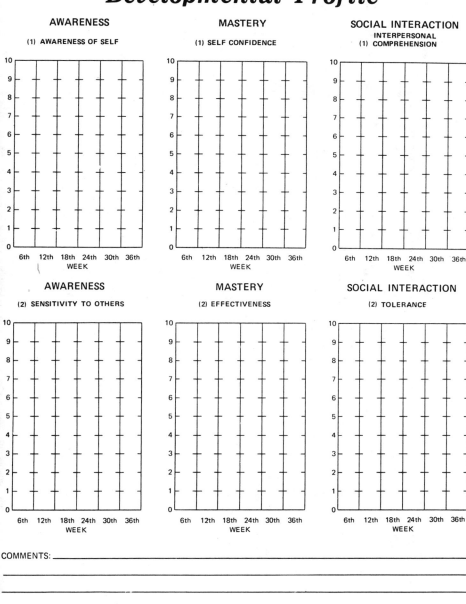

AWARENESS
(1) AWARENESS OF SELF

MASTERY
(1) SELF CONFIDENCE

SOCIAL INTERACTION
INTERPERSONAL
(1) COMPREHENSION

6th 12th 18th 24th 30th 36th
WEEK

AWARENESS
(2) SENSITIVITY TO OTHERS

MASTERY
(2) EFFECTIVENESS

SOCIAL INTERACTION
(2) TOLERANCE

6th 12th 18th 24th 30th 36th
WEEK

COMMENTS: _____

_____

_____

INSTRUCTIONS: At the end of each six week period, the teacher should make use of the following scales to analyze the child's development. Using the descriptions given, he should be able to determine the number most indicative of his perceptions of the child. This number can then be entered on the appropriate scale, and as subsequent numbers are recorded, any developmental trends should become apparent.

AWARENESS

(1) AWARENESS OF SELF

The aware child knows how he feels, what he thinks, and what he is doing. Although he is conscious of himself, he is not self-conscious, insecure or embarrassed. This awareness does not produce anxiety. He accepts and can acknowledge how he really feels, thinks, and acts.

(10) Very aware; always conscious of his feelings, wishes, fears, and the meaning of his behavior (positive or negative).

(8) Most of the time aware, ready to acknowledge what he feels, thinks and does. Only occasionally uses denial.

(5) Often aware of his feelings, behavior and thoughts, and willing to recognize them as such. However, often reacts without awareness or uses denial.

(2) Usually unconscious or unaware of himself. Denies his real feelings and thoughts, and cannot recognize his own actions for what they are.

(0) Unconscious; full of denial; completely unable to recognize his

MASTERY

(1) SELF CONFIDENCE

The confident child is eager to try new things. He is self-assured and realistic when coping with challenge. His acceptance of himself permits freedom of expression which is natural and uninhibited, without being dramatic or exhibitionistic.

(10) Always eager to try anything that is new. Approaches challenge with assurance and reacts freely and naturally.

(7) Most of the time seeks out and meets new and challenging situations with confidence. Generally reacts freely and naturally, but is inhibited upon occasion.

(5) Usually tries anything new that is presented to him, but seldom seeks out challenging situations on his own. Often is inhibited rather than free and natural in his expression.

(2) Frequently avoids challenges, but will deal with them when encouraged. Responses are inhibited and stilted.

(1) Almost always shies away from challenges. Requires repeated encouragement before reluctantly

SOCIAL INTERACTION

INTERPERSONAL
(1) COMPREHENSION

This trait assesses the child's understanding of how one person's behavior causes approval or disapproval of that behavior in another person.

(9) Very high-comprehension. Child almost always recognizes the effect of any given behavior.

(7) Usually comprehends what the second person's reaction will be to the first person's behavior.

(5) Sometimes perceives the interpersonal effects, but just as often fails to comprehend how one person's behavior affects another person's attitude.

(2) Seldom comprehends interpersonal interaction. Usually at a loss in being able to see how one person's behavior affects another person's reaction.

(1) Virtually no comprehension of how a person's behavior causes attitudes in other people. Almost always fails to comprehend the interaction.

The tolerant child recognizes and accepts individual differences. He accepts and gives full regard to others who have different feelings, thoughts, and reactions than his own. But he does not necessarily approve or yield to their influence.

(10) Extremely tolerant. Understands and accepts differences as natural. Tolerates a very broad spectrum of feeling, thoughts, and behavior in others.

(7) Reasonably tolerant about individual differences.

(4) Mildly tolerant, but tends to not accept certain natural variations.

(2) Usually intolerant. Tends to regard people who differ from him as being unacceptable, even wrong.

(0) Very intolerant. His way of feeling, thinking and reacting is the only way that he can accept. People who are different are completely unacceptable.

Published by:
Human Development
Training Institute
7574 University Avenue
La Mesa, California 92041

The effective child copes appropriately. He is emotionally stable, and flexible enough to successfully implement his own desires or meet the external demands of his environment.

(10) Always deals appropriately and successfully with his inner needs and external demands. Flexible enough to shift approach, yet stable enough to maintain direction.

(7) Typically gets his needs met. Usually able to accept and adjust to changing circumstances.

(5) Often successful, but frequently fails to get his needs met. Has trouble shifting from original viewpoint or behavior. Realization of a need to shift may be upsetting to him.

(2) Mostly ineffective, but occasionally successful in his efforts. Usually unable to adapt to new information or demands and is upset and loses his bearings when circumstances change.

(1) Rarely succeeds in his efforts. Rigid. Very unresponsive to new information or demands. Generally agitated or immobilized by change in circumstances.

The sensitive child is concerned about the well being of other people. He readily ascertains what others are feeling and adjusts his behavior in ways that are thoughtful and beneficial to them.

(10) Acutely aware and very concerned about other people's feelings and reactions. Readily modifies his behavior in response to this awareness and concern.

(8) Most of the time aware and concerned about how others are truly feeling and reacting. Generally modifies behavior in accordance with his concern for others.

(5) Often aware and concerned, but in many instances seems unaware and relatively unconcerned about other people's feelings and reactions. Frequently his behavior generates negative feelings in others.

(2) Usually unaware and disinterested in what other people are feeling but can recognize what is going on in others when directly called to his attention. He seldom responds to the feelings of others.

(0) Insensitive and unconcerned as to what is going on in and with other people. Tends to pursue his own behavior no matter how it may affect another person.

such as teachers and school psychologists, to use in carefully structured research models testing the results of a variety of educational
curricula, usually including the Human Development Program.
The Developmental Profile is reproduced in this Chapter.

Articulating the Program in the
Self-Contained Classroom

In the nine years in which we have been doing circle sessions
with students and talking to teachers and counselors about their
circle sessions, the fact has become evident that no one correct way
exists to carry out the Human Development Program in the
classroom or in any other setting. In fact, within a few guidelines
relating to the environment, time, space, age and number of group
members, etc., one might say that *the correct way is any way that
works* for any particular teacher (or leader) and class (or group).
Magic Circle Activity Guides and the Innerchange Leader's Manual
both present guidelines and strategies that have worked for a number of teachers and leaders. Major items of structure need to be
considered.

Group size and composition. Since time is taken to focus on
the feelings of each participant who wishes to speak in the session,
and to allow group members to listen reflectively to one another,
the group will need to be kept relatively small. We have generally
seen that any number from seven to twelve usually works best.
When the number reaches thirteen or more, to give group members
enough time to express themselves and to hold the interest of the
students who are not verbally participating is difficult. Many students are generally capable of somewhat extensive verbalization,
depending on their age and a number of other factors. This ability
should be used to advantage as much as possible and not stifled
because of time constraints.

Each group should be as heterogeneous as possible with respect
to sex and the racial and ethnic backgrounds of the students. Sometimes a group will exist in which all of the students are particularly
reticent. In this case the leader should bring in an expressive student who will spark the others to verbalization. Reticence is a more
common problem in groups of junior and senior high school students than it is in groups whose participants are in the elementary
grades. For this reason the Innerchange program has designed a

156

number of Preliminary Activities in each growth area (Awareness, Mastery, and Social Interaction). Most Preliminary Activities can be completed by students independently, thus in relative privacy a student can become somewhat familiar with the flavor of Innerchange and prepare for participation in the circle session.

Although the need for occasional changes in the composition of groups should be anticipated, membership should be stabilized as quickly as possible and should remain stable.

Time and space. Circle sessions last approximately twenty to thirty minutes at most grade levels. At first, interest may abate before twenty minutes have elapsed and the teacher may decide to end a session sooner, but usually the reverse is true, and a problem arises of carrying out all of the steps within a thirty-minute time period. For those classes with more relaxed schedules some sessions have lasted forty-five minutes or more and interest has remained high throughout the session. Generally speaking, the students, with repeated experiences in the circle, become comfortable and highly motivated to express themselves, to listen reflectively, and to discuss the meaning of each session.

We make few recommendations to leaders of circle sessions regarding times of the day for conducting the sessions, but we will mention some of the times that classroom teachers have held sessions and found those times to be satisfactory for them. Often, the circle is conducted in the morning as an initial activity, thereby setting a positive tone in the classroom for the remainder of the day. Many teachers prefer to hold the session at the end of the school day as a kind of "coming together" before going home. Some teachers conduct circles at other feasible times throughout the day depending on the scheduling of other activities and tasks. Once a time is established it should remain as stable as possible so that the students will know that the session is something on which they can depend.

With respect to scheduling, many teachers have carried out the Magic Circle as part of their social studies curriculum and/or language arts program. The process involved in the circle session has been seen by many as "social studies in perhaps its purest form." And the fact that the session is a language program, and much more, is apparent. For subject area teachers at the junior and

157

senior high school levels, the Innerchange Leader's Manual contains information and suggestions regarding ways to combine the Innerchange program with (1) specific subject areas (to achieve confluence) and (2) specialized programs, such as career education, drug abuse, and crime prevention.

Since classrooms and other settings vary greatly in the amount of space available, we make few recommendations along these lines. Generally, a circle session may be carried out wherever space permits and few or no distractions occur. (A discussion is presented in the Magic Circle Activity Guides and the Innerchange Leader's Manual regarding the achievement of these conditions.) Most teachers seem to prefer having the students use chairs rather than sit on the floor, since the participants seem to be less apt to invade one another's space while seated in chairs. However, many groups do sit on the floor and some teachers (and/or leaders) conduct sessions with children out-of-doors with everyone seated in a quiet, secluded grassy area.

How often should circle sessions be held? The more often students are exposed to the circle session process and to the issues being discussed, the better the end results will be. This fact is particularly true due to the developmental nature of the topics which build understanding in the students in a sequential manner. *The Program should be carried out daily, or as close to that frequency as possible in order for the most benefits to occur.*

We are aware that large classes, overcrowded schedules, and other pressures facing the teacher at first make this task difficult. For those teachers in typical classrooms with twenty-eight to forty-eight students who recognize the importance of including in the curriculum an affective/confluent educational program such as the Magic Circle or Innerchange, ways can be developed to offer a session daily. Some plans that have been used successfully by many teachers for involving as many students as possible are described in the Magic Circle Activity Guides and in the Innerchange Leader's Manual.

In preschool and kindergarten the teacher works with no more than twelve children (preferably less) at a time in single circles. (Conditions are optimal for following this plan when a teacher assistant is available.) This plan may be carried out effectively in

158

all of the grades. Answers to such questions as, "What do I do with the rest of my class?" are supplied in the Magic Circle Activity Guides and the Innerchange Leader's Manual. (See Figure 3.1.)

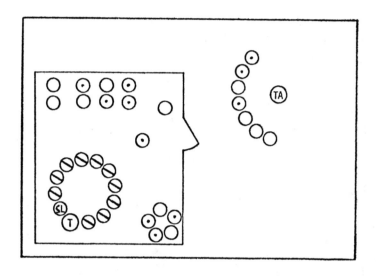

(T=Teacher, TA=Teacher Assistant, SL=Student Leader)

Figure 3.1. Teacher meets with one group in a single circle at a time. An assistant works with the other children in the class.

For teachers who wish to involve as many students as possible but who have limited time, another plan is suggested. (See Figure 3.2.) This format begins with the single circle. Then a small outer circle of well-controlled students is added. The number of students gradually increases until three groups are meeting at once with one group verbally participating in the inner circle while the other two groups listen and observe in an outer circle. When the session is being reviewed and the culminating questions are being discussed *all* of the students in both circles are free to become involved verbally. Each day the groups alternate so that each participant is involved at some level everyday and personally involved at the verbal level every second or third day. This plan may be found to be particularly stimulating at the advanced unit level in junior and senior high school.

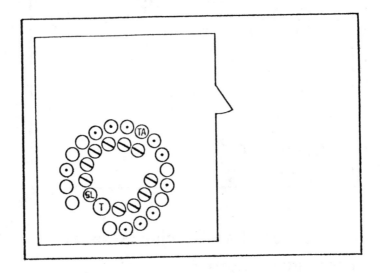

Figure 3.2. All students are involved in each session, either as a member of the inner or outer circle. Groups alternate.

Three additional plans involving student leaders are suggested and are further articulated in Levels V and VI Activity Guides and in the Innerchange Leader's Manual. Procedures for expanding student leadership are also described so that the students may meet in their groups independently if time does not permit the teacher to meet with each group each day. (See Figures 3.3., 3.4. & 3.5.)

160

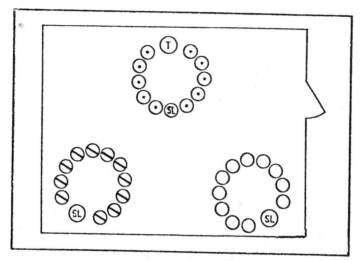

Figure 3.3. Three groups led by students meet at once. Teacher circulates. (Fifth grade and beyond only.)

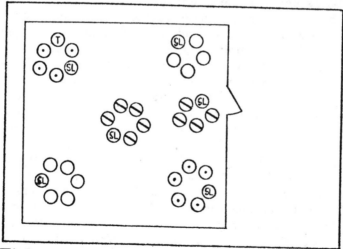

Figure 3.4. Three groups are divided into six smaller groups led by students. (Fifth grade and beyond only.)

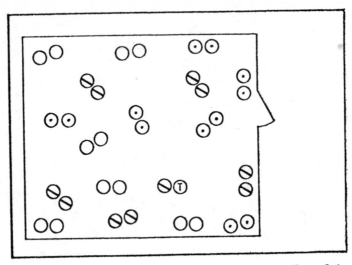

Figure 3.5. Another student leadership variation: Dyads. (Fifth grade and beyond only.)

Why student leadership is important. We believe that every human being (barring those having considerable sub-normal intelligence) has leadership potential and that the optimum time for energizing this ability is in youth. We have seen in countless classrooms that students are very capable of effectively leading their own circle sessions. The fact has been noted that students' leadership abilities are likely to transfer to other school and community functions following the practice they have gained in leading circle sessions. Often, if students are not given an opportunity to experience successful leadership practice in their youth, having to be responsible for a group effort or "getting up in front of people" later on in life is likely to be a frightening experience. For this reason, student leadership has become a significant component of the Human Development Program. The safe, accepting atmosphere of the circle session is a good place to begin to develop strong leadership functions. Then, as students grow and mature they may choose to lead in certain situations and follow in others. The option of leadership will always be available to students who know that they have led successfully in the past.

Parents and Community

Due to the ever-increasing, positive trend toward parental and community involvement, teachers and school administrators are urged to inform the community of the objectives and format of the Human Development Program as it is instituted in the school, or, better yet, prior to its institution. We recommend that invitations be extended to parents and community members so that these individuals might visit and hear about the program and see it in action. If feasible, circle sessions should be held in which the parents and community members are participants. This practice has been successful in a number of schools and is highly recommended. The "Warm Fuzzy" Awareness topics presented in this Chapter are generally well suited for this kind of demonstration.

A Final Word to the Reader

Although to provide you with enough information to carry out the Human Development Program over an entire school year is impossible, our hope is that we have described enough of the "basics" of the Program to help you decide whether or not you are interested in starting the Magic Circle or Innerchange in your school (if you are an administrator) or classroom (if you are a teacher). Teachers at the elementary level will need the Activity Guides at their grade levels to supply them with the information needed to sustain the program over the period of a school year. Secondary school teachers will need the Innerchange packages for either junior or senior high school. Each package contains complete sets of instructional materials, individual student activities, and the Leader's Manual. The Magic Circle Theory Manual (a separate publication available to teachers) and the Innerchange Leader's Manual provide the fundamental theoretical understandings that circle session leaders need in order to conduct sessions in accordance with the general principles of the Program.

If you are a teacher and you do plan to institute the Program, the list of "warm fuzzy" Awareness topics in this Chapter and the sample topics listed below will provide you with enough circle session subjects to enable you to start conducting circle sessions right away.

Awareness topics:

"A Time When I Had A Good Feeling About Someone"

"A Wish of Mine that Came True"

"Something that Made Me Feel Good and Bad at the Same Time"

Mastery topics:

"Something I Like To Do"

"I Taught Someone To Do Something"

"A Time When I Felt Proud of Myself"

Social Interaction topics:

"I Did Something that Sparked Good Feelings in Someone"

"Someone Did Something that Sparked Good Feelings in Me"

"We Made Room for One More"

Prior experience in affective techniques in the classroom will be helpful in carrying out the program, and special training in the Human Development Program will be even more helpful and is highly recommended.

As you experiment with your first circle session, you are likely to be encouraged by the feeling of magic and excitement created by the students as they experience the sense of sharing and belonging that the circle format and procedures seem to generate. You also will be encouraged by seeing the process work smoothly and systematically with leadership abilities you already possess and can feel confident about using.

We have seen that the Human Development Program has helped students to develop their personal effectiveness and to succeed academically. And we have seen educators who use the Program enjoying their jobs more and becoming more like "producers" who know that their product is valued. They are seeing the students as their "consumers," taking the students' wants and needs into account and inviting the students to contribute to the learning activities of each day from their own personal experience. We feel that the Program provides an experience for circle participants in which they will accept and appreciate their own humanness and the humanness of others. Our hope is that these feelings will lead to enjoyment and celebration, and a habit of personal and shared growth.

164

REFERENCES

Bessell, Harold, Ph.D. The content is the medium: The confidence is the message. *Psychology Today.* January, 1968.

Bessell, Harold, Ph.D. Human development in the elementary school classroom. *New perspective in encounter groups.* San Francisco: Solomon and Berzon, Editors; Jossey-Bass, Publisher. 1972.

Bessell, Harold, Ph.D. *Methods in human development theory manual.* Human Development Training Institute. San Diego, California: Revised, 1973.

Borton, Terry. *Reach, touch, and teach.* Student Concerns and Process Education, McGraw-Hill Book Company, 1970.

Brown, George I. *The live classroom, innovation through confluent education and Gestalt.* Penguin Books, 1976.

Castan, Frances. Alternatives to corporal punishment. *Scholastic Teacher,* Junior/Senior High Teacher's Edition, September, 1973

Coopersmith, S. *The antecedents of self-esteem.* San Francisco: W.T Freeman and Co., 1967.

Elbert, Weldon. Change in headstart teachers following HDP training in Odessa, Texas. *HDCP research Bulletin,* II, a mimeographed report, Human Development Training Institute, San Diego, California, 1970.

Helfat, Lucille. The gut level needs of kids. *Learning,* II, No. 2, October, 1973.

Jackins, Harvey. *The human side of human beings, the theory of re-evaluation counseling.* Seattle: Rational Island Publishers, First paperback printing, July, 1972.

LaChapelle, Dolores. Teach children to love themselves—or God help their neighbors. *The Catechist,* a religious education publication of the Catholic Churches in the U.S.

Palomares, Uvaldo, Ed.D. Desegregating people's minds. *The Civil Rights Digest,* a quarterly report from the U.S. Commission on Civil Rights, Summer, 1969.

Palomares, Uvaldo, Ed.D. and Rubini, Terri. Human development in the classroom. *Personnel and Guidance Journal,* LI, No. 9, May, 1973.

Palomares, Uvaldo, Ed.D., Trujillo, Miguel and Ball, Geraldine. *Bilingual education and the human development program,* a monogram printed by Human Development Training Institute, San Diego California, 1973.

Patterson, C.H. *Humanistic education.* Prentice-Hall Inc., 1973.

Rogers, Carl R., Ph.D. *On becoming a person, a therapist's view of psychotherapy.* Sentry Edition, Boston: Hoghton Mifflin Company, 1961.

Rogers, Carl R., Ph.D. *Becoming partners: marriage and its alternatives.* A Delta Book, Center for Studies of the Person, La Jolla, California: First Delta Printing, August, 1973

Rubin, Louis R. *Facts and feelings in the classroom.* Walker and Company, 1973.

Saavedra, Carlos, Rivera F. and Cordova, H. Curriculum and materials for bilingual-bicultural Education. *The Nional Elementary Principal,* I, No. 2, November, 1970, p. 56.

Simpson, Elizabeth L., *Humanistic education: an interpretation.* Ballinger Publishing Company, 1976.

Weinstein, Gerald and Fantini, Mario D. *Toward humanistic education, a curriculum of affect.* Praeger Publishers, 1975.

4

PSYCHODRAMA, ROLE PLAYING AND SOCIOMETRY LIVING AND LEARNING PROCESSES

Carl E. Hollander

Editor's Notes:

In Hollander's Chapter, the author applied psychodrama and sociometry to the individual as "methodologies or learning processes." Psychodrama can be a highly personal technique used chiefly for the benefit of an individual participant, although other persons in a group may share in the actor's reliving of a situation. If a psychodramatic technique was used in the schools to bring about a particular environment, the attempt would be, in the main, to help specific individuals change personal environments, with the hope that through personal changes their primary function (whether as students, teachers, administrators, or other school personnel) would become more effective.

Another dramatic technique, which involves directly more than one person at a time, is role playing. The capacity of this process to assist in "spontaneous problem solving, information gathering, and the alternatives for living and learning," is the benefit group members may derive by becoming involved in roles similar to their own of responsibility within the school system, but playing unfamiliar roles and thereby identifying with points of view of other persons with greater compassion and understanding. As examples, students might play the roles of teachers, administrators, or students, or students might play the roles of administrators or counselors.

The primary advantage of role playing is that players who experience being in other roles and associating with other role viewpoints develop a communication understanding of the roles of other school personnel. Since role playing is a pertinent technique used to assist individuals or groups in becoming accustomed to unaccustomed roles, it can be employed effectively to change roles and statuses within a system, or to alter a formal organizational structure in which personnel learn to accept different responsibilities or work procedures. In other words, role playing is a useful technique that acclimates persons working in a system to change certain behaviors to meet appropriate environmental changes.

An exciting application of role playing for teachers is in classroom instruction. Hollander describes numerous examples of the academic areas of history and social studies, literature, mathematics, biological sciences, and mental health.

Hollander stated that sociometry "provides structure to measure systematically interpersonal networks within a group." Techniques for the assessment of such interpersonal networks are valuable tools for effecting the environmental influences emphasized in this Book: changes in individual needs, values, or motives; changes in the social structure of the school, including roles and statuses of people and the accompanying norms governing behavior; and changes in the formal organizational structure of the school, involving its purposes and the responsibilities associated with various roles and statuses, communication channels, and work procedures.

ABOUT

THE

AUTHOR

CARL E. HOLLANDER

Carl Hollander, the 35th Certified Director of Psychodrama, Sociometry, and Group Psychotherapy: Moreno Institute, was co-founder and president of Evergreen Institute for Human Development and Family Growth from 1966 to 1972; Colorado Center for Psychodrama, Sociometry and Sociatry from 1972 to the present time; and Hollander and Hollander, Inc: Marriage, Family, Relationship and Individual Counseling, from 1974 to the present.

Hollander has seved as a consultant to schools, universities, mental health centers and a long list of other agencies. His active memberships include American Society of Group Psychotherapy and Psychodrama, American Association of Marriage and Family Counseling and American Sociological Association.

Recognition has been given Hollander in *Who's Who in the West, Who's Who in the United States, Men of Achievement* and *International Biography*. Monographs and articles written by Hollander occur on therapeutic recreation, psychodramatic process, sociometry, religious education, role playing, and video tape use for learning and groupings in classrooms.

Hollander resides with his wife and four children near Englewood, Colorado.

PSYCHODRAMA, ROLE PLAYING,
AND SOCIOMETRY: LIVING
AND LEARNING PROCESSES

CARL E. HOLLANDER

For me to describe a process about action-learning is a paradoxical endeavor and immanently difficult. Perhaps to avoid over-intellectualizing, as is the case when writers describe action phenomena, my clearest thinking will result if my writing talks with you directly (rather than "teaches" you).

This Chapter should entertain you, charm you, and hopefully transmit to you what has been one of the most important discoveries of my life: how to combine into one process the use of psychodrama, role playing, and sociometry. My use of these processes began in 1962 and has steadily expanded in range and depth of power; but do not be so zealous after reading this Chapter that you will try to see if my process really works. Like a palate of oils, like a golden trumpet, or like the most beautiful raw piece of alabaster marble, psychodrama and sociometry must be gently tested and repeatedly plied before the artisan can know the true beauty of the combination. No book of art worth its salt will delude its readers by pretending to "teach" art from its pages. At best the book will describe an ideal, pave the way to an art form by clarifying a vocabulary, or describe the process by which art evolves. In any event upon completing the segment about psychodrama and sociometry, *you*

171

will not know how to direct a session with confidence. That paradox will occur after you have been a member of a training workshop and tried your hand repeatedly at directing a psychodrama session. To discourage your immediate use of psychodrama is difficult since action is the most useful method for optimal learning.

Both psychodrama and sociometry can be classified as art forms: my encounter with an important definition of art was Philip C. Beam's, about eighteen years ago while a student at Valparaiso University. Although he was paraphrasing Curt J. Ducasse, Beam shed a new light on the definition when he said, "Art is the controlled objectification of feeling." (Beam, 1958, p. 114) When asked, "What can art do for us?" Mr. Beam (p. 6) answered that it can "clarify, intensify, and interpret the meaning of reality." Beam's reality consisted of two parts: the inner subjective reality, and the cosmic or external reality. Because psychodrama is an art form that agrees with Beam's definition, psychodrama may be defined as "the controlled objectification of feelings;" or, to state it in more detail, psychodrama is a process through which feelings are concretely and systematically portrayed in order to increase the intensity, clarification, and meaning of the actor's inner and outer world. The actor may be either you or me. The scene may be any scene from your biography at any period of your life. Once the important characters who occupied that time and space with you have been clearly introduced, the "canvas" is ready. Psychodrama paints that "canvas" by re-enacting the essence of that scene and bringing into clarification the feelings you held during that scene. Frequently, re-enactments create great intensity and meaningfulness of a situation: hence, life experiences can be acted and/or re-employed to develop new learnings from our biographies. You would agree that each person is the sum total of his entire biography. As that person grows older, a broader lense of understanding develops through which to make new sense from things around us. Also, a person becomes better equipped to review various events in the past and to become updated through existential lenses.

A powerful incident occurred between Daniel, my son, and me shortly after he had turned four years old. As we were driving across Denver on a balmy October afternoon, I began to share with Daniel my warm feelings about being with him and the golden autumn trees. "Everything seems so filled with love, today, Daniel," I said. He responded,

"Daddy, where did the Stegoraurus and Anklyosaurus go? Would the Triceratops really kill a Tyrannisaurus Rex?" Seeing that we were each talking out loud but not at each other, I said, "Daniel you're tuning me out!" He responded immediately. His face had an astonished look; one of surprise mixed with confusion. He said to me, "Daddy, what's a ningme?" I admitted my ignorance. He countered again with, "Yes, you do! You just said it." "No," I said, "I didn't say that. You must have misunderstood me." "No!" he argued. "You did say ningme!" After rewording our conversation both within myself and with Daniel, I realized what had happened. He had heard, "You're tuning me out" as "You're two ningme out." Daniel knew he wasn't two years old; yet, the note of irritation in my voice doubly amplified the word "out." What he heard was his "loving" father calling him two years old and all but ordering him "out." How often words become misconstrued among people of all ages!

All people are capable of talking with sense by using the symbols called "language," although frequently subtle references are formulated as castigations about those who "obviously don't make sense." To overhear indirectly or to hear quite openly one person referring to another as "that person's crazy . . . dumb . . . sick . . . stupid . . . bad . . . or . . . inappropriate" is almost commonplace. Ask what motives underlie these labels of behavioral categories, particularly if the labeler, like the one being labeled, also, in fact, "makes sense." One tenet, mentioned earlier, is that each person is the sum total of an entire biography; that is, every experience of life becomes a party of the "now" person, predisposes current perceptions, and acts as the foundation for future learning. If this point is true, then the labeler is revealing something by making perjorative inferences about the person being labeled or categorized as "crazy, dumb, bad, sick, stupid, and inappropriate." The person who is quick to define categories with which to label others (which do not apparently "make sense") has had little or no life experience from which to understand, appreciate, empathize, or tolerate the one whose life experience is being exposed. This behavior also may reflect that the labeler has been exposed to something too threatening to be comfortably encountered. Frequently, to create categories and labels for people is easier than to examine "the others" closely. An examination may be akin to developing a file cabinet that has six drawers, all of which contain powerfully painful unknown contents. Rather than risk opening the drawers and examining the contents, to paste on labels is easier and evermore refer to the interior by affixed labels. Likewise, learning frequently is interrupted by the labeling technique. Too often the label interrupts rather than nurtures the heuristic process. Witnessing the aforementioned references about the nonsensical person can be a painful travesty of life in that making such an evaluation subtly casts the recipient into a dehumanized social sector. Equally as tragic is the social pressure that is sustained when enclaves of other people adopt the label and cooperate in the categorizing that contributes to dehumanization, and often to isolation and/or rejection.

Imagine as you refer to Figure 4.1 that with each new experience (emotional, spiritual, social, and rational) new lenses are developed through which to view and make sense out of one's life and the lives of others (shaded area). Also, imagine that a biography begins at the point of conception rather than birth. *During the course* of living, each person intersects with someone whose life experiences exceed our personal experiences. The areas between that person's experiences and ours are unshaded and reflect entire segments of life totally alien and apparently meaningless to any prior investment. If our heritage has been fraught with rules, has judgmentalized "right vs. wrong" ways for living, and has developed a lack of trust and respect in human differences, then the judgmentalized labels of "crazy, dumb, bad, sick, stupid, and inappropriate" are applied.

The excitement of living comes by seeking out the unkown. Similarly, taking risks by pursuing the enigmas that likewise challenge spontaneity is exciting. As a person lives and matures, this question becomes a challenge: Am I open and available to investigate and encounter that which my lenses do not as yet see, or am I only looking at those things which my lenses will permit me to see?

Everyone lives by internal logic and a set of values that collectively underscore an unique living process; which, in turn, suggests that everyone lives according to a set of processes. At times our separate processes can be articulated clearly; at other times, these processes are not clearly definable. Further, in the discovery of our personal processes three functions are required: *an experiential integration for self awareness, a fusion of self awareness with skills and*

174

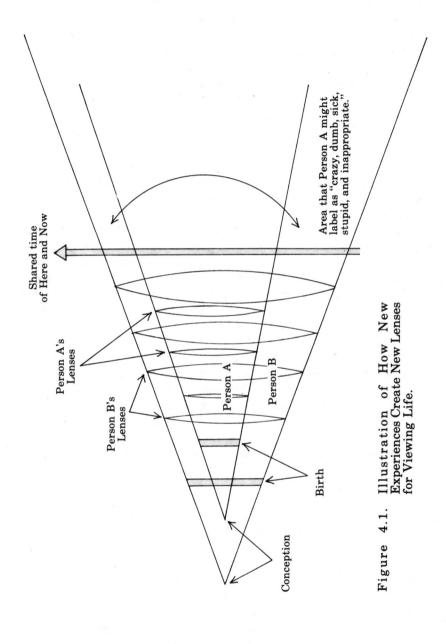

Figure 4.1. Illustration of How New Experiences Create New Lenses for Viewing Life.

knowledge, and a willingness to risk experiencing the unknown. Each person must become alert to a set of personal processes that develop: (1) more clarity in his/her communication, (2) more acceptance of self as a person, and (3) more power to achieve those goals, which fuse with greater creativity in thinking.

Author's note: I trust from my personal growth and the skills that I have acquired, that methods exist which facilitate the discovery of those experiences emanating from life . . . pleasant and painful.

Because life is dynamic (i.e., always changing and in flux rather than remaining static and secure) the methodologies employed in daily thinking must be similarly dynamic and experiential. Two methodologies, or learning processes, that help to integrate personal processes are *Psychodrama* and *Sociometry*. In effect, psychodrama and sociometry parallel the metaphor of an x-ray machine employed to view inner physical functions; for both methodologies generate a powerful force to create the lenses that view the inner workings of a person's mind and to assess the strength and limitations of a person's functions that alter or accommodate to the surrounding environment.

Author's note: Fortunately, I have given up teaching my children anything and have opted to learn as much as I possibly can from them. The way my sons (Michael, Daniel, Joel, and David) reflect the ways they make sense out of this world and its circumstances, the greater the contrast I am exposed to with regard to the ways I attempt to understand the same circumstances. I often realize that my sons, my friends' children, and I have never updated certain portions of our lives.

Often unwittingly, our existential environment is seen through the remote eyes of that five-year-old, or of a teenager dying within us, without consciously trying to unlock the painful experiences of the past or to release the feelings that are encapsuled as a result of those painful early experiences. To update our experiences with contemporary lenses is crucial. Growth and maturation often are retarded when early, painful experiences compete with existing energies and inhibit those experiences from becoming more creatively placed. (Ergo—*incomplete terminations*

176

interfere with new beginnings.) In order to experience optimal creativity, each person must sever the emotional controls from the past in order to savor more fully the moment at hand.

This Chapter is about psychodrama, role playing, and sociometry as each relates to learning, creativity, and health. Please enjoy it!

PART I

LEARNING IS A CREATIVE PROCESS

Author's note: Psychodrama is the most powerful learning process I've ever witnessed. Many educators and clinicians who do not feel basically "together" or fairly well integrated seek powerful methods and processes to bolster their rather tenuous footholds on life. These people are like playful children who believe carrying a large weapon means safety. So, in prelude, the power in a psychodramatic process emanates via the skill, power, and wisdom of the user, not merely via the media.

I want to share with you a few words about a strong prejudice. Everywhere I look people seem to want shortcuts: instamatics, instant foods, microwaves, and supersonic time. Unfortunately, those who live by this "time-pressure sword" are similarly dying by it. My personal discomfort and anger are directed at people who have become technique and gimmick-directed. Whenever a high power and vogue technique is marketed, all eager, powerless folks run after the wagon like the itinerate medicine man who upon each visit brought bigger and better bottles. Eavesdropping on conversations among these "helpers" we hear terms like "hot seat," "effectiveness," "encountering," "primal," and "my thing" until we catch on there's a new jargon developing—a shorthand, if you will, that reflects the supersonic era of gimmicks and techniques for human feelings and human processes. Because I am beginning to sound as conservative as Reich's Consciousness II people, I want to add a note of clarification: these "supersonic facilitators" have failed to grasp the most important societal-environmental factor—"people-helping."

A process is a "path," not a "place": the evolutionary flow inherent in growth and development—dynamic rather than static. Process is a natural cycle of "events" that seeks a systematic order and tends to build upon itself. If interrupted by disease, crises, or external forces, the natural characteristics of the system—be they animal, vegetable, mineral, or cosmic—strive to return to basic rhythms and characteristics. If unable to return, what is left intact begins to regenerate a balance based upon remaining strengths. Every human being lives by an accumulative process. In order to sustain that process, each person requires an awareness of the surrounding environment and the processes of other people who make up that environment. The clearer we are in understanding of our processes, the clearer the understanding is of the processes of our friends, family, co-workers, students, counselees, and enemies (and the clearer we will be understood by them).

Over the past fifteen years my experience has been that people who have *not* dared risk knowing the unknown of their innermost lives (i.e., those sanctuaries within each of us which are private) are most apt to look for shortcuts and techniques. This rejection, fear, or reluctance is a form of subtle protection: "If I won't go into your process, I won't have to get into my own;" or "I can only go as deeply in your process as I have gone into my own." Techniques and shortcuts are powerful when adroitly employed within someone's process; however, each technique/shortcut becomes a lever to obviate the truth should it be utilized without attending consciously to the person's process.

Recently, the "guitar phenomenon" (this is my terminology) that regularly occurs during psychodramas and among individuals became conceptualized through the following situation:

> During a recent psychodrama training workshop, a dynamic and bright married woman of twenty-nine began to reveal her anger at her husband for their eight years of misery and miscommunications. Taking us into her home by simulation, she set the scene of her family room and all its furnishings. The room was in a state of disarray and reflected her loss of involvement with its maintenance. She presented her husband to the rest of us by assuming his posture, language, and overall demeanor; then became her husband and through his identity told us his side of the

"marital story." Upon concluding his introduction, someone in the audience was selected to portray him as depicted.

The scene commenced with Dave lying on the floor watching television. Ann began the dialogue by announcing that she had reached her level of discontent and desired a divorce; he was too phlegmatic! Dave saw only in Ann what he wanted to see rather than what she "knew" to be her "true self." Dave accused her of encroaching upon his freedom and "laying her thing" on him. As the emotional debacle was released, Ann became aware of familiar feelings that reached into her early biography. She felt "bad" for not making Dave happier. He registered his discontent about her lack of motivation to make the marriage work. As she experienced the feeling she was partly returning to a similar scene with her parents. Simultaneously, Ann stated that she seemed to be repeating a process when talking with Dave similar to experiences she recalled from her parents' arguments. Three central themes became apparent.

1. The insecurity of anger was triggered by another person who seemed passive, disinterested, and ungiving.

2. The feeling of accountability was developed because of failure to bring relief to a situation of pain.

3. The reliving of the experiential process revealed how present conflicts repeat parental processes learned during childhood.

Relating the family-room scene revitalized memories of the second scene: Ann was five years old. She introduced the essential characteristics of each parent; then selected a man and woman in the audience to portray her parents. The theme of their argument was explained, and Ann, as a five-year-old child kneeling upon the floor, began to respond to their anger. Crying pleadingly, the five-year-old Ann began by promising to eat all her food, to pick up her toys, to go to bed on time: thereby successfully diverting the anger between her angry, arguing parents. As their focus was diverted, so was their anger momentarily abated; however, young Ann cognitively integrated her parents' process as terminated and the anger arrested (rather than momentarily interrupted.) Given this power of intervention, young Ann built into her "logic-of-life" that she could "patch things up" and resolve conflict and pain whenever she wanted. An important point to share here is that Ann's mother was the vocally irate parent; her father was characteristically passive and not, as a rule vocally angry. He welcomed Ann's interventions and used her comments as escape routes from an attacking wife; hence he socialized in Ann an obligation to divert conflict and arguments to such a degree that he reinforced this "logic-of-life" message in Ann's process. Seeing the similarities in both life-styles—i.e., her parents' and her own as a married woman—confronted Ann with the need to update her process used as a five-year-old and to accept alternatives for living acceptable to her current age.

When the psychodrama enactment was concluded, people in the audience (Ann's group) were weeping and spontaneously vocalized similar feelings and events in their lives. Their stirrings of associated feelings and events were affective (not cognitive) identifications, triggered by Ann's psychodrama. Now, "guitar theory" can be defined as a process common to and among individuals in which the spontaneous release of a feeling in one person vibrates that "string" (or feeling) in others. Just as the complementing strings of two guitars will vibrate together when in tune, so do people at an affective level vibrate and share a common identification. Ergo—*Spontaneity begets spontaneity because all people have essentially the same repertoire of feelings and likewise have a common communication link.* As my personal consciousness of myself expands at both the emotional and rational levels, I am more available to understand my own "vibrating" and spontaneous feelings as well as those of other people. Too, the realization that my consciousness must expand before the other person's will be clear to me.

In psychodrama groups that meet regularly, for one psychodramatic theme to trigger a similar theme in subsequent psychodramas is usual. Therefore, commonly related themes (by the same individual and/or different individuals) seem to evolve as a stream of associations develop; and succeeding psychodrama sessions can be traced to psychodramas completed by other group members, even as far back as a week or two. If techniques are used arbitrarily (without respect for each involved person's unique process and the group's evolving association of feeling), the overall individual and collective processes become unclear and violated.

When beginning this stream of thought, my concept was that no basic shortcut gimmicks to or through someone's process exist; this follow-through is imminent. Each involved person must be ready (warmed up) to expose an area of spontaneous feeling, suffering, and/or pain before a full purge or catharsis can ensue. Subsequent to the catharsis, ample time to eventuate meaningfulness or cognative integration of that feeling with a life-style of that moment (updating our past with our present) is required. As one area within us is exposed to ourselves and in time integrated, other parts of us begin to unfold within our private process. For example, by uncovering a feeling of anger, the reaction is to make some form of logical sense while working through the feeling. Usually the associated dynamic that resonates will be a feeling of helplessness that will require integration, and that feeling likewise will trigger other associated feelings of helplessness. Perhaps after integrating further, feelings of strength, power, and/or renewed awareness of one's assets will surface; and uncovering of the process will make an individual extremely sensitive to similar processes with others.

Therefore, feelings within a person that are initially identified and explored develop into a simple awareness of similar feelings in others. Later, these feelings may be "seen" as part of a greater system of feelings that must expand the personal awareness level before the systems level can devote similar feelings in others. Each system relates to other systems within us, and these awarenesses help us respond at a third level to the processes of similar systems in others. These levels of awareness seem to follow from the simple to the complex and become further differentiated when traveling from person to person, depending upon the varying contexts of life experiences.

As we live we are consistently facing challenges which require understandings. The understanding cannot be appreciated fully until the experiences are felt optimally. Once one engages the episode, the requisite integrating understanding can ensue. That each person continues to sojourn into the unknown recesses of the intuited, imagined, the past, present, future, the feelings and perceptions, and of course the novel ideas of our time is imperative to growth.

PART II

PSYCHODRAMA

Psychodrama* is a learning process. Unlike the classical theatre of the Greeks, psychodrama is spontaneously produced without written and prescribed roles. The method is designed systematically for individual and group expression of perceptions and feelings through total involvement. Although difficult to describe, psychodrama encourages immediate action, spontaneous involvement, and self-directed discovery as media for growth. By dramatizing life situations, an individual can actually discover and affirm the truth of learning alternatives, for no limit is imposed on what experience can be selected for a psychodrama.

For example, in a *hospital or clinic* for emotional disorders, an individual can act out fantasies, delusions, illusions, personal conflicts, or any segment of life (from birth to death). Once upon the psychodramatic stage, the individual can portray pain; or demonstrate the desired situation as though that pain were not present, A loved one from the past who has died can be invited back through someone in the group who "stands in" for the deceased, at which point the individual can complete portions of the interpersonal termination process.

In *correctional institutions*, psychodrama may be utilized to explore alternative life styles, to rehearse alternative methods for the efficacy of rage release, to learn the depth of the rage, to practice social integration upon parole, to explore building new relations, and to terminate mental association with former styles of crime. Often inmates choose to talk to a son, a daughter, or a spouse who has not been seen in years by asking prison staff or inmates to play the roles of family members.

Introduced to the world on April 1, 1921, at the "Komoedien Haus," a theatre in Vienna, by J. L. Moreno.

In *schools,* students may be asked to portray stories, historical events, literary figures, social processes, and educational content from the physical sciences. Any of such portrayals can involve the student physically, emotionally, and intellectually; and such portrayals can dispel the boredom of "at-the-desk" lethargy learning.

In the section on *Role Playing,* specific examples are listed that lend themselves to the psychodramatic process as well as to role playing. Educational counselors often use psychodrama to help a counselee put into action the concerns that are uppermost in the person's conflict; also psychodrama is often employed in group and individual counseling.

The two primary goals of psychodrama are (1) to provide maximum emotional involvement (i.e., a catharsis) wherein the individual can spontaneously release feelings which relate to his/her reasons for participating in the psychodrama; and (2) to develop a personal process for bringing together a deeper, broader, and more understandable appreciation of each experience. Technically, these goals are called, respectively, the *catharsis of abreaction* and the *catharsis of integration.* The ultimate goal, however, is to pursue the truth through sponaneous dramatic methods.

LANGUAGE OF PSYCHODRAMA

Like so many processes and theories, psychodrama has its own unique vocabulary. Following are some of the basic terms utilized in psychodrama communications and the basic concept of each:

Audience: the people observing the drama; the collective of people that selects the topic, theme, and feelings to be portrayed in the psychodramatic or role-playing situation; the group members who through their sociometric identification select the protagonist.

Auxiliary ego(s): the other actors (the cast) in the psychodrama; substitute characters in the protagonist's life (e.g., a mother, a father, a friend, a spouse, and so forth); those people who are helpers and perform in the drama to elicit spontaneous expression which otherwise the director would need to employ interview techniques to elicit; people selected from the audience to portray significant roles for the protagonist.

Catharsis: the relief that accompanies the spontaneous expression of feelings; the purging; the release from blocked expressions.

Catharsis of abreaction: the first technical goal of psychodrama; the flowing forth of buried feelings related to a specific event; the emotional apex of the psychodrama.

Catharsis of integration: the second technical goal of psychodrama that follows the catharsis of abreaction and reflects the integration of cognative and emotional processes. It is the incorporation of insight with feelings and begins a closing or termination relief.

Director: the trained psychodramatic practitioner (often counselors, teachers, therapists, and clergymen) who guide the psychodrama; the catalyst of action; the person responsible for following the psychodramatic process to a conclusion; the chief, or leader, of the group.

Double: a specialized auxiliary ego; a person who acts as the private thoughts, feelings, and perceptions of the protagonist; an extension of the protagonist's identity; someone who offers support to the protagonist; the person who mirrors the body postures and is seen and heard as being one with the protagonist.

Integration: the process of connecting feelings and perceptions to thoughts and circumstances; making sense out of one's feelings and processes, such as behaving, communicating, feelings, thinking and so forth. The four parts of integration are: (1) the relief that accompanies making sense out of a personal conflict (i.e., often the remission from suffering, confusion, and ambivalence); (2) the process of returning the protagonist to the audience at the conclusion of the psychodrama; (3) the sharing of feelings by the audience members after a psychodramatic enactment; and (4) the introduction of new alternatives for expressing feelings or solving problems that can be rehearsed in the psychodrama.

Protagonist: the central character in the drama; the person whose topic, theme, and feelings with which the group can most readily identify; the sociometric star; the client; the principal student in the psychodramatic or role-playing situation.

Role Playing: the spontaneous enactment of a particular situation or event; an action-learning process; a method for defining social, emotional, intellectual, spiritual, and physical roles.

Sociometry: the science and art of human relations; the systematic measurement of interpersonal relationships; the greatest umbrella of group dynamics; the system of assessing interpersonal networks and linkages; the process through which socialization occurs and is measured.

Stage: the locus of the action; the front of the classroom; the counselor's office; the classical psychodramatic stage; the place open and available to permit action.

Warm-up: a required process for generating spontaniety; a readiness to act, feel, think, and perceive; the introduction to the actual psychodrama; the preliminaries of a scene in a psychodrama or role-playing situation; the preparation process essential in art, music, athletics, sex, and all phases of life.

Other terms and concepts that require elaboration will be explained in the context for readers who are relative newcomers to psychodrama, role playing, and sociometry.

THE PSYCHODRAMATIC PROCESS

The purpose of this section is to present to inexperienced psychodrama practitioners and trainees a macroscopic and microscopic approach to the methodology of the classic psychodramatic process. The styles or techniques which are commonly employed will not be presented, as a bountiful volume of techniques exists among other psychodrama resources (Moreno, 1964, pp. 233-246). Instead, emphasis will be placed on viewing the process by which a psychodrama develops, proceeds, and concludes. The intent is to propose a systematic method to help others understand the developmental evolution of a psychodrama session. To date, only a few models for training exist whereby newcomers can receive an overview of the total process as well as follow the separate stages of a psychodrama. Through the Hollander Psychodrama Curve* (Hollander, 1974) a new avenue is being provided to assist the trainee and trainer in their tasks.

The process has been employed at the Colorado Center for Psychodrama, Sociometry, and Sociatry in Denver, Colorado, and with beginning training groups, advanced seminars, workshops, and psychodrama consultations throughout the United States and Canada. The range of consumer disciplines may include clinicians, educators, social scientists, religious leaders, businessmen and women, correctional staff personnel, and government personnel. Through the use of a graphic paradigm (the Hollander Psychodrama Curve) trainers and trainees are enabled to reify an abstract and at times intuitive process.

THE CURVE

Borrowing and transforming the concept of the normal curve into a variant that resembles a pyramid, the Hollander Psychodrama Curve attempts to denote the bilateral symmetry that exists among all population activities so long as the three-part temporal processes of warm-up, action, and integration are fulfilled; thus the Curve is divided into three horizontal parts. In addition to the horizontal continuum, a vertical dimension is employed. The vertical concept denotes the emotional qualities which exist as one proceeds from the *warm-up* through *integration* (Figure 4.2). These continua remain theoretically the same for any activity, be it birth, learning, teaching, therapy, athletics, counseling, music, lovemaking, communicating, or developing interpersonal relationships.

Although the Curve places emphasis upon the classical psychodrama per se, it also applies to the developmental sequence employed in sociodrama and role playing discussed in the following section.

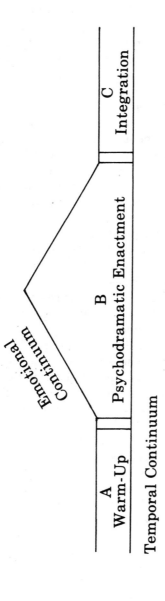

Figure 4.2. Triad of Vertical and Horizontal Dimensions.

187

Calling upon a few examples, clarification may occur. Beginning with the birth process, a warm-up period is gauged by the state of readiness the individuals of the family and the collective family emotionally develop. Many tacit adjustments are required. Such issues as, "What position did I hold as a child in my family?" and "How did I respond to my brother or sister who held the position that corresponds to the position of our expected baby?" "Does any unfinished business with my siblings (or parents) exist that might unwittingly become transferred and projected to the new baby?" Throughout the nine months, anticipated plans are rehearsed and changed. The effect the child will have on the marital relationship, the geography of the household, the economic budget, and the other relationships within the home must be scrutinized with sincere sobriety. For if these issues are left until the child is born, crises and anxieties ensue which create acrimony and a less than fecund environment for the child to enter. Incomplete warm-ups leave incomplete processes and likewise complicate life. Physiologically, the pregnancy may be marked with severe periods of anxiety, counterpointed with rest periods which if continued generate a rhythm to which the unborn child is constantly accommodating, and from which the child is learning. Responding to erratic adrenoline infusions, arhythmic heart sounds, temperature changes, muscle tightness variance, stomach and intestinal gas sounds that amplify or recede, combine to influence the neonate's learning about life. Once the neonate arrives, the birth drama marks the emotional catharsis awaited for nine months. The acceptance of the child into the family denotes the beginning of integration; inclusion as a person, family member, obligation-dependent, and as a fantasy that for nine months could not be ascertained until the moment of birth and the subsequent periods after birth.

Lovemaking, too, proceeds from a warm-up through integration. Lovemaking is a co-creative process requiring certain warming-up conditions within the relationship that are fructifying. The lovemaking act is the catharsis of that warm-up and, if completed successfully, initiates a reaffirming closeness or integration.

Teaching, too, follows the emotional-temporal continuum. Each teacher's style, pace, and circumstances vary; nevertheless, a preparatory period exists when the educator's personal level of readiness transfers to the students, the environment, and the material; a feeling of teacher-spontaneity comes to life (warm-up). The actual presentation, the delivery to the class, is the enactment of this feeling of spontaneity (drama). Finally, the sharing of feelings, thoughts, and perceptions with others builds the avenues that bring students into a shared arena with the teacher; and the presentation permits a meaningful level of teacher-student understanding to be reached that was not present at the outset (integration).

THE WARM-UP

The warm-up position along the continuum may best be described as the process of activating or locating a person's spontaneity. The warm-up is the "operational manifestation of spontaneity" (Moreno, 1964, p. 52), and, as the manifestation, acts as a catalyst for creativity. Without the necessary ingredients for spontaneity, creativity would be virtually non-existent. The completeness of the warm-up period determines the propensity for creativity. Incomplete warm-ups result in incomplete psychodramas and other life functions. Further discussion of "spontaneity" and "creativity" is in the section on *Sociometry*.

The warm-up period is dissected into three micropart subdivisions: the *Encounter,* the *Starters or Phasers,* and the *Sociometric Process.* The motivating basis for all forms of interpersonal experiences is the *Encounter,* a word derived from the French word "rencontre" and the German word "begegnung." Because "begegnung" does not translate easily to any single Anglo-Saxon word, its meaning implies "meeting, contact of bodies, confronting each other, facing each other, countering and battling, seeing and perceiving, touching and entering into each other, and sharing and loving" (Moreno, 1960, p. 15). *Encounter* means the deepest level of communication on a face-to-face basis in which people by individual choice fully experience each other, without coercion or interference by external authorities. These individuals intuitively reverse roles with each other, and each is existentially present to the other in time and space.

The *Encounter,* or "begegnung," takes place in two parts during a psychodrama: (1) "self," (2) "other." The "self" encounter occurs when the individual spontaneously becomes aware privately of physiological or psychological readiness; and asks, "What is going on within me?" or "What am I warmed-up to?" The "other" (or me-you, you-me) encounter is based on sociological and sociometrical principles. During the initial moments of a psychodrama, the director (chief therapist, catalyst, and leader) symbolically asks, "Where is my relationship with you?" and "Where is your relationship with me?" (thereby investigating relationships within and among the group or audience). When optimal spontaneity is experienced at "self" level and "other" levels, the director is prepared to investigate the sociometry of the group.

If the director experiences anxieties either personally or among the audience which are impeding the flow of spontaneity among the audience to the degree that resistances are blocking the expression of the group, *"starters"* must be found through which the anxieties can be expressed and externalized. Action at a physical level is one means of relieving anxieties. Since anxiety develops in the absence of spontaneity, directors often draw upon the repertoire of physical *"starters"* to avert anxiety development.

Implementation by "starters" identifies the second microscopic subdivision—the *Warm-up Phase.* Some examples of "starters" that are useful physical methods for helping individuals to begin interacting are spontaneity tests, (Moreno, 1964, pp. 117-121), situational tests, group exercises and games, and changing the seating arrangements. (Spontaneity tests are a specialized form of play in which novel situations are introduced to individuals in the audience who are invited to meet the situation as an "impromptu" experiment.) Because participants frequently enjoy themselves during the spontaneity tests, their underlying resistances are revealed frequently.

Once the residue of anxiety is dissipated from the audience and director and spontaneity is evident, the group is prepared to deal creatively with issues which heretofore were locked. The point at which the group members begin to interact and co-act marks the termination of the *Warm-up Phase* and the beginning of the *Sociometric Process.* When the audience does not require "starters" and feels warmed-up to begin the session, the director should avoid artificially introducing activities that may be perceived as unnecessary techniques.

In the Sociometric Process, the interpersonal placement and communication pathways which are accessible via sociometric methods become evident (Moreno, 1951, 1953, 1956, 1960). Through these channels of spontaneous interaction

1. the group's wishes are identified,

2. the theme to which the group needs to relate is disclosed,

3. the isolates and rejectees are revealed, and

4. the sociometric star (or protagonist) emerges.

An example of this process occurs when the director invites the people who appear warmed-up for a psychodrama session to stand where the audience can locate them visually. Next, those who have remained seated are asked to rise and go spontaneously and honestly to the person who appears most warmed-up *and* with whom personal identification, feelings, and/or circumstances can be shared. Every member, then, is encouraged to make at least one selection by "putting a hand on the shoulder" of a primary choice. The overall effect is a living action-sociogram of the total group network that includes the individual linkages, the isolates, and ultimately the person chosen as the protagonist. The *warm-up* period is fulfilled when the protagonist emerges from the audience and is ready to work with the issue upon the designated stage or action area. (See Figure 4.3.) As the protagonist moves to the stage and begins spontaneously to work with the director, the psychodrama action (or second part of the total process) begins.

THE PSYCHODRAMATIC ENACTMENT

The psychodramatic enactment begins as soon as the protagonist has warmed-up (1) to the psychodrama stage and (2) to the situation in which the group is to become involved.

Because the protagonist has been selected by the group to be their ambassador (i.e., to represent the prevailing psychodrama theme), the participants move away from the audience to the stage. Frequently, the protagonist requires time to overcome any nervousness engendered by being alone on the stage with only the psychodrama director, who must exercise tenderness and patience to help the protagonist feel trust and spontaneity. As the stage often is foreign to the protagonist, ample time to become acclimated to the new locus is an essential. Once the director, the protagonist, and the stage are united as friends, the action is ready to begin.

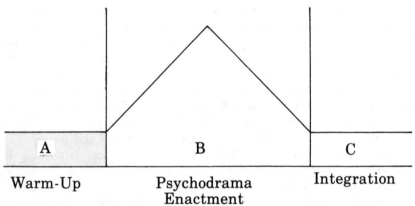

A	B	C

Warm-Up   Psychodrama   Integration
           Enactment
1. Encounter
2. Phase
3. Sociometric
   Process

Figure 4.3. The Three Divisions of
the Warm-Up Period.

Since the protagonist is an expert on his own life, the decision to define in more detail the theme to be enacted as well as the emotional depth limitations is a personal choice. As soon as the theme is defined clearly, the director asks the protagonist to set the stage of the scene to be visited. The following dialogue is an example of a psychodrama scene:

Tom: I've been preoccupied with my graduation and feel sad about leaving home—going to college. I feel that my mom and dad are going to be so lonely when I leave. You see, I'm all they have and their entire lives have been centered around me.

Director: Tom, I know terminations are hard. I remember how mixed up I was when I left for school. In fact, I remember crying on several occasions over the same issue. Tell me, Tom, when did you first become aware of your sadness?

Tom: Well, I've been thinking and planning for college for a long time . . . two or three years. However, it was during Christmas vacation that it really hit me!

Director: Tom, why don't you use the card table, the folding chairs, and whatever else you need in this room to show us that scene. As you place the furniture in the room, describe what you're doing so we can become as much a part of your room as you are. Try to describe even the remotest detail—pictures on the wall, the Christmas tree—if it's in this room—and its decorations, and any other item that is of particular importance to you. Do you understand what I'm asking you to do?

The protagonist describes the scene, and physically establishes the objects in their appropriate places. Tom concretely represents the furniture, pictures, windows, draperies, doors, closets, and color schemes used in the parent's home. Auxiliary objects are used to represent the real objects—folding chairs may become a TV, a couch and so forth. As the protagonist positions the articles, the audience and director warm up to the same room (i.e., they begin to see it through the protagonist's eyes). As the protagonist is encouraged to arrange physically the furniture and objects, an exploration of feelings is not pursued; instead, the protagonist is being encouraged to re-enter the environment emotionally where many feelings were aroused. Anxiety about "performing" before peers is simultaneously dealt with by encouraging physical effort such as lifting of objects, carrying them, and walking about the stage. As the initial scene is set, so, too, is anxiety being dissipated.

Generally, a wise decision is to permit the protagonist to take as much time as required for scene-setting. The moment of spontaneity is usually existentially visible, and that is the signal to proceed to the next task; namely, establishing the time.

Director: Tom, I'm here in your living room in Denver, Colorado, with you and must say it is certainly warm and comfortable. I can see your Christmas tree and the beautiful decorations, some of which date back to the early married years of your mother and father; your stereo; this red print couch; the windows, here, overlooking University Boulevard; the picture of your grandmother, and so forth. Tom, what time is it when we are in this room?

Tom: It's Christmas Day about four-thirty in the afternoon. I've just returned to this room after a phone call from my friend, Don.

Seasons, dates, and hours are temporarily important to the warm-up since the sociometric placement of relevant "others" is strategically linked to one's life. Individuals are linked by associations to both time and space; that is, as a person recalls a time period, a person, or a particular location, simultaneously a vital link is made. As time and place are experienced, weaving the significant people into the action becomes easier; and as time, place, and people merge to complete the picture, a greater potential for emotional involvement and a clarification for both rational and emotional integration follow. "Rational and emotional integration" means the ability of the protagonist to recall events in detail and at the same time link personal feelings to those events.

Including the people in the scene is the final task of scene-setting. Often the actual relatives, friends, and so forth, are not present when the protagonist embarks into psychodrama; therefore, members of the audience are asked to substitute for the missing actors. When the audience members are asked to be "stand-ins," the personalities and characteristics of the auxiliary they are to represent must be identified.

Director: We've taken care to establish your living room, Tom. We know the time is four-thirty in the afternoon and you've been on the phone with Don. Right?

Tom: Right. The phone call wasn't as important as what my mom and dad were saying when I returned.

Director: I'd like to see and hear your mother and father as they're talking. First, I want to meet these two fine people. In order to do this, Tom, I'd like to introduce a psychodramatic procedure called the "self-presentation." What I'd like you to do, Tom, is to go to the part of this room where your father is and take on his identity. Be him. Talk as he talks, gesture as he gestures, use his phrases, and, as your father, tell us about yourself. What's your father's name, Tom?

Tom: His name is the same as mine: Tom. *(Tom crosses the room, and positions himself upon the red couch. He physically takes on an attitiude of sadness—slumped shoulders, long face, arms resting on knees, and a down-at-the-floor look.)*

Director: Hello, Tom. I understand that you and your wife are having a discussion. You look a little sad. What's the matter?

Tom as father: Well, you see, young Tom is a senior in high school; and this is his last Christmas at home. All my life I've thought about his education, his interests, and tried to see that he had what he required; and what I've just begun to realize is that I hardly know my own son; I've been too busy to share my time. *(Tom begins to cry.)*

Director *(waits until tears abate)*: Tom, I'm also feeling sad that you're so "heavy hearted." Before we go further into your sadness, I'd like to know more about you. For example, what do you do? What is your relationship with your wife? What sort of hopes do you have for your son, Tom? Also, tell me anything that is important to you that you would like me to know.

(As the father, Tom proceeds to respond to the questions. Spontaneously, the perceptions he has of his father are revealed while the audience watches. Tom portrays many facets of his father's personality and the audience knows full well that "the father" being presented is an amalgam of Tom's perceptions of the father's actual characteristics. What is of

195

central importance is Tom's perceptions of his father's conflicts and his understandings of the father's situation. After Tom, as father, finishes talking, Tom is asked to select from the audience someone whom he'd like to be the auxiliary-ego for his father. His choice comes to the stage and assumes the exact physical position of the father, hands on head, elbows on knees, sitting upon the red couch looking down toward the floor. Tom does a self-presentation of his mother in essentially the same manner until a clear picture of her is completed; then he selects someone in the audience to be her auxiliary-ego.)

As the auxiliary-egos represent people in the protagonist's social atom, their performances and behavior support the warming-up experience of the protagonist. Auxiliary-egos are asked to portray the people whom they represent as close to the protagonist's depiction as possible. Once auxiliary-egos reproduce the role as described by the protagonist, an important aspect of the psychodramatic process is to encourage the people who are portraying roles to introduce their honest feelings into the role in order to expand the reality of the character. Hence, "canned" or "acting" roles become role-taking and role-creating experiences instead of hollow enactments.

The initial psychodrama scene begins at the protagonist's "reality" level. As a general rule, people seek their comfort level in daily experiences. Therefore, as people tend to function where they are comfortable, the first scene in a psychodrama places the protagonist and auxiliary-egos at or near the operational level of spontaneity; not directly at the core of a conflict. Warm-ups begin at the periphery and graduate to more intensity as they develop. The more complete the warm-up, the more complete and realistic the entire psychodrama session. *Incomplete warm-ups result in incomplete psychodramas.* As the first scene evolves, the protagonist shows how "his/her life really is." The values of the initial scene are many. For example, the director learns from the first scene the biases and assumptions rationally and emotionally maintained by the protagonist. From this array of information, the director develops his/her initial assessment of the multiple implications of the psychodrama.

For example, Tom reveals that his parents have affixed vocational aspirations (as expectations) for him to achieve. Father is subtly projecting the unmet aspirations of his youth upon Tom. Father and mother have expressed greater disenchantment with their relationship. Father is spending more time away from home in order to make more money to support Tom's education; thus Tom feels a burden of responsibility for his parents' unhappiness. Tom does not aspire to become the marine biologist his father has expressed, for he is worried about success versus failure in such an unfamiliar environment. Too, he feels ill-prepared and afraid of living indepently for the first time; and is sad about leaving his friends, his home, his style of life for eighteen years, and, most painfully, his girl friend. Internally, he is in that "What's it-all-about?" struggle within himself; the "gut" feelings "men don't show." As the director makes mental notes of these issues, he must decide, with Tom, which thread of this fabric is the central issue to follow. Through the process of the other scenes in the psychodrama, the answer to this issue becomes clearly defined.

The length of the first scene is gauged by the time it takes the director

1. to understand and explore the essence of the problem,
2. to synthesize a "diagnosis," and
3. to create an atmosphere of permissiveness that nurtures a feeling of trust, integrity, and feedom. Gleaning the essential data from the first scene paves the way for ensuing scenes.

Moving from one scene to another in a psychodrama requires experience with accurate timing; including perception of the protagonist's readiness to accelerate beyond the emotional level of each scene, clarity of director about issues being portrayed, tolerance of audience for the emotional depth established by the protagonist, thoroughness of explanation of theme in each scene, and degree of overall learning possible in each scene. Remember, the quest is for the spontaneous truth as it unravels in the process. Many times the flow from one scene to another is stated clearly by the protagonist; other times the flow rests upon the timing acumen of the director to suggest, always with the permission coming from the protagonist.

197

As the protagonist moves from scene to scene, the movement through the process going from the periphery (i.e., from the most obvious), to the center, then to the most hidden and difficult areas of the pursuit and integration. While moving from the periphery to the center of the quest for integration, exactness of substantive detail becomes less significant than the emotional qualities related to the experiences. By encouraging only the crisp essence of an experience, the director catalyzes the action and interaction toward an emotional apex. As the spontaneity increases throughout the psychodramatic process, the affective climax becomes apparent to everyone present. By offering patience, kindness, and firmness, the director encourages the protagonist to release in action those emotions which have remained unexpressed and unintegrated. Frequently, a protagonist becomes frightened by the surge of feelings beginning to well up to the surface and experiences acute ambivalence regarding their release. Protagonists often have described that moment as the turning point in the session, and have equated this point as the greatest risk faced during the entire process. Protagonists often feel abysmal fright, and need absolute assurance they will not be abandoned and someone will be present who "will and can" midwife them through the experience. The ambivalence felt by the protagonist is referred to as *resistance*, and for the director to recognize this resistance and respect it is absolutely essential. If the protagonist is violated at this juncture, and the need to be cautious is attached, abused, judged as "bad," or some similar innuendo, the remainder of the psychodrama will certainly be enacted under duress. Therefore, when the protagonist manifests resistance in drawing to the emotional climax, the director has several options

1. to become firm and supportive, and to encourage completion of the "catharsis of abreaction,"
2. to detour the route undertaken, and to suggest an alternative that will achieve the apex from some other direction, or
3. to take the time to work consciously with the resistance.

Whichever the choice, the director must be sensitive to the emerging emotions.

The director is by no means passive during the psychodrama, yet often remains unassuming and tacit in behavior. The director's role is to be alert to even the most cursory nuance of details, adding through action helpful infusions that concretize what the protagonist is saying in abstract concepts, and frequently highlighting and amplifying for the audience and those in the psychodrama enactment the full impact of the situation being presented.

For example, Tom says, "I'm torn between doing what I want to do, Dad, and what you want for me. I feel stuck and can't make up my mind." Director: "Dad, I'd like for you to hold Tom's left arm and pull in that direction while telling Tom you want him to go to college, to be a marine biologist, and to do all that you never had the opportunity to do when you were a boy. I'd like to ask Frank to be your double, Tom, and to be that internal part of you that represents what you want to do and opposes your father. Frank will take your right arm and pull opposite your father. Together I want both forces to pull and talk aloud about the two poles between which Tom feels torn ."

Picture the director as the maestro of a symphony. While each person plays a particular instrument with aplomb, the maestro cues, with calls of amplification, diminution, acceleration, and retardation that builds to a climax and works for an aesthetic integration. The "team" is allowed to utilize its se-arate skills and play its parts to enrich the theme and the total process. Although the composition being played may not be the creative genius of Beethoven, the maedtro's contribution is evidenced through a selective ability to maximize the performance of the available musicians. Such is true with the director in a psychodrama.

The initial scenes of a psychodrama are exploratory and disclosing in nature. Efforts to make total meaning are discouraged; for as the process is permitted to evolve, the meaning becomes cumulative and accretionary. The emotional apex of the psychodrama is that point which frequently signals the half-way point of the session. At this point the exploration and validation of the theme has been achieved, the height of emotional spontaneity reached, and the second half of the psychodramatic process begins. Once the emotional climax has been achieved, the director assists the protagonist in "closing down" the drama. (See Figure 4.4) Rather than working on every theme that surfaces in the pyschodrama, as often happens, even in closing the director continues to focus upon the theme that seems most pronounced; otherwise, the director and audience will be inundated with a "psychodramatic medley" which compounds, clouds, and creates unnecessary fatigue for everyone present. The "other themes" will be grist for other psychodrama sessions. The director begins finding ways to integrate and provide closure in the remaining second half of the psychodrama.

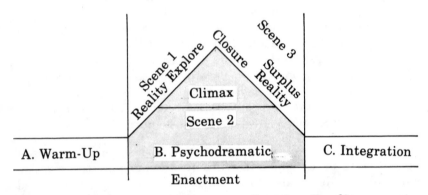

Figure 4.4. Reality — Climax — Surplus Reality
in Psychodramatic Enactment.

Although each session has the potential for vitalizing many other psychodramas, the director needs to be aware of time and energy limitations. Psychodrama as a process is dynamic and, like life, is constantly in flux. The director knows that only a small cross-section of life can unfold during a single psychodrama, and that which is expressed must be integrated by the protagonist before being introduced to another.

The final stages of the psychodramatic enactment require the application of three principles: (1) surplus reality (Moreno, 1953, p. 85, & 1965, pp. 211-216); (2) renewed spontaneity and alternative creativity in learning; and (3) emotional, intellectual, and social integration. Surplus reality refers to those events which are possible in a psychodrama but not actually possible in everyday life. Although everyone employs fantasy-type depictions in dreams in the form of hopes and aspirations, or in "Walter Mitty"-type daydreams, specific dreams per se are not living realities that most people define as common phenomena. Therefore, in psychodrama the opportunity is afforded to place into the dimension of the experiential rather than the abstracted dream dimension a person's private thoughts and feelings.

For example, the utilization of future projections, past reincarnations, or talking to a deceased person via some auxiliary-ego are forms of surplus reality. Another example is what Tom would do if he could envision his future and see through action what he would be doing if he chose each of the alternatives that were discussed earlier. How would his life be if he decided to pursue the marine biologist career chosen by his father versus the life he would have, should he pursue his own choice? One rehearsal scene might permit Tom to share his true feelings with his father, knowing the difficulty of the process of uniting the feelings with his father and son into communicable understanding. Both possibilities are called *surplus realities* because each remains in the realm of realities that "could be." "Surplus" realities are contrasted with the "givens," which Tom had as options at the beginning of the psychodrama, and place more "realities" at Tom's disposal than when the session began.

Surplus reality refers to the enactment that is possible only in psychodrama—not in everyday life, and permits the extension and expansion of creativity given the discoveries made available through psychodrama; a form of life rehearsal and life fulfillments that provide opportunities to experience one's dreams, hopes, and needs, which in life are not forthcoming. A protagonist is encouraged to confront and talk to himself, a method used to complete psychodramatic ego-repair (i.e., to forgive self, to assess personal assets, to relinquish interpersonal debts, to redefine one's identity, and to find alternative ways to expand and become more spontaneous).

201

Psychodrama is enacted to provide creative and productive objectives. One ethic inherent in the methodology is the suppression of destructive behavior; therefore, no session may conclude with a destructive act, such as suicide or murder, nor may the session terminate in an artificially contrived manner (i.e., if the protagonist doesn't believe in the method). Using the surplus reality concept, the protagonist is directed toward a positive or productive closure feasible within life's purview. In such closures, the protagonist experiences several levels of integration: spontaneity training, role training, and an aesthetic expression of his/her creative potential.

Earlier the statement was made that the entire second half of the psychodramatic production is integrative in nature. The integrative process occurs at three central levels:

1. the exposed feelings of the protagonist are worked through and resolutions begun;
2. the protagonist and auxiliary-egos are integrated into the sociometry of the audience; and
3. the members in the audience are given time to share and integrate their feelings of awareness as identified with the psychodrama.

As Tom passed from scene to scene in the action, he retrogressed to age five and recalled that he "always wanted to please his parents" so he would earn their love. His earliest recollection of this innate urge came as he was preparing to leave home to enter kindergarten. As the scene developed, Tom was struggling with his anxieties over leaving his parents, his fear of going to a strange school and being essentially "alone," and his desire to do what was "right." Through the drama it was revealed that his crying was met by a petulant reproach from his teachers who said that "big boys don't cry." The conflict between his feelings to please or to run produced a scene parallel to that which occurred earlier when his father was pulling one arm and his double pulling on the other. In essence, the scene was the source of an incompleted process—a process in which Tom cut off his spontaneity and opted to be a "big boy" and not cry.

The outcome of this scene was that Tom confronted his teachers in anger and told them that they had no right to order him to stop "feeling his sadness." Simultaneously, Tom realized that he had harbored the belief that becoming angry and feeling sadness placed him in jeopardy of losing his parents' love. He continued to express himself openly and spontaneously. The anger erupted, his tears flowed, and his intense conflict was unlocked and released. Using surplus reality, Tom at eighteen had a heart-to-heart talk with Tom at five. He embraced the five-year-old via a double and assured him he was still lovable when he cried in his experience of anger or fear, and that he (Tom) would love the little five-year-old even if he did "show" his feelings. Tom reversed roles with the five-year-old Tom and answered himself from his younger self: "You know, Big Tom, if you cry, you're lovable, too;" and another tender, genuine embrace ensued with his five-year-old double. Then Tom looked up at the director and said, "You know, Carl, all this time I've been withholding my feelings from my parents because I feared they'd reject me; and I don't really think that's true."

The closing scene showed Tom rehearsing how he wished to tell his parents the truth by taking their roles, via role reversals. He engaged them in dialogue that made sense until he clearly replicated what he believed his parents would say and feel. He integrated the meaning of the conflict he initially presented. The psychodramatic enactment concluded.

INTEGRATION WITH AUDIENCE

Once the psychodramatic enactment is concluded, the auxiliary-egos return to their seats in the audience; the director and protagonist sit side-by-side in front of the audience; and the third segment of the process, *Integration,* begins. (See Figure 4.5) Three steps are included in this section: audience sharing, interpersonal dialogue, and wrap-up.

Because the protagonist gives a great deal of himself/herself to the audience and feels very vulnerable, an essential component is for the *audience to share in a like manner.* Therefore, the director informs the group that the protagonist is to remain silent and listen

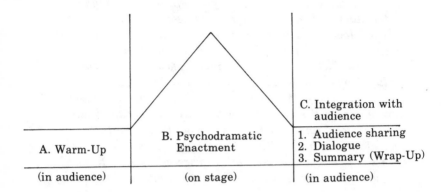

Figure 4.5. Integration Steps.

while all persons in the audience report their own feelings, as openly and honestly as they are able. As the protagonist listens to the reports of how others identified with the dilemma, the shared vulnerablities among everyone present are recognized. Questions, analyses, interpretations, and criticisms are discouraged. Should these occur, the director encourages the audience member to convert the interpretation, question, criticism, and analyses into personal statements. The sharing is important for two reasons:

1. As in all life experiences, one association triggers another, and in doing so uncovers areas in the "memory bank" of each person which, in turn, releases emotionally loaded material (similar to the "guitar" theory mentioned previously). For example, listening to a musical composition may recall memories of childhood experiences, unrequited love experiences, or special relationships with people. The same phenomenon occurs in psychodrama; the audience vicariously lives through the protagonist's experiences and catharsis.
2. As the protagonist emerges as the theme carrier and leaves the audience, a physical and emotional separation occurs on the way to the stage. Consequently, the

204

audience sociometry is changed, and the protagonist risks isolation. The efficacy of the *Integration* segment is the catalyzing of group cohesion and a reassimil_tion of the protagonist into the audience. As the audience members share their feelings, the protagonist learns that nearly every member of the audience can identify with the theme of the session. Through this process the protagonist receives validation that no isolation has occurred; instead a great deal of love and respect has resulted (Barbour, 1972, pp. 132-137).

The second part of Audience Sharing is the *dialogue*. Once each person's associated life experience has been related, open dialogue follows. This dialogue is equivalent to a group discussion, to group psychotherapy or counseling, or to a didactic training in sociometric group dynamics. Since the first part of the audience integration is self-disclosure and is by design a time when questions and answers are discouraged, the dialogue portion permits this interactivity among "the others" in the group, but not to or with the protagonist. The major emphasis in the dialogue is on open interaction among group members and the feelings which these individuals need to expose. Usually, staff members act as co-therapists or discussion facilitators and encourage the group to plot its own course and take time to come "full circle" with the theme they selected to explore. This process is consistent with the role of the director in the psychodrama in that the director *follows* and assis+s, rather than leads, the dialogue discussion. The group receives reification for its strength during the dialogue period and re-enters into the experience that "a group takes care of its own members." Reification of strength is subtly developed when the group chemistry or group personality increases in cohesion and members learn that a group determines its members and members determine the group.

Infrequently, a director or a protagonist is unable to complete the integration during the action part of the drama. Whatever the reasons may be for incomplete integration, the built-in mechanism of the Audience Sharing segment furnishes alternative insurance. Closure occurs for the protagonist while sitting with the audience and listening to its sharing, dialogue, and wrap-up. The novice director thereby may be assured that the protagonist will not be left without adequate closure and integration should an incomplete integration exist in the psychodramatic enactment. The essential element in the total psychodramatic process is trust; and with trust, the process will function faultlessly. Certainty and reliability in the process comes only with many hours of psychodrama involvement. Trusting this process evolves with practice — just as miles of skiing are required before that process can be trusted.

The concluding segment of the process is a summarization or wrap-up. This summary may be presented by the director, the protagonist, or someone in the audience. Often, a verbal summary is not required; rather, the director merely may ask, "Would anyone else like to share anything before the drama is closed?" The concluding comments move from an affective to a cognitive focus. As the audience members integrate their feelings, experiences, and thoughts into a congruous whole, they simultaneously insulate themselves against the possibility that anyone will leave in "psychodramatic shock," or in a state of incompleteness, pain, or panic. One method to use in seeking closure is to encourage members to become more cognitive in the utilization of their intellectual processes.

PSYCHODRAMAS IN SUMMARY

The Hollander Psychodrama Curve has been designed to facilitate the training of psychodrama practitioners. Because psychodrama is applied by the educator, the counselor, the theologian, the social scientist, and the clinician, the Curve is depicted as generally lending breadth for multi-disciplinary application. By design psychodrama is geared to those individuals interested in classical psychodrama; yet, the process is equally applicable for those using sociodrama, role playing, ethnodrama, axiodrama, or group process.

The greatest strength of the Curve is its visual usefulness because the Curve permits both a partial and a total analysis of classical psychodrama. In addition, the newcomer to psychodrama is presented with the symmetry by which sociometry, psychodrama, and group processes are integrated. Furthermore, the Curve may be utilized as a paradigm which professional and student practitioners may use to review and gain understanding of psychodrama sessions.

All too often the psychodrama neophyte falsely assumes that a few sessions are adequate preparation for directing the process. An introduction to the total process and dynamics of psychodrama via the Curve may encourage this individual to be more circumspect about precipitous assumptions, which may result in the neophyte giving more time and energy to professional preparation.

Although upon first impression, the Curve connotes the presence of a terminal point in a psychodrama session, a finale is never consummated. Each session is potentially an extension of, or forerunner to, additional psychodramas. Therefore, the Curve is only one facet of a dymanic process consisting of a continuum of similar curves. The Hollander Psychodrama Curve is not intended to be static; rather, the Curve is an objectification of a dynamic process having many parallels to the dynamic process of life (See Figure 4.6). The discussion proceeds by focusing on role playing in the next section as a practical method for action learning.

PART III

ROLE PLAYING

A classroom in which the emphasis for learning is on (1) active involvement, (2) emotional and cognitive integration, and (3) spontaneous expression is a classroom in which happy teachers and students are working as co-learners. The individual learners are not secondary to the lesson, its content, or the learning process. The learner is not the "mug" into which the "jug" pours wisdom or knowledge; rather the learner is being freely encouraged to experiment and test out the mysteries of life and maintain zeal for learning. Role playing is one example by which students and educators can co-learn and experience "fun."

Before describing the methods for using role playing, consider for a moment an area of learning prior to the introduction of a child to an institutional school. Play-qua-play is one form of learning. Through play activities children "try-on" their environment. They become the people, animals, and objects which surround them. With fervor, they assume the characteristic feelings, mannerisms, value systems, logic, and so forth inherent in the identities which they assume. For children, as with many adults, identity can only be actualized when it is tested. Children are natural testers. They test through the media of games, pretense, fantasy, and experiment by imitating the characters to whom they have been exposed. For children, environmental testing is the method by which learning

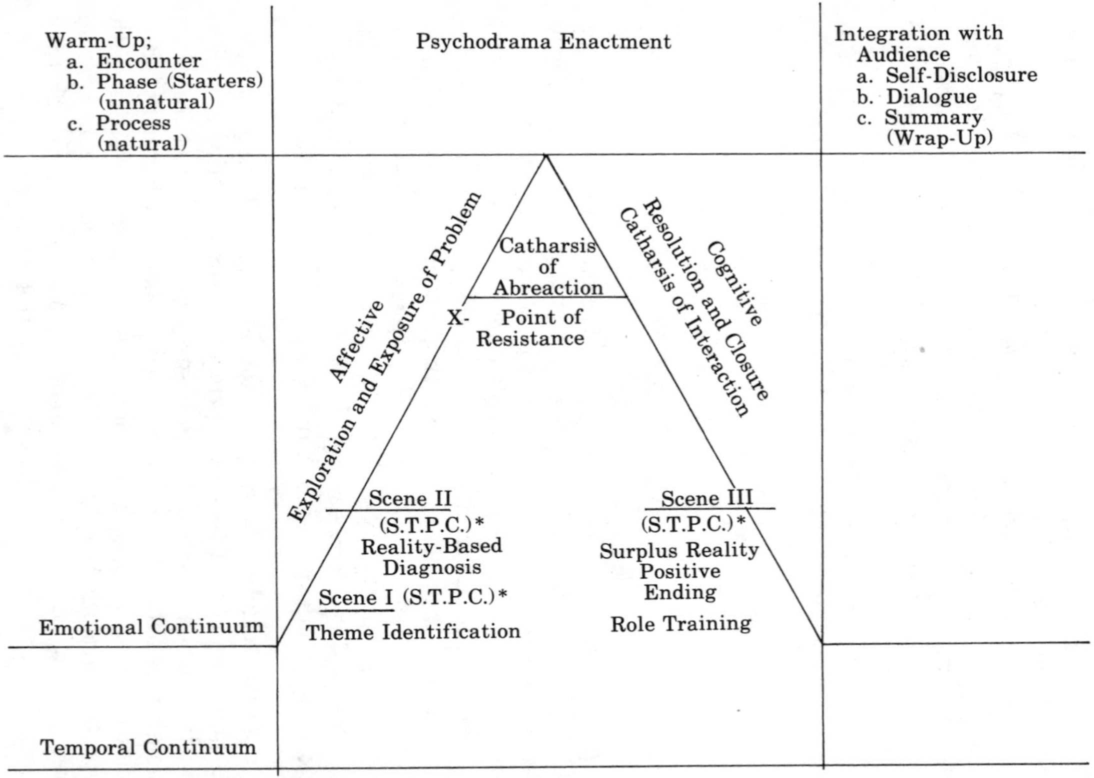

Figure 4.6. The Hollander Psychodrama Curve. *S.T.P.C. – Scene, Time, People, Circumstances.

occurs. Playing-out an experience requires spontaneity and creativity. The emergence of a "self" is a beautifully creative process. The development of a multi-dimensional self is likewise tested over and over again as children rehearse "themselves" in play. Yet, before the creativity of the child can fructify into a fuller person, an essential component is to support the child's experimental efforts in learning about the concepts of environmental space, time regulations, interpersonal strengths, and personal creativity. Whenever a child's learning capacity is not exercised in these areas, experiences lack fulfillment and individual confidence does not maturate as the child relates to life. For this reason, play is essential to the development of the child evolving into adulthood.

Incomplete play experiences leave incomplete children; and incomplete childhood testing via play results in incomplete adults. This phenomena is reminiscent of the discussion of the psychodramatic process; namely, that incomplete warm-ups leave incomplete dramas and integration. "The extent to which people allow themselves to warm up to an event determines how fulfilling, complete, and creative the act that follows will be" (Leman, 1973 & 1976).

One of the earliest cultural shocks occurs when a child begins school. Play and fantasy methods are regulated systematically and limited upon entering the formal learning environment. The child is required to accommodate and assimilate to a myriad of stark realities:

1. Organized activities
2. A pack of other children
3. A set of rules and expectations defining behavior
4. Foreign "work" and play paraphernalia
5. A novel environment
6. Time regulations and limitations
7. An environment in which every article is "on loan" and none "mine"

These realities confront the child "all at once with nothing first" and force the child to either retreat and/or regress in order to accommodate to the shock. Too little warm-up time is provided for the child in preparation for the environmental change of school; yet, warm-up is absolutely essential to survival in school. Often the child is confused and overwhelmed, and responds with fear and resistance.

In the throes of these cultural crises, children survive; in fact, children use the same survival process as chicks in a pen use when the shadow of the hawk falls upon them: they flock together and continue to play. Fortunately, children are resilient and recover quickly from a crisis experience. Nature and life seem to have blessed them with that wonderful gift of spontaneity that catalyzes adaptability.

As stated previously, without an adequate warm-up to school, children meet the novel environment with anxiety, mistrust, and suspicion. The rules and expectations placed on early school-age learners result in feelings of imposition. Adult teachers are viewed by the children as the authors of this learning experience that inordinately manipulates their spontaniety. Actually, action-oriented learning which was predominately exercised in their life of play is being transformed into cognitive and phlegmatic learning. The excitement of life and its discoveries are being reduced as the learning time per day in school is being structured and increased. Children articulate the emotional message, "You expect me to live your way, and that's foreign to me; I can't be me and live your way." Children need to be met and encountered on their own terms; to be known as individuals in and for their own rights. Guiding child encounters requires the learning of new methodologies and concepts by the pedant, particularly in the areas of children's values, attitudes, and, above all, feelings. Children are affective learners, and will, if permitted, self direct their learning through play, according to Sharon Hollander (1976).

Maximum growth occurs when an individual is intellectually, physically, emotionally, and spiritually involved and can utilize his/her life experiences to incorporate new learnings and make sense out of what he/she is currently experiencing. When a teacher is faced with a class of thirty or more students, as so often happens in our classrooms today, he or she is faced with the task of making information relevant to each of those students in terms of his or her life experiences. Not only does each student have unique life experiences, he/she also has a unique process of learning—his/her own way of thinking things through, of incorporating new ideas and information, of responding. The task of making information relevant to all thirty students with thirty sets of experiences and thirty

210

individual processes of learning seems overwhelming to most educators and, at times, impossible. To "feed" the "student" information and to evaluate the "learning" by requiring the student to send back what the teacher has expressed frequently is easy. The following material illustrates an example of what can occur in such a situation.

The teacher is standing at the head of a fourth-grade class explaining to her thirty-five students the concept of the American family. Most students come from middle-class homes. The time is 10:00 a.m. and the students have been unusually attentive and cooperative; it is one of those days when there is a good feeling in the classroom. She goes on ".... the average American family lives together in a house. Each member has different duties for which to be responsible. The mother may cook, clean house, take care of your clothes, help you get ready for school. The father may go to work and make money to buy food, clothes, and toys. The children may empty the garbage, set the table, and keep their rooms clean. They each do something to help the family live together, and each feels a part of the family. Each member depends upon the others and in this way learns how to get along with them. The family teaches you how to get along with people, helps you assume responsibility for when you grow up." The teacher asks for the childrens' responses.

In her classroom, fifteen of the students come from homes where their parents are either divorced or separated; four have lost one of their parents through death; three live in apartment houses; twenty of the childrens' mothers work; three of the students' fathers are diagnosed alcoholics and unable to work; five of the students never clean their rooms; and the pattern could go on and on.

A girl speaks up, "It's like we all need each other for something . . . that's how it is in our family. I do the dishes, and I get an allowance. Except our dog, Snuggles, doesn't do anything; but we still love him." The class is silent, and slowly those students whose home was described begin to grasp the concept of the interdependence of the family and talk about it. The others, believing their families to be typical, feel self-conscious, guilty, and many actually believe that if they pick up their rooms more often, they, too, will be average and "OK."

The teacher has described a family that even for middle-class America is slowly becoming a myth. Some of the students have confused "average"* with "normal"* and have confused "get along with"* with "don't be angry, loud and spontaneous."* She has alienated many students in her class and unwittingly made it very difficult for most of her students to appreciate the "value and functions of the American family,"* (*Quote marks have been added by the author.)

Mrs. Hollander concludes her thought with the belief that each of the thirty-five students and the teacher are experts on family relations. In fact, no one "right" answer exists to define a reality. Grand theories too often discount the particular realities and foster unattainable ideals. Teachers might consider role playing the life experiences of their students in order "to activate the wealth of experiences within each child's repertoire." In 1934, Dr. J. L. Moreno introduced "role playing" in *Who Shall Survive?* Upon its revision, he refined his ideas in these terms: "Role playing may be considered as an experimental procedure, a method of learning to perform roles more adequately . . ." "Role playing is an act, a spontaneous playing, ..." (Moreno, 1950, p. 84)

Role playing is exciting because it is very simple. The learner shares in the learning by being physically, emotionally, and intellectually involved as a person; certainly not passive nor dependent. Neither is the teacher imbalanced with extreme responsibility and over activity. Now, as teacher an essential component to the role-playing process is for you to develop a warm-up, that is, an environment of trust devoid of criticisms, judgmental comments, and censorship. An atmosphere of unconditional positive acceptance is crucial for students to feel the permission to disclose their spontaniety. Spontaniety is the mediating quality of role playing; the spark of each individual's uniqueness that amplifies the role being portrayed.

Once an environment of trust has been established, the teacher needs to be aware that as a role model, others are being socialized to these norms. The teacher's fears, anxieties, and spontaniety will carry over to the others involved. Role playing is as free and productive as the teacher will permit himself/herself to be and consequently will allow others to feel.

Role playing can be employed in almost every class once the foregoing variables have been given attention.

Author's Note: You are only limited by your own creativity and spontaneity. If the teacher is flexible and imaginative, no limit exists to what can be introduced with role-playing methods.

ROLE-PLAYING STRUCTURE AND IMPLEMENTATION

Begin the role-playing session with a clear introduction of the purpose. Often people need the introduction as a warm-up period in which to begin gauging whether or not they can become attuned to the situation and the actors. Students commonly become concerned over the degree of accuracy with which they are role playing the parts. Therefore, the teacher needs to clarify (1) the definition of the role-playing situation and the roles for each of the actors; and (2) the fact that each individual brings an uniqueness compiled from special life experiences to the enactment, and that biases are valuable to the role portrayal. No two people will play a part in exactly the same manner. Allow the role player to feel the spontaniety of the moment and to flow with the events. Once a person begins to "act" in the theatrical sense (i.e., with artificial affectations that are more stereotyped than sincerely felt), such pretense indicates the spontaniety and creativity in the role-playing situation has been lost. Role playing is not a training session for "actors," it is a medium used to direct spontaneous problem solving, information gathering, and the alternatives for living and learning.

Permit the learners to volunteer for the roles that are required for the session. Involve the role players in some of the scene details, e.g., furniture for the scene, closeness and distance of participants to one another, and time of enactment. Also, introduce the characteristics of the role players. When the individuals of a class feel that they have shared in the details of the role playing, they, in turn, will feel greater commitment to the action.

Once the role-playing situation is defined, four mechanical considerations follow:

1. *Establish the scene.* Set the scene in detail by using chairs, boxes, and tables to represent the accoutrements of the scene. Permit the students to explain spatial details that

213

will facilitate a rich feeling of the locus for enactment; the more tangible and concrete, the more realistic.

2. *Establish time.* Seasons of the year, month, and hour often reveal a mental set from which the situation can be appreciated. Is the occasion a birthday, an evening after supper, or the anniversary of a special event?

3. *Define the circumstances of the situation.* Is an historical event taking place, e.g., the enactment of Joseph as he is sold into slavery by his brothers would encourage the students to describe the clothes that were worn, to perceive time without modern technology, and to recall the values upheld by the family regarding the statutes of men and women. How did the Jewish community exist under the threat of Pharaoh?

4. *Select the student actors.* Permit each student to warm-up to the part by interviewing for the role.

Proceed by employing the present tense rather than by referring to past referents (as is done in psychodrama); in other words, orient the interview to the "here and now." The role-playing enactment may begin by clarifying any questions and saying, "Now, go ahead." Remember, the more physical the action, the greater the spontaniety. As teacher, step away and permit the students to carry the responsibility until concluded.

The time limit for the role playing may be defined by the abilities of the actors to maintain the flow of the action. If an impasse is reached or the spontaniety lost, the instructor may invite the actors to rejoin the audience (rest of class). Role playing also may continue according to time limits announced in advance. If adequate time is available, the session can be trusted to close naturally by the role players. In the event that the session concludes because of an impasse, whatever the reason, the actors and audience can unite to finish the details of the action by open discussion. If the session concludes naturally, the entire class is encouraged to discuss points of interest apropos to the theme of the role-playing session. The instructor might paraphrase students' lives or the roles with which they identify.

A critique of the actors is dispouraged as this process tends to violate the atmosphere of trust, unconditional positiveness, and spontaniety. Judgmental comments, as "Michael did better than Calvin," are likewise discouraged. In role playing each actor employs his/her perceptions and background of experiences to create the role he/she portrays. Therefore, presumably each student would act out the role differently than any other student.

Listed below are some recommended role-playing situations:

Class	Role-Playing Situation
History (Secular or Religious)	a. Moses, Aaron, and Israelites receiving the Ten Commandments.
	b. Lincoln and Douglas debating issues of the nation in the nineteenth century.
	c. Jesus with the disciples (e.g., at the Last Supper).
	d. "The Good Samaritan."
	e. General Robert E. Lee signing the surrender of the Southern States at Appomattox Court House.
	f. A discussion among Colonial revolutionaries prior to the War for Independence.
	g. The Battle of the Alamo.
	h. The view points of Crazy Horse, Sitting Bull, and George Custer; and the events leading up to the battle at the Little Big Horn in Montana.
Literature	a. Steinbeck often employs marine animals to highlight messages in his novels, and these animals could be portrayed.
	b. In a chair before the class a literary character(s) could encourage free discourse between the character(s) and the class.
	c. F. Scott Fitzgerald could be invited to talk with "Gatsby," Sally Carroll of "The Ice Palace," and George Hannaford of "Magnetism."
	d. A dialogue could be initiated between his mother and "Lord Randal."
	e. A debate could occur between Christopher Marlowe and William Shakespeare.

f. Short stories the students have written could be staged. (This device is particularly helpful if characters need depth and dimension.)

Developmental Anatomy

a. Use clusters of students as anatomical parts by running streamers among them; then have parts of the circulatory system traced by assigning one or two people to act as drops of blood. Encourage animation in Walt Disney fashion for each role as well as in the dialogue.
b. Use a model similar to "a" to show how an aneurism develops in a prescribed area.
c. Use a model similar to "a" to show the birth process.

Social Studies

a. Portray a parole board in session.
b. Enact the state legislative process of initiating a bill through committees, etc., into a law.
c. Be the President of the United States (or Secretary of State, or an energy administrator), receiving a telephone call.
d. Demonstrate norms, mores, and folkways as processes of socialization.
e. Lead a discussion about ways a complex organization dehumanizes its employees.
f. Develop a "grapevine" for circulating school rumors.
g. Enact a coy girl on her first "date."

Mathematics

a. Use individuals of the class as units, tens, hundreds, and so forth, and demonstrate elementary arithmetic (actually carry a person as a unit to the person who is a ten.)
b. Create a store scene between customers and sales people. Explore numbers and monetary concepts.

c. Use streamers as points on a plane; then explain the laws, axioms, and theorems of geometry. Encourage anthropomorphic dialogue within the role playing.

d. Use individuals as measuring units, to concretize length, to tell time, and to measure liquid.

e. Create a stock brokerage firm in which a regular investor is buying and selling shares of stock via stock exchange board listings.

Biological Sciences

a. Place a mineral, a rock, or the elements of a geological process in an empty chair and ask students to talk to that item (the students are to be other rocks, minerals, etc.).

b. Demonstrate how red sandstone is formed.

c. Demonstrate the process of uplifting and faulting in the mountains.

d. Demonstrate how a plant grows.

e. Demonstrate ecology in action.

Mental Health

a. Demonstrate what happens in a family prior to, during, and subsequent to a divorce.

b. Demonstrate how mental hospitals contribute to chronicity among patients.

c. Demonstrate a counseling session as the session might be conducted ideally; then how not to conduct the counseling session.

d. Demonstrate "being-with" a patient in order to assist the patient as a person.

e. Demonstrate a group session as a counseling or therapy process.

f. Be a person in need of help and ask the class to identify what you need or what would be most beneficial to you as a person.

217

The examples listed certainly are limited; add to the list and experiment freely. Remember ability to employ role-playing methodologies is limited only by a willingness to risk being spontaneous.

Generally, role theorists make three assumptions about role playing according to Mann and Mann, 1959, pp. 64-74:

1. Role-playing experience increases role-playing ability. (Role playing is defined in terms of the size of the role repertoire and the effectiveness of the role enactments.)
2. Role-playing *experience** increases interpersonal adjustment. (Interpersonal adjustment is defined in terms of role-playing ability and the situational appropriateness of the roles that are performed.)
3. Role-playing *ability** is positively related to interpersonal adjustment.

Role playing is a process. Like psychodrama, role playing includes the warm-up, the enactment, and the sharing. The central difference between role playing and psychodrama is the degree of emotional depth and the training required for the leader or director. Role playing is usually situational and pre-designed; psychodrama evolves from the known to the unknown. Role playing, although excellent for problem solving, is not directed at emotional catharsis; the psychodramatic process examines complex emotional situations and requires intensive formal training to utilize. Role playing and psychodrama both include sociometry, described in the following section as a process for interpersonal relationships.

PART IV
SOCIOMETRY

The primary aims of psychodrama and role playing are to facilitate those avenues which will integrate a person's life into a creative design, to help that person feel personally powerful among peer collectives, and ultimately to feel membership and separateness

---

*The italics are those of the author.

within the world at large. Sociometry is the generic term used to . . . "describe all measurements of societal and interpersonal data." (Bain, 1943, p. 212)

SOCIOMETRY AND LEARNING*

One young person, e.g., Bobby, is consistently chosen last in gym class. When the coach announces the activity, "basketball," "pom-pom-pull-away," "red-rover-red-rover," or "dodge-ball," invariably the two captains selected as alternating choosers select everyone to be on one team or the other. As the least skilled person or the least liked, Bobby is chosen last; moreover, he knows, as do the others, that if the teams are limited to seven, he would be left on the sidelines. So, after consistently being chosen last, his behavior predictably begins to change. He begins to come to class late, usually after the teams are chosen. He says that he forgot his gym shoes; becomes injured more frequently in the game; or gets ejected from the game for aberrant activities (breaking rules and so forth). Bobby is a sociometric isolate, struggling for membership and a sense of integrity. Certainly every teacher has encountered a Bobby, and I am sure many can identify Bobby's dilemma. With the use of sociometric lenses the dynamics for understanding and aid for Bobby becomes evident.

Three of the most important questions each person asks throughout life are

1. Who am I?
2. Where do I fit?, and
3. How well am I functioning?

An individual needs to appreciate those uniquenesses from and commonalities with those around him/her. Without this sense of identity and this sense of separateness and togetherness, no person can acknowledge him/herself favorably, nor link with others in a meaningful way. The proclavities for appreciating and accepting oneself (and others) directly correlates with productivity and

---

*This section has been co-authored with Sharon L. Leman-Hollander and is an extrapolation, in part, from "Sociometry," *Sensorsheet,* (Winter, 1973.)

creativity. Therefore, any person who has a low self-concept can be expected to have severe difficulties with learning.

Sociometry is based on the concept that individuals must have a specific number of people with whom they can meaningfully relate or feel close to in order to experience their creativity and power, i.e., self confidence. Sociometry provides the structure to measure systematically interpersonal networks within a group; in other words, to identify the "social winners" and "social losers." Teachers and other in leadership positions have the power to influence the sociometric process of a class and thereby enhance the learning of its members. Therefore, the concepts of the three social atoms—the psychological social atom, the collective social atom, and the individual social atom—must be understood fully by teachers in order to appreciate optimally sociometry as a behaviorial measurement.

THE PSYCHOLOGICAL SOCIAL ATOM

The "psychological social atom" is the smallest number of individuals that each person absolutely requires in order to function in life. The psychological social atom generally (but not always) includes oldest, dearest friends or relatives; this social atom is tantamount to one's vitality. Without these vital people, life swings into a crisis pattern instead of a growth pattern. Everyone varies in the number of vital people required for his/her psychological social atom, the number may be two, five, or seven . . . when one's psychological social atom size falls below that which is required, energies redirect themselves toward locating people to fill the void. This search pattern exists as a priority, often at the expense of all other activities. For example, Mike's psychological social atom may include his best friend, his brother, and his mother. Should his best friend move away from the city, every attempt will be made to maintain emotional contact with his friend. Should this prove futile, Mike will experience severe emotional disequilibrium because of the social disequilibrium. Mike's overall behavior will reflect his crisis, and his capacity to be creative will be replaced by an all-out attempt to re-establish his psychological social atom size of three. One poignant feature of those people in our psychological social atom is the depth of intimacy we feel toward them and they toward us. They can reciprocate great emotional involvement at

220

more levels with the other than anyone else. Essential variables for the relationship are depth, breadth, need, and reciprocity. Likewise, each person can role reverse with the other intuitively, emotionally, spiritually, and socially.

The feelings associated with these special individuals are organic (i.e., the people comprising the psychological social atom are experienced as vital organs providing sustenance to one's life). If one individual is removed through death, geographic change, or interpersonal disassociation, the resultant sensation is shock, grief, and disequilibrium. The desperation that accompanies psychological social atom death* is tantamount to one's own death—beginning outside oneself and concluding within; that is, psychological social atom death may precede and correlate with one's own illnesses and ultimate physical death. To acknowledge the pain involved consciously is extremely important when marriages dissolve, when people grow old, when people retire, when people geographically relocate: to name only a few examples. Everyone involved in these examples—children, parents, spouses, and friends—may all be afflicted with tremendous shock and/or threatened survival if a member of the psychological social atom is involved. To hear or read about an elderly married couple who has no one left in their lives but each other is not uncommon. When one member dies, the surviving member has no psychological social atom remaining. Within weeks, the community learns that the survivor, too, has died.

COLLECTIVE SOCIAL ATOM

From conception onward, human beings always are connected to an invisible and informal social network, referred to as *sociometric linkages*. With rare exceptions, everyone alive has a tie to another person who, in turn, is tied to another, and so on. Through growth and time these linkages, or associations, take on form and structure called *collectives*. Each person reaches a point in life when identity by affiliation with a collectivity becomes important—be it Cub Scouts, Little League, dancing school, a play group, the family, "the club," kindergarten, pre-school, or nursery school. Later, as adults, the collectives develop into more complex organizations, such as place of employment, family, civic groups, religious

*Psychological social atom death refers to a total dissolution of all members such that the number is reduced to zero.

221

affiliations, peer group, recreational organizations, educational enclaves, political memberships, professional groups, and so forth. From childhood through adulthood, certain groups of people become more important than others; in fact, a few collectives are regarded as essential and vital, not merely "primary," as Charles Hart Cooley (1962, pp. 23-31) alluded. The collective social atom is responsible not only for the socialization of the individual, but also, like the psychological social atom discussed previously, for the qualities of intense and reciprocated need. *The collective social atom is that aggregate of people and activity absolutely vital to one person's existence at an emotional level.*

Just as the psychological social atom was defined, the collective social atom consists of "the smallest number" of collectives to which a person requires membership in order to feel sociostasis (i.e, socio-emotional equilibrium). An emotional attraction to the collective exists in the same sense of need that prevailed in the psychological social atom with the exception that the collective is a cultural entity and not a human entity.

Collective social atoms are the structures which provide linkage into the community for the individual, the avenues by which individuals relate to others in a meaningful way, and the lifelines which meet needs for growth and maintenance of growth. Collective social atoms provide a structure within which an individual can be spontaneously expressive and creative. The feeling that accompanies and relates to a collective social atom is "I'd do almost anything to be a member here!"

Sometimes, unfortunately people perjure their values in order to retain a linkage in the collective social atom particularly when their available options are too few. As valuable as integrity is, a person will violate that integrity for a collective social atom particularly when he/she requires one for emotional survival; yet loss of integrity or values are not concomitants for membership in collective social atoms. However, collectives engender a feeling of tremendous commitment; and some people do, in fact, forego identity, values, and integrity when a collective social atom requires this action. Some notable examples are the values imposed by the teenage culture, the cultures of ethnic and racial ghettos, poverty communities, professional organizations, police departments, and armed forces. Teenagers (and, of course, others) turn-on together with "grass" or hallucinogens even though they know them to be ill-advised, illegal, and/or harmful. Adults and youth may "sniff coke," or "do smack," in order to "get-down" with a group of friends. In order to behave professionally, many men and women accept the obligation for others before they have completed the process of being responsible for themseleves—in the name of "helping." Police and armed forces personnel kill in the name of their cause or role. These paradoxical activities, of which everyone is capable, become more likely if the collective social atom supports these norms or criteria for membership. Conversely, when the collective social atom nurtures creativity, the people who have sociometric linkage within it experience tremendous surges of power and growth.

A collective social atom of a nine-year-old might look like the one for David that is illustrated in Figure 4.7. Although collective social atoms are basically small, the point is likely that many types of groups or affiliations exist in one person's life. David, the nine-year-old portrayed in Figure 4.7, belongs to Cub Scouts, Hebrew School, a fourth-grade class, and a Little League soccer team; yet, his family and a core-group of play peers, in this example, are the most vital parts in his life. Should either his peer group or family dissipate suddenly (or gradually), his activity in all the other affiliations would appear sub-standard; in fact, he might manifest gross learning difficulties at school. Until he finds a substitute or replacement for his dissipated collective social atom, he will exert his energies into this activity (i.e., replacing it). Also, David's behavior probably will appear to be emotionally, socially, intellectually, and even physically impaired. Once he completes the required grieving process *and* redevelops his lost collective social atom, his activity in the other areas predictably will regenerate.

INDIVIDUAL SOCIAL ATOM

The "individual social atom" is the "smallest number of people" that a person requires within the collective or the affiliation in order to feel emotionally linked to it. Reflecting upon David, as a nine-year-old, he is a member of a soccer team; however, the soccer team is not one of his collective social atoms, but the team membership is important for him to desire inclusion. Upon closer analyzation of the team, David has two buddies who stand out as more important than anyone else on the team. Both friends, Joe and

223

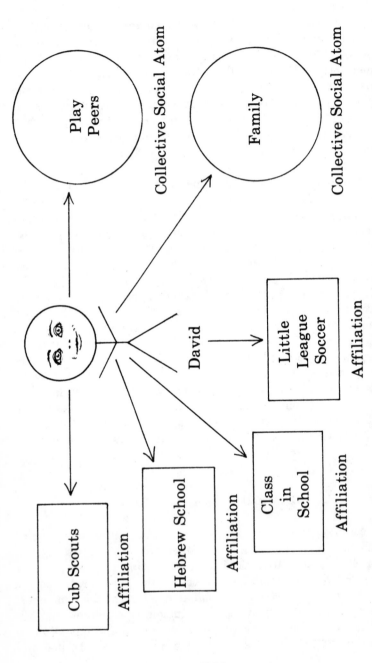

Figure 4.7. Important Affiliations and Collective Social Atoms of a Nine-Year-Old Male.

Patrick, are part of his individual social atom. For Joe and Patrick to qualify as part of David's individual social atom, several criteria must be met:

1. A feeling of reciprocation must exist between each boy and David such that they can feel into the real essence that is truly David and he feels each of them, as well. In psychodramatic terms, each boy truly role reverses with David and he with each of them.

2. David affectively knows that he can be spontaneous with Patrick and Joe and reciprocates the levels of spontaniety of the other two.

3. Through their relationships David feels and demonstrates his creativity.

4. Their interlocking relationships provide David with a feeling of cohesion which in turn must work in opposition to a feeling of isolation and/or rejection from the soccer team.

5. A feeling of satisfaction exists with David in relation to his social atom size of two people, otherwise, if David's social atom size were only one (instead of two), either Joe or Patrick would be less important to David in the soccer group.

6. David must be able to ask for and receive certain kinds of support from the other two; in other words, the relationship must meet certain specific needs.

7. If in David's situation Joe and Patrick were to leave the team, predictably David would (1) choose to stay but begin trying to link two new boys into his individual social atom; (2) lose interest in soccer and manifest sub-standard team playing, higher incidence of absenteeism, and accident-proneness; or (3) terminate affiliation with the team.

Although the applied individual social atom related to David and could apply to all children, the principles stated apply to adults and teenagers as well. Every individual needs to establish an individual social atom in every group to which he/she belongs. For everyone to learn the specific number of people needed in order to experience and express maximum spontaniety and creativity is essential. If a person requires five people in a social atom and the number falls below that, uppermost in personal actitivies will be

225

the search to locate a replacement for the absent number. For students the spontaniety required for learning is reduced while searching; and they appear less attentive and/or mentally available at class sessions.

Individual social atoms are critical for survival—be the atoms academic, professional, or at times physical. When the number of members in one's social atom (psychological and individual) drops to zero, crises develop. Some of the most dramatic examples exist during periods of adjustment to relocation (e.g., transference to another school, incarceration in prison, admission to a hospital, commitment to a nursing home, housing replacement to urban renewal projects, and change in family ties—children going away to college, getting married, or establishing families).

If new social atoms are not developed, death may soon follow. In the school environment, academic death may result from failure to achieve grade standards. In prisons, death frequently occurs by suicide. In nursing homes, death may result from immediate and continuous physical deterioration. In urban renewal, increased crime and delinquency, alcoholism, and illnesses are evidenced. Children leaving home frequently exacerbate parental depression and that may escalate to family discord and/or divorce. Such losses may conceivably predispose one to physical illnesses.

In summation, every person in this culture requires a specific number of people to respond to their manifold needs. Some of these people are those who know us most intimately and have an appreciation for our biographical evolution. These people are vital and can appreciate our emotional vitality and vulnerabilities—our psychological social atom. Likewise, centers exist for social contact with a variety of role definitions. These places afford us with anchorage, i.e., a sense of stability which acts as a geographic territory that is called "ours." These small enclaves provide us with reference groups that have ties to other groups in such a way that we feel a community relatedness. These units are our collective social atoms. We identify with them as actual social structures and in a different vein, as cultural entitites. The third social atomic structure (the individual social atom) relates to the actual people who are members of the associations, groups, and collectives to which we belong. These individuals are the few who by their presence help us to continue feeling motivated and enthused. These are the special persons who can console, commiserate, and support us whenever we feel the need. They are our individual social atoms.

226

SOCIOMETRIC NETWORKS

In addition to the human need for social atoms, an equally important need for sociometric network linkages exists. The classroom provides an excellent structure to examine further the concepts and importance of sociometry. As a student chooses other students to be part of an individual social atom, many criteria are used in the selection process. Concurrently the student begins to form networks throughout the classroom. Some students receive and send many choices to other students; others send a few; some, send no choices at all. Choices may be positive, indifferent, neutral, or negative, and may or may not be reciprocated. The classroom may be diagrammed (Figure 4.8) to indicate student preferences when asked (1) With whom would you *most* like to sit to discuss the assignment? or (2) With whom would you *least* like to sit to discuss the assignment?

The significant people in the diagram (Figure 4.8) are Dick, John, and Dan. Dick is a sociometric isolate; a person within the group who receives no choice from his peers on any criteria. Unchosen both negatively and positively, Dick is a peripheral person not connected to the netowrk because he neither chooses nor is chosen; therefore, he is powerless to effect any affirmative influence in the class.

John is a sociometric star, a person within the group who is most often chosen according to a particular set of criteria, and a person who frequently responds in kind to those who choose him. As the sociometric star, he has a capacity for perceptual and emotional sensitivity and can feel and respond to the processes of other people. His character is reflected by a centrality established according to group norms, by an emotional, intellectual, or social position, and by a capacity to carry great power or skill informally in a specific area of response.

If John received the highest number of choices and the highest volume of reciprocated choices, and was singularly outstanding on all or most criteria, he would be charted as a sociometric leader— not merely a star. Some of the following criteria might exist in a classroom: With whom would you most like to study? ... Do a paper? ... Have lunch? ... Sit and visit socially? ... Play football? ... Share your feelings? ... Walk to and from school?

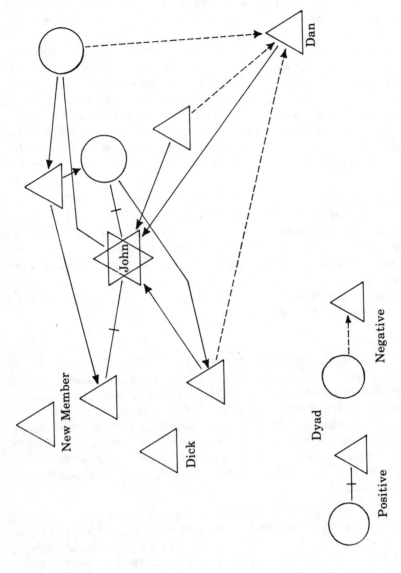

Figure 4.8. Diagram of a Sociometric Network Linkage.

To establish viable criteria is extremely important prior to the administration of a sociogram. A sociogram should not be viewed as a popularity contest, for it is a measurement of specific criteria that assesses each individual and develops networks along specific dimensions. Criteria, to be reliable and valid, require the answers of involved individuals to be truthful and spontaneous. In addition, the criteria must be related to the actual implementation of the individuals' responses. If criteria are manufactured or hypothecated, answers become less relevant and therefore less meaningful and valid. For example, if improbable criteria—such as, "With whom would you most like to sit on a bus should we travel to Chicago?"—were used, students knowing that the trip was unlikely would tend to fabricate responses and thereby invalidate answers.

Dan in Figure 4.8, is a sociometric rejectee; a person who receives an unexpected number of negative choices from peers. Dan's position is similar to the isolate's in that he is a peripheral person vis-a-vis the class. However, a rejectee is consciously rejected from membership or linkage within the network; an isolate is not responded to at all—just seems to blend into the "woodwork."

Given the previous classroom sociometry, a teacher may accurately assume that John holds a tremendous amount of informal power to influence the learning and growth in the classroom. Dan holds a different form of power, the power to interrupt the learning process while remaining powerless to affect affirmative class decisions. Dick is busy directing energy toward finding group linkages, not toward learning. Until each member in the class makes and/or receives reciprocal choices, the point can be assumed that the class energies will be directed toward that end, and students will place higher priorities on that activity than on the lessons imposed or introduced by the teacher.

TEACHER INTERVENTIONS TO FACILITATE LEARNING

If the teacher provides an atmosphere in the classroom of spontaniety and freedom from judgment, students are enabled to form linkages with peers and fill social atoms. Students require time and space for this process. Frustrations frequently revolve around the teacher's need for classroom control, which often requires an inordinate amount of both teacher and student energy. The "loss of control" as described by teachers is very often an active movement among students to develop social networks, to reveal existing social networks, and to test indirectly linkages with one another. Another description of this process is that the students are warming up to one another in order to expand their sociometry, the most important priority before moving into the classroom drama of learning. The teacher, akin to a psychodrama director, who flows *with* rather than *against* the students (or audience) enhances availability to participate affectively in the classroom situation being disclosed.

For teachers to reap the benefits of their professional power, they must learn how to identify where the powers in their classrooms lie. Although the schools and the school systems formally ascribe nominal power, i.e., leadership authority, to the classroom teacher, no intrinsic guarantee exists that the students will reciprocate and confirm that role to the teacher. Impotent teachers like impotent students are socialized to the dilemma ... each in part by the other. Educators who are available to the informal networks created among their students are usually educators who can cite where they fit in their respective faculty networks. Such educators understand and appreciate the process of power sharing and will respect rather than fear the power in the classroom.

One of the crucial variables for the teacher to use in finding the most powerful people in the classroom (stars and leaders) is the student social networks. As the isolates and rejectees in the class develop and become apparent, the affective teacher is in a position to integrate them. One powerful method available to integrate peripheral people, particularly those in a position concomitant to learning difficulties, is to combine them with the apparent sociometric stars and/or leaders, or with students who are already linked or close to the stars. Concretely, the teacher must avoid linking rejectees and/or isolates to one another; for, as these links develop, enclaves or pockets of resistance form to interrupt the total class process because the isolates and rejectees who have little decision-making and interpersonal influence maintain a tremendous disruptive power.

One advantage of being aware of this system is that the teacher knows where to place the most energy when disquieting episodes disrupt and erupt within the class. A rejectee can become particularly disruptive as the recipient of a large number of negative sociometric choices.* Such disruptions are signals of distress, of crisis feelings and of a need for help—even at the price of becoming the class clown or cynic. If this strategy occurs, the teacher must confront both the rejectee and the group directly in an attempt to develop an understanding of the position of the rejectee in the class context, and to establish some rationale for the initial rejection. This settlement is necessary before lessons begin. Class cohesion is in indication of an atmosphere totally conducive to spontaniety and learning. When isolates and rejectees persistently exist, cohesion is reduced significantly and optimal learning blocked.

A student caught in the process of changing schools requires time and encouragement to link into the social networks. As a teacher becomes more adept at identifying the sociometry of classes, the disequilibrium felt by a class and a newcomer can be removed more quietly and quickly. Often the new student is apt to link with an isolate or rejectee who is, in desperation, reaching out, too, for someone—anyone. If this linkage develops, the newcomer is caught in a position of isolation or rejection with the older "class member." To avoid such dilemmas, the teacher can reduce the social distance among new, isolated, and rejected students by bringing two polarized positions together (e.g., the new student with the star). Again the fact is emphasized that the most powerful integration agents for peripheral people are the sociometric stars, the leaders, and the people most closely related to them.

As an educator, my assumption is that students cannot be made to learn, and that essentially a teacher cannot teach a closed mind. A student learns when the content presented makes sense in terms of personal life experiences, when the student wants to know the content, and when the student feels comfortable in the group sociometry. Every individual gravitates toward those situations which provide the greatest opportunity for spontaneous expression, and which permit the continued seeking for companions who are willing to share. Sociometry is a democratic process of, for, and by the people that enables each person to form interpersonal linkages and to nurture mobility. All people require psychological, individual, and collective social atoms in order to survive socially,

---

*These choices are demonstrated through class activities rather than on standard sociometric tests.

physically, emotionally, and intellectually; therefore, learning is directly related and influenced by sociometry and the development of social atoms.

TELE-TRANSFERENCE-EMPATHY

Sociometry also includes the concept of *tele;* the phenomena that envelopes spontaneity, creativity, and cultural conserves. *Tele,* a term used by Moreno, is central to sociometry, and often characterized by reciprocation. *Tele* originated from the Greek concept for "far" or "far off," and, as applied by Moreno, means to feel into distance to perceive the real attributes of another person. To this author *tele* is the feeling two people have for one another because they are able to sense intuitively the actual processes operating within one another. Also, *tele* is the cement which holds relationships together. Telic sensitivity is the smallest unit of feeling that can be measured by a sociogram; and though it cannot be measured directly (like intelligence and personality factors), its manifestations can be measured. According to Northway and Detweiler (1956, pp. 271-286), "Tele is the fundamental factor underlying our perceptions of others." The high degree of mutuality found in sociograms is usually due to *tele,* for *tele* binds people together to form social atoms.

Moreno asserts that relationships cannot be built or maintained through projections. Transference, for example, is a process of establishing a relationship in which the primary mechanism is projection. For example, Tom sees in Bob certain characteristics of his brother, Steve. Because of the similarities, Tom tries to develop a relationship with Bob based on the characteristics of feelings about his brother, Steve. As soon as Tom discovers that Bob refuses to be Steve, his brother, or respond as Steve does, Tom begins to lose interest in that relationship.

Similarly, empathy (one-way tele), or empathic sensitivity, projects one's personal feelings into the *tele* process in an effort to share in feelings of another person. Perhaps the other person does not have the same feelings. A person who is able to empathize with another person may be able to take injurious advantage of that person, or to make that person dependent upon him/her through "empathic cunning." "This is why training of empathic ability as in the case of psychopathic individuals frequently leads to the opposite of what is expected." (Moreno, 1965, p. 21). Empathy generally occurs among counselors and therapists with their clients. In these situations the client is seen, heard, felt, and respected for whom he/she is but cannot reciprocate intuitively into the counselor which leaves the individual feeling in imbalance and denuded to the other. These examples work against relationship building because they are too one sided and obviate a telic and sociometric bond. Therapists and counselors, in order to overcome this situation, are required to disclose their human dimension (needs, values, feelings, opinions, and intellect). Relationships built upon transference and empathy do not last. For an empathic or transference relationship to be redirected into a telic relationship is possible.

Tele, I believe, is trainable and can be further developed in everyone. This author equates *tele* to intuition. *Tele* is a nonrational and almost reflexive inner sense that is present in children, but atrophies as one passes into adulthood. Because to validate the authenticity of *tele* or receive feedback about it, is so difficult most people "unlearn" and devalue its utility (often fear that the opprobrium will cost them valuable relationships).

PART V
LIFE-PROCESS CURVE

Life is a weaving together of one's spontaniety, creativity, and cultural conserves. When each flows cyclically into the other, life has meaning.

Psychodrama, role playing, and sociometry are means for us to assist others in their life flow. Let's examine spontaniety, creativity, and cultural conserves to understand how each flows cyclically into the other, forming a life-process curve.

SPONTANEITY

Spontaneity is defined in two parts by Moreno (1934, p. 42): "a novel response to an old situation or ... an adequate response to a new situation." Therefore, depart with me from the usual style employed in this Chapter and let's develop a novel form in contrast!

(Q.) What are the characteristics of spontaneity?
    (A.) Spontaneity is related to the *moment;* has defined *parameters;* a specific goal: *creativity; adequacy* (i.e., to time, space, circumstances, and people); *novelty* (i.e., a quality of newness, freshness, originality, and the energy

233

to activate one's warm-up to the expression of feelings—
"S-Factor").

(Q.) How does spontaneity relate to anxiety?

(A.) Spontaneity relates to the present moment; anxiety relates to the future. In the absence of spontaneity, anxiety arises. Anxiety creates a "blocking" phenomenon that requires physical action for release. Anxiety lacks clear parameters and seeks its own release as its goal. Anxiety calls forth familiar and often inadequate rather than novel and adequate ways for release.

CREATIVITY

(Q.) What is meant by creativity?

(A.) Creativity is the externalized by-product of spontaneity; the validation of a person's power; a unique synthesis and integration of an idea, feeling, perception, and interaction with one's environment; the process of birth and growth; in summary, the potential possessed by everyone. A person is not required to paint as Van Gogh, compose as Beethoven, write as Steinbeck, or think as Einstein to be considered creative.

CULTURAL CONSERVE

(Q.) What is "cultural conserve"?

(A.) Cultural conserve is a process of preserving that which was created, a process whereby the art, literature, music, language, values, and relationships that form a culture are reproduced systematically. Cultural conserves can be viewed as the internalized social heritage of society and the "distinctive way of life of a group of people, their complete design for living." (Kluckhohn, 1951, p. 86) From our internalized cultural conserve repertoire we draw new energies to create.

For life, growth, and health to exist, the process is necessary to weave together a person's spontaneity, creativity, and cultural conserves so that each flows cyclically into the other as is illustrated in Figure 4.9.

234

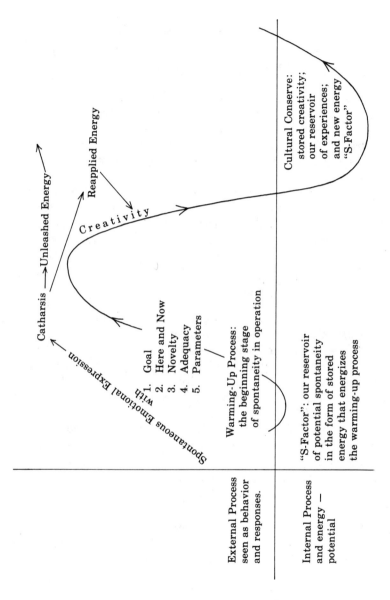

Catharsis →Unleashed Energy→

Reapplied Energy

Creativity

Spontaneous Emotional Expression
with

1. Goal
2. Here and Now
3. Novelty
4. Adequacy
5. Parameters

Warming-Up Process:
the beginning stage
of spontaneity in operation

Cultural Conserve:
stored creativity;
our reservoir
of experiences;
and new energy
"S-Factor"

External Process
seen as behavior
and responses.

Internal Process
and energy —
potential

"S-Factor": our reservoir
of potential spontaneity
in the form of stored
energy that energizes
the warming-up process

Figure 4.9. Life-Process Curve.

PART VI
CONCLUSION

Psychodrama, sociodrama, and role playing were originally group therapeutic methods modeled after life. Today, because of their flexibility they are used throughout the world as learning vehicles in all kinds of institutions—Mental Health, Educational, Corrections, Religious, Business, Industrial, Government, Family, and Armed Service. A person is not a collective of isolated segments but an operative synthesis of personal totality: physical, emotional, rational, social, and spiritual. In order to benefit fully from learning, a person requires total involvement in the learning process. Psychodrama, the process and the theory, engages the individual at every personal level and encourages the expansion of each level in order to enhance the reservoir of personal power. Calling forth energy (S-Factor), each person becomes more alive to such personal power (spontaniety—creativity) and learns to integrate flexibly into an environment that is spatial, temporal, and interpersonal. All experiences of an individual are considered real—be they hallucinations, fantasies, dreams, wishes, perceptions, feelings, interactions, or thoughts; and each experience can be concretely enacted in a psychodrama.

In order to maximize learning, the understanding of temporal and spatial sociometry is essential. A human being is a social being and requires social inclusion. Failure to become grounded in sociometric networks and social atoms creates crises and pain. These events subtract energy from, living at the creative level and bring about behavior geared more for survival than for growth. Psychodrama enables the individual to discover psychological, individual, and collective social atoms; to develop sociometric linkages, and to function via alternatives offered in these spheres. Every individual requires a catharsis to purge the toxity of suppressed feelings; and catharsis can only occur when spontaniety is available and congruent with both the individual's warming-up process and environmental rhythms. However, catharsis for catharsis sake is insufficient. One must learn to integrate cognatively feelings, values, and perceptions by acting out creatively fresh methods most harmonious with each person's needs.

Psychodrama seeks out the truth and strives to sustain it. Learning seeks for truth, also. Since Psychodrama is a learning process and can be tempered to any environment; no special professional field is the sole possessor of its use. Certainly extensive preparation is required of someone wishing to practice psychodrama and sociometry. Central to becoming a director or practitioner is the acquisition of knowledge about theory and skills involved in the process, and the discovery of personal truths that comes by experiencing the psychodramatic process directly as a protagonist time after time. Learning psychodrama is no different than learning life; it must be lived through with its pains and pleasures untitil knowledge begins to transfer into wisdom. Justice Oliver Wendell Holmes made this statement: "Life is action and passion: I think it is required of a man that he should share the action and passion of his time at peril of being judged not to have lived." He was excitingly confronting and wise! Imperative to a meaningful life is that individuals realize they are what they believe and believe in what they are, that they do what they believe and believe in what they do, and that they do what they say and are able to say what they do.

Author's close: this anecdote is true! It occurred several years ago while I was a staff member at the Fort Logan Mental Health Center. As was usual, on Thursday afternoons I left my office in the Administration Building, crossed Oxford Avenue and walked north to the Geriatric Division of the Center. Upon entering the unit, I found the staff and patient members sitting in a semi-circle awaiting my arrival to "lead" them in their weekly psychodrama session. On that day, however, I was greeted by a kind old man whose name was Mr. Riley. He and I had been together in the Thursday psychodrama sessions for several months and had come to respect and, in our ways, love each other. "Carl," he said, "can we do something different today?" Feeling he had something in particular on his mind, I asked him to share his idea. He suggested that the twenty-two people in attendance sub-divide into small groups, discuss a theme that was important to them, then in turn play-out their vignette as a role-playing situation. As there was general agreement with Mr. Riley's idea, we proceeded to enact his suggestion.

One group, in particular, stood out that day. When they took the stage each person brought his chair, or wheelchair; then placed the chairs together in pairs so that

237

each pair was arranged in rows, one behind the other. Mr. Riley announced, "We are sitting on a bus taking a tour of Paris, France. I am the bus driver and tour guide." He assumed his position at the front of the paired passengers, and with his imaginary microphone began describing the sights. As he narrated the tour, the passengers maintained a chronic din of complaints. As he pointed to The Louvre, he said, "On your right, ladies and gentlemen, is the classic art museum of antiquity, The Louvre. Isn't it magnificent!" The passengers responded to their comfort rather than the classically beautiful Louvre. They made such statements as "I'm uncomfortable." "Who's smoking?" "How long is this ride going to take?" "I hope the fee is worth the trip!" Riley continued, "And up ahead of us, ladies and gentlemen, is the Arc de Triomphe—that's Napoleonic in vintage. Can you believe how beautiful and well preserved it is!" The passengers continued to complain. Then Mr. Riley addressed them with "Look over there! There's the Eiffel Tower, the engineering hallmark of Paris. Isn't that majestic!" Still the passengers complained. "Now, ladies and gentlemen, we're going up into the mountains." (Pause) "We're now seventy-five miles from Paris or anywhere ... My God, our road is slipping away!" At this point the patients and staff who were role playing the passengers responded to Mr. Riley. "Oh, he's lying to us." "Well, why doesn't he get out and do something!" "I'm just going to sit here until he takes care of it." "I want to go back." "I'm afraid!" "You know, we might die here!" The final response to this last statement was— "C'est la vie."

I recall feeling tears in my eyes and hearing weeping from a few people scattered throughout the room. As is the procedure after action, I asked the members of the audience to share their feelings. I received many gifts as these aged people spoke. To paraphrase their words, which reflected so much wisdom and foretold what I as a thirty-year-old man had to look forward to, they said "There are so many classical things in life to experience—like the Eiffel Tower, The Louvre, Arc de Triomphe—the friends and family who mean so much, the kind words or gesture that someone offers, the little bits of sharing. Yet, so many people spend life complaining about every little thing, and pass by these lovely classical moments. Everybody one day will be seventy-five miles (i.e., years) away from the source where their trip began. Will we bemoan our fate by saying, 'I'm not really at the end of my road; it's a big lie.' or, 'I'm somebody else's responsibility and want to be taken care of?' or, 'I want to reminisce and live each precious moment in reverie.' or, 'Yes, I'm going to die here but—Oh, I've lived!' I, too, ask these questions, then answer, "Life's classical moments are too precious to miss."

The challenge of the gift these old people shared with me and which I now share with you is: What will we say when we face that time and space of life's termination!

REFERENCES

Bain, Read. Sociometry and social measurement. Sociometry, August, 1943.

Barbour, Alton, The self-disclosure aspect of the psychodrama sharing session. *Group psychotherapy and psychodrama,* Vol. XXV, 4, 1972.

Beam, Philip C. *The language of art.* New York: The Ronald Press, 1958.

Berne, Eric. Review of Gestalt therapy verbatum. *American Journal of Psychiatry,* Vol. 126, 10, April, (1970).

Cooley, C.H. *Social organization.* New York: Schocken Books, 1962.

Hollander, Carl E. A process for psychodrama training: the Hollander psychodrama curve, (Monograph). Littleton, Colorado: Evergreen Institute Press, 1969, revised for Colorado Center for Psychodrama, Sociometry and Sociatry, 300 E. Hampden Ave., Englewood, Colorado 80110, 1974.

Hollander, Sharon L. See Leman, Sharon L.

Kluckhohn, Clyde. The study of culture, Daniel Lerner and Harold D. Lasswell (Eds.), *The Policy Sciences,* Stanford: Stanford University Press, 1951.

Leman, Sharon L. Action learning. *Sensorsheet,* a co-publication conceived by the Environmental Studies Project and the Earth Science Teacher Preparation Project, funded via National Science Foundation. Boulder, Colorado, Box 1559, 80302: Newsletter No. 10 (Winter, 1973). Revised as Sharon L. Hollander for Colorado Center for Psychodrama, Sociometry and Sociatry, 300 E. Hampden Ave., Englewood, Colorado 80110, 1976.

Mann, J.W. and Mann, Carola H. The effect of role-playing experience on role-playing ability, *Sociometry,* 22, 1959.

Moreno, J.L. *Group method and group psychotherapy.* Bacon, New York: Beacon House, Inc., Sociometry Mono., No. 5, 1932.

Moreno, J.L. *Who shall survive? a new approach to the problem of human inter-relations.* Washington, D.C.: Nervous and Mental Disease Publishing Co., 1934.

Moreno, J.L. *Sociometry, experimental method of science and society.* Beacon, New York: Beacon House, Inc. 1951.

Moreno, J.L. *Who shall survive?* Beacon, New York: Beacon House, Inc., 1953.

Moreno, J.L., et al. (Editors), *The Sociometry Reader.* Glencoe, Illinois: The Free Press, 1960, reprinted from *Who shall survive?,* 1953.

240

Moreno, J.L. *Sociometry and the science of man.* Beacon, New York: Beacon House, Inc., 1956

Moreno, J.L. *Psychodrama,* Vol. I. Beacon, New York: Beacon House, Inc., 1964.

Moreno. J.L. Therapeutic vehicles and the concept of surplus reality. *Group Psychotherapy,* XVIII, 4, December, 1965.

Moreno, J.L. *Psychodrama,* Vol. III. Beacon, New York: Beacon House, Inc. 1969.

Northway, Mary L. and Detweiler, Joyce. Sociometry in education: children's perception of friends and non-friends. in J.L. Moreno, (Ed.), *Sociometry and the Science of Man.* Beacon, New York: Beacon House, Inc., 1956.

Schutz, William. *Here comes everybody.* New York: Harper and Row, 1971.

RECOMMENDED READINGS

Bischof, Nedford, J. Moreno, (Chapter 10), *Interpreting personality theories.* New York: Harper and Row, 1964.

Blatner, Howard A. *Acting in: practical application of psychodramatic methods.* New York: Springer Publishing Co., 1973.

Corsini, Raymond J. *Roleplaying in psychotherapy—a manual.* Chicago: Aldine Publishing Co., 1966.

Eisenstadt, Jeanne Watson. Personality style and sociometric choice, (Monograph). Washington, D.C.: NTL Institute for Applied Behavioral Science, Associates with the National Educational Assoc., No. 3, 1969

Haas, Robert B. *Psychodrama and sociodrama in American education.* Beacon, New York: Beacon House, Inc., 1949.

Hawkins, Frances Pockman. *The logic or action: from a teacher's notebook.* University of Colorado, Boulder, Colorado: Elementary Science Advisory Center, 1969.

Hollander, Carl E., and Moore, Charles. Rationale and guidelines for the combined use of psychodrama and videotape self-confrontation, *Group Psychotherapy and Psychodrama.* Vol. XXV, No. 3, 1972.

Moreno, J.L. *Psychodrama,* Vol. II. Beacon, New York: Beacon House, Inc., 1964.

Moreno, Zerka T. Psychodramatic rules, techniques and adjunctive methods (Monograph 41), Beacon New York: Beacon House, Inc., 1966.

Yablonsky, Lewis. *Robopaths.* Baltimore, Maryland: Penguin Books, Inc., 1972.

5

LEARNING HOW
TO ASSESS
HUMAN GROWTH
THROUGH SYSTEMATIC APPROACHES

Thomas C. Froehle

Learning How to Assess Human Growth Through Systematic Approaches, as presented by Froehle, clearly defines the importance of assessment in improving learning environments: (1) analyze the problem to establish a goal; thus a person or group specifies initially just what needs to be accomplished; (2) decide how to reach the goal most efficiently; then (3) determine how people involved in effecting the change or solving the problem may determine when the goal has been achieved. Approaching growth and development in this systematic fashion increases the control of a person or group over the environment it plans to develop.

The problem-solving process recommended by Froehle is similar to the communication process of encoding, transmitting, channeling, and decoding. Whenever one or more persons assume responsibility of bringing a particular environment or change into being, the first step is to communicate the problem situation accurately. A problem assessment and goal analysis make accurate communication interpretation possible. Since most changes in an educational environment are dependent on the actions of people, such changes must be analyzed in terms of specific behaviors or performances people must follow for the goal to be achieved. Therefore the goal-analysis procedure for bringing about changes in an environment or for problem solving requires actions or performances to reach a specific goal. Froehle defines a performance as an "observable behavior, something that people can see or hear or detect that another person does."

Another essential element in this performance is for the persons or group intending to change an aspect of an environment or to solve a problem to "see" when the goal has been reached; in brief, "the end product must include precise statements of measurable objectives," otherwise no way exists to determine whether the goal has been achieved, and the change consummated.

245

Of course, during the assessment process different types of objectives may be considered as vehicles for reaching the goal change; however, "In assessment of consequence-based objectives it's what the receiving person, the consumer, knows, does or can do that counts." Assessment, then, rather than being a beginning or end step in the process of solving problems or effecting environmental changes, is an ongoing process that necessitates wording objectives in terms of the actual terminal performance desired.

Regardless of the situation, the first step in systematic problem solving is to specify precisely what behavior(s) we want to establish, under what conditions it is to occur, and what constitutes minimum performance level.

Actual measurement (or assessment of how a consumer is progressing toward the agreed-upon goal) by a counselor, teacher, parent, principal, or any person trying to effect change is of utmost importance in determining whether or not the consumer has been helped to accomplish the change. Since such accountability is professionally significant, a helper must be concerned not only with post-assessment of the end product, but also with pre- and process assessment. These four types of assessments are classified by Froehle as (1) attitude objective, (2) knowledge objective, (3) skill objective, and (4) consequent objective.

ABOUT

THE

AUTHOR

THOMAS C. FROEHLE

Thomas C. Froehle recently completed a federally funded research and development project in competency-based counselor education. Although the initial focus of that project was the development of a performance based training program for counseling/consulting specialists for Inner-City Schools, it has since been incorporated into the master's degree Block program for counselor trainees at Indiana University. Dr. Froehle's current writing efforts center around an article on Competency-Based Training for Psychoeducational Consultants which will be published as a major article in a forthcoming special issue of the *American Personnel and Guidance Journal.*

In addition to considerable writing about Competency-Based Learning and Competency-Based Education, Dr. Froehle has developed numerous training materials which honor the tenets of Competency-Based Learning. These include separate training manuals for Criterion Referenced Instruction in Counseling Techniques, Laboratory Practice and Individual Appraisal.

Dr. Froehle's current professional focus centers around research questions concerning the efficacy and efficiency of various instruction and training procedures in counselor education. Of particular interest at the moment are the areas of video/computer assisted procedures for training and self-supervision and the area of individual student aptitudes for these and for the more traditional training procedures.

Thomas C. Froehle is an associate professor of education at Indiana University.

LEARNING HOW TO ASSESS HUMAN GROWTH

THROUGH SYSTEMATIC APPROACHES

Tom Froehle

This Chapter is written to a particular audience. Members in that audience share the fact in common that they are "change agents." Included in the label "change agent" are those countless teachers, parents, counselors and other helpers who influence change in people or in more complex bodies such as organizations and institutions. Out of respect to the varied membership of that audience, an attempt will be made throughout this Chapter to use examples familiar to teachers, parents, counselors, and similar change agents. For convenience however the term "client" has been chosen to refer to the *person or organization* which is the recipient of the change agent's helping efforts. The term "client," then, will be used interchangeably with pupils in a classroom, student teachers in a university seminar, children within a household, clients in a counseling agency, and recipients of help in other settings.

THE WHY FOR WRITING THIS CHAPTER

The most basic commonality among change agents is the fact that their helping efforts are most appropriately governed by client need. Said another way, client welfare, however defined, is the ultimate criterion of change agent worth. In this Chapter *client welfare* is defined as the amount of congruence between "What Is" and "What Ought To Be" for the client. This definition is illustrated in Figure 5.1. By the same token, the discrepancy between the two situations determines the degree of the client's problem or the strength of the need.

249

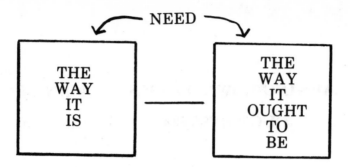

Figure 5.1. Need definition.

Once needs have been identified in terms of discrepancies, one can then generate goal statements and measurable objectives which, if accomplished, will produce a reduction of needs over time. In Figure 5.2 a change strategy (Function 2.0) has been added. The function is to reduce the discrepancy between "What Is" and "What Ought To Be" as illustrated in Figure 5.1.

The three-part sequence in the proposed scheme may be viewed as an hypothesis which states: "If the change strategy of choice is properly implemented, then the situation produced will more closely resemble the desired situation." Problem solving then can be viewed as hypothesis generation and hypothesis testing. We, of course, do not know that a problem has been solved or a need satisfied unless the solution of "change strategy" actually produces the desired situation. What follows then is that the effect of the change strategy is judged by the measured difference between the post-treatment condition (The Way It Ought To Be) and the pre-treatment condition (The Way It Is). In Figure 5.3 is illustrated a possible post-treatment condition, in this case what seems to be a near solution.

Operating under this model, competent change agents are defined as persons capable of reducing the difference between "What Is" and "What Ought To Be." These change agents have the ability to devise and to implement change strategies leading to the solution of client problems and realization of client goals. A person is competent in a *particular area* to the extent that he/she is able to effect efficient solutions to problems in that *particular area*.

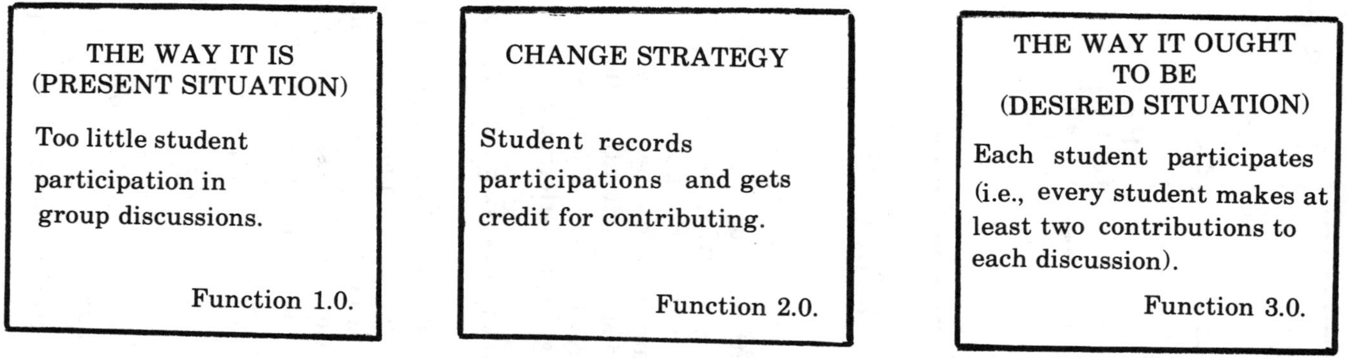

THE WAY IT IS
(PRESENT SITUATION)

Too little student participation in group discussions.

Function 1.0.

CHANGE STRATEGY

Student records participations and gets credit for contributing.

Function 2.0.

THE WAY IT OUGHT TO BE
(DESIRED SITUATION)

Each student participates (i.e., every student makes at least two contributions to each discussion).

Function 3.0.

Figure 5.2. Systematic Problem Solving.

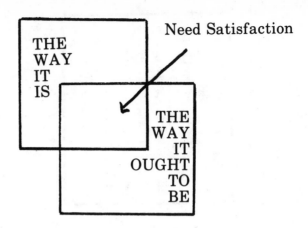

Figure 5.3. Solution definition.

This Chapter was written in the hope of promoting change agent accountability. More specifically, the Chapter was written to provide change agents with those skills needed to assess client needs, to translate need statements into measurable objectives and to develop feedback mechanism to monitor the attainment of objectives. These skills are regarded by the author as requisite to competent and accountable change agent performance.

CHAPTER OVERVIEW: SOME OBJECTIVES

This Chapter has two sections. In the first section on goal analysis, procedures are described which might be used to analyze situations where change is desired and to set goals and objectives for change. The second section contains assessment procedures to better enable the change agent to assess progress toward as well as the accomplishment of goals and objectives.

After reading the first section of this Chapter you should be able to do the following:

1. Distinguish between goals and objectives on the basis of their degree of specificity.

2. Identify the distinguishing characteristics of performance terminology.

3. Differentiate performance from non-performance terms (i.e., abbreviations).

4. Distinguish between statements which describe phenomena in performance terms and those which do not (i.e., from statements which use abbreviations of performance).

5. Translate abbreviated statements into statements characterized by performance terminology.

6. Distinguish between criteria-referenced outcome objectives and criteria-referenced experential objectives.

7. Distinguish among four types of criteria-referenced outcome objectives: cognitive, affective, performance, and consequence-based objectives.

8. Correctly classify examples of each type of criteria-referenced outcome objective.

9. Identify the four components of criteria-referenced outcome objectives using the Mager (1961) paradigm.

10. Formulate criteria-referenced objectives based upon general statements of helping intent.

After reading the second section of this Chapter on assessment procedures you should be able to do the following:

11. Define and provide an example of pre-assessment, process assessment and post-assessment procedures.

12. Describe differences between "evaluative assessment" and "diagnostic assessment" and between "end point assessment" (i.e., summative evaluation) and "periodic assessment" (i.e., formative evaluation).

13. Describe major differences between norm-referenced assessment and criteria-referenced assessment.

14. List the three measurable attributes of human performance (frequency, duration, intensity) and describe the relative advantages and disadvantages of each.

15. List the characteristics of a performance graph and correctly interpret each characteristic.

16. Describe the components of a behavioral baseline.

17. Differentiate, from examples of baselining, those procedures which are more or less obtrusive.

18. Identify specific ways that baselining procedures might influence the performance which is being measured.

19. Interpret correctly data reported on a performance graph.

20. Construct a performance graph which reports baseline and intervention data.

PART I
GOAL ANALYSIS

In this Chapter a differentiation is made between the terms "goal" and "objective" on the basis of their degree of specificity (Ryan, 1969; Armstrong, *et al.*, 1970, Froehle, 1976). Within this framework, goals tend to be identified by very broad and general statements open to many interpretations. Goal analysis is the technique by which objectives that constitute the meaning of the goal are identified. Said another way, the object of goal analysis is to figure out how to know when a goal is achieved. Once one knows the objectives that collectively define the goal, one will be in a better position to decide upon appropriate change strategies.

One very common misunderstanding about goal analysis should be pointed out, that is the all-too-common practice of describing goals not in terms of outcomes, but in terms of procedures used to achieve those outcomes. This practice is not what goal analysis is all about. Goal analysis does not attempt to figure out how to achieve particular outcomes. By the same token, goal statements (i.e., the product of goal analysis) should talk about ends rather than means. Said another way, a goal statement should describe an outcome (i.e., student understanding of cultural differences) rather than a process (e.g., to help students develop an understanding of cultural differences). The former statement describes what the goal state looks like when the goal is achieved, while the latter implies something about how the goal is to be achieved.

```
┌─────────────────────┐
│ HAWD - 1            │
│ How Are We Doing?   │
└─────────────────────┘
```

On the space provided, identify with the letter "G" the statements which meet the criteria for goal statements as discussed so far in this Chapter. Identify with a "P" the statements which describe a process.

_____1. To win the baseball world series.

_____2. To attempt to teach Russian to third grade children.

_____3. To end the fiscal year with a balanced budget.

_____4. To have children spend more time reviewing their corrected papers.

After you complete HAWD-1, you may want to check your responses against suggested responses. For your convenience, suggested responses are presented in the HAWD-1 footnoter.

In Figure 5.4 is illustrated the focus of evaluation for process and for outcome objectives. In Figure 5.4, the framed box signifies the point at which evaluation takes place to see if the objectives have been met. In the first column series, the emphasis is placed upon criteria-referenced *activities* or procedures. This column contrasts with the outcome column series where the focus of evaluation is upon criteria-referenced *outcomes* or products.

Determining whether a statement describes what a goal outcome is when achieved or whether the statement implies how the goal is to be achieved (i.e., a process) is not always easy. Critical within that determination is the time frame in which the statement is construed. For example, earning a straight "A" grade average might be a goal for a particular eleventh grade student. In this example, the academic year is the time frame for the goal statement and the point of evaluation is the end of the academic year. Within an extended time frame, earning straight "A's" during high school might in fact prove to be the principal explanation for the student being awarded a college scholarship. Under this extended time frame, high school academic achievement might better be described as a means to an end (or goal) than as an end in itself. What this illustrates is the fact that today's short-term goals may be means to

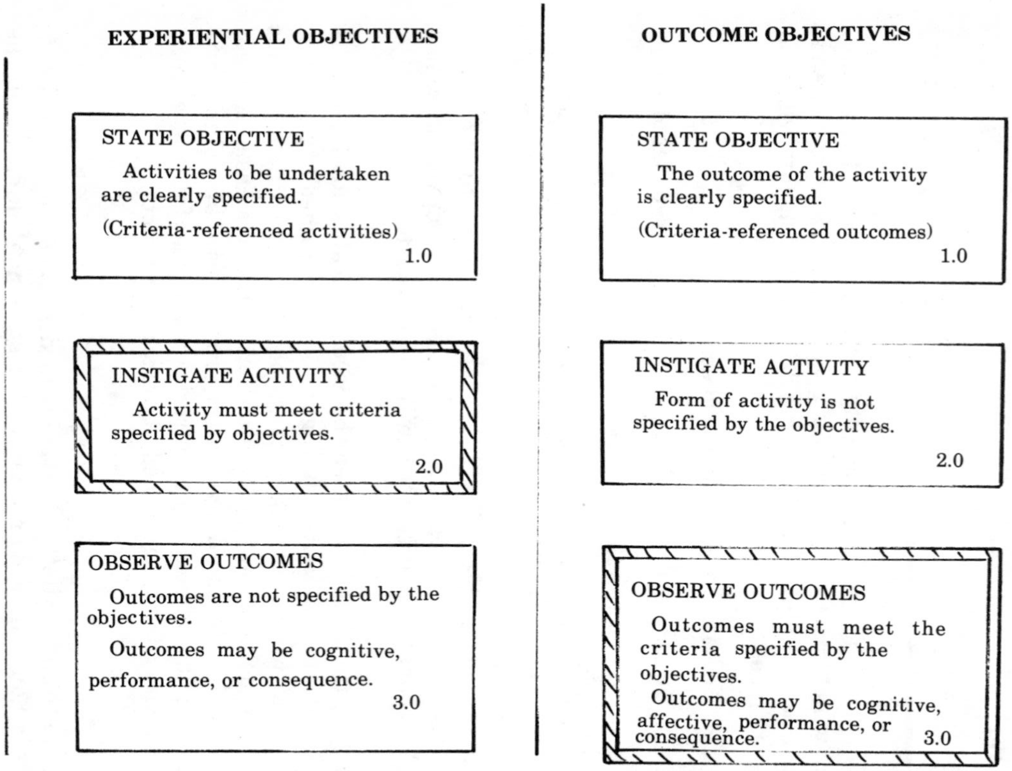

EXPERIENTIAL OBJECTIVES

STATE OBJECTIVE

Activities to be undertaken are clearly specified.

(Criteria-referenced activities) 1.0

INSTIGATE ACTIVITY

Activity must meet criteria specified by objectives. 2.0

OBSERVE OUTCOMES

Outcomes are not specified by the objectives.

Outcomes may be cognitive, performance, or consequence. 3.0

OUTCOME OBJECTIVES

STATE OBJECTIVE

The outcome of the activity is clearly specified.

(Criteria-referenced outcomes) 1.0

INSTIGATE ACTIVITY

Form of activity is not specified by the objectives. 2.0

OBSERVE OUTCOMES

Outcomes must meet the criteria specified by the objectives.

Outcomes may be cognitive, affective, performance, or consequence. 3.0

Figure 5.4 Focus for Evaluation for Experimental Objectives and for Outcome for Objectives.

tomorrow's long-term goal. This point is made lest the reader conclude that goals and means to reach goals are easily differentiated. What confounds the matter even more is the fact that in the final analysis, human intentionality determines whether we are dealing with a goal or with means for achieving a goal.

Any number of procedures have been proposed to facilitate goal analysis. In the Kurpius and Christie Chapter of this book are described several possible procedures. While procedures may differ, the end product typically manifests certain fixed characteristics. The reader is referred to Chapter 1 for a discussion of these common and unique characteristics.

Whatever goal analysis procedure is employed, one thing is certain: the goal analysis procedure requires accurate communication among parties to the analysis. In the next section of this Chapter are proposed some methods for increasing accuracy of communication in goal analysis procedures.

ANALYZING GOAL DESCRIPTIONS
IN TERMS OF PERFORMANCE

For accurate communication to take place, a necessity is for the language used to have common meaning to all persons trying to communicate with one another. For most of us, that language includes descriptors, labels, and "abbreviations" which are used to describe closely-related behaviors, attitudes, and so forth. Words like hostile, empathic, interested, motivated, depressed, or resistant are short-cut ways of summarizing many things that a person does. Because of their summarizing nature, these terms are potentially very economical and efficient communication tools. In fact, without access to such abbreviations, everyday conversation would be unduly drawn out. Little wonder that such a sizeable portion of the language arts curriculum is given to teaching the meaning of and the common usage of these labels.

HAWD-1.   1.   G   2.   P   3.   G   4.   P

Words which are available to describe human goals and human experience fall into two categories, those that name what can be observed (performance) and those that stand for a range of performances (abbreviations) but which cannot be directly observed. To be able to distinguish between performances and abbreviations of performance is important. Mistaking an abbreviation for a performance can lead to errors and misunderstandings in interpersonal communication.

Abbreviations

An abbreviation is a name for a cluster of apparently related performances. Abbreviations of performances are quite useful. Using a single word such as "happy" allows us to convey information about a cluster of related performances in an abbreviated way. Another useful function of performance abbreviations is that abbreviations suggest particular kinds of component performancs. The following citation from the American Personnel and Guidance Association's (1962) policy statement, *The Counselor: Professional Preparation and Role,* can serve as an example of use of abbreviations:

> Commitment to Individual Human Values. The counselor has a primary concern for the individual as a person whose feelings, values, goals, and success are important. The counselor respects and appreciates individuality including the right and need of those whom he counsels to find their own best values, to determine their own goals, and to find ways to achieve these goals. He is concerned with facilitating this process in a manner that is helpful to the individual and society.

This statement identifies no observable performance, nothing that a second party might use as evidence of any degree of commitment. How can one determine if the counselor:
—has a primary concern . . .
—respects and appreciates individuality . . .
—is concerned with facilitating . . . ?

These abbreviations are only broad suggestions of those observable counselor performances that might be taken as evidence of counselor "commitment." These abbreviations cannot be used as criteria of commitment or evidence of commitment since they are not directly observable. (Lauver, 1971)

Performance

A performance is an observable behavior, something that people can see or hear or detect that another person does. Performances are those behaviors that people do that can be observed. As an example, observable counselor performances that might be included in the abbreviation "respects ... individuality" from the previous American Personnel and Guidance Association statement are as follows:

—says "Do your own thing."
—says "There's something to be said for your point of view."
—argues for dumping the dress code.
—joins the American Civil Liberties Union.
—makes relatively few "You should ..." statements.

Observable performances such as these provide a means of defining an abbreviation such as "respects ... individuality" much more precisely.

```
HAWD - 2
How Are We Doing?
```

In the spaces provided, indicate with a T or F whether the statement is true or false.

_____1. Performances can be observed reliably by more than one person.

_____2. An abbreviation is an observable behavior.

_____3. Performances are inferred from abbreviations.

_____4. Statements of abbreviation are more precise than statements of performance.

_____5. A performance is an observable behavior.

_____6. Abbreviations are inferred from observed performance.

_____7. Statements of performance are more precise than statements of abbreviation.

_____8. Abbreviations can be observed reliably by more than one person.

After you complete HAWD-2, you may want to check your answers against those suggested in the HAWD-2.

The next section of this Chapter focuses upon an illustration and some associated exercises in differentiating between performance and non-performance terms. The exercises are designed to help you apply your knowledge of the difference between abbreviations and observable performance.

In Figure 5.5 is illustrated the distinction between abbreviations and observable performance. The shaded center circle represents the abbreviation "depress" while the outer circle is made of possible performances which may be used as evidence of "depression."

In everyday communication one might use the abbreviation "depressed" (inner circle) to describe another person on the basis that one or more of the performances (outer circle) were observed. And of course, the abbreviation "depressed" might be used to describe another person where related but not the same performances were observed.

Three points should be made about the example illustrated in Figure 5.5. First, observable performances similar to those which appear in the outer circle are the only evidence available to others. "Depressed" is an abbreviation or label for a cluster of such performances. "Depression," the center circle, cannot be directly observed.

Second, the unobservable, or private behaviors (center circle), are available to others only through performances. (I infer or guess that you feel depressed from observing your performance of crying and from hearing you say "I'm depressed.")

Third, the performance components of "depressed" listed in the outer circle in Figure 5.5 do not constitute a comprehensive definition of depression. Those performances that are meant by any one person who says "I'm depressed" are unique to him. Whoever must "understand" another person must determine what performances that person is abbreviating with the word "depressed." For this reason the compound descriptor "performance examplar" is sometimes used in place of the simple term "performance;" the term serves to remind one that reference is made to an example performance, i.e., to one of a range of possible performances.

HAWD-2.   1. T   2. F   3. F   4. F   5. T   6. T   7. T   8. F

Figure 5.5. Observable Components of the Behavioral Abbreviation: Depressed.

To test how clearly you understand what has been communicated about abbreviations and observable performances, underline the performances in the following list:

1. Love   2. Say   3. Hostile   4. Enter   5. Laugh   6. Touch
7. Appreciate   8. Kiss   9. Like   10. Turn

When you finish, check your performance with the HAWD-3 footnote.

You are correctly discriminating performances and abbreviations if you did not underline words that do not name any performance that one person can do and another person can observe. The words that do not make a performance are abbreviations for a range of possible performances and therefore should not be underlined.

For each of the following four statements write A in front of each abbreviation and P in front of each performance.
Example: Charlie is *lazy.* I know because . . .
     P he picks up none of his materials.
     A he doesn't want to help.

1. Paul *is* a *motivated* teacher. I know because . . .
    _____he likes kids.
    _____he prepares detailed lesson plans.

2. Peg *likes* her work as a secretary. I know because . . .
    _____she arrives before 8 a.m.
    _____her morale is good.

3. Pam *appreciates* help. I know because . . .
    _____she understands how important it is to her.
    _____she says "thank you."

4. Pete is *hostile.* I know because . . .
    _____he comes to class late.
    _____he likes to make trouble.

Ask yourself, "Could I see or hear this performance" before checking the answers in HAWD-4 footnote. If not, try again and then check your performance. Give yourself a pat on the back if you have four yeses.

**HAWD - 5
How Are We Doing?**

In the space provided, supply a performance that might be included in the abbreviation given in each of the following statements. The first one, an example, is completed for you.

> Example: We can agree upon which of two men is hostile because the hostile man .. *is shouting obscenities*.

1. You can determine which of two men is sad because the sad man can be seen _____.

2. Robert has initiative. I know because he _____
   _____.

3. Martha is the classroom clown. More than anyone else in the room, she _____.

See the HAWD-5 footnote for comments.

CLASSIFICATION OF CRITERIA-REFERENCED OBJECTIVES

Regardless of the approach to goal analysis employed by the change agent, the end product must include precise statements of measurable objectives. As shown previously in Figure 5.4, the objectives which are generated through these procedures may be categorized as either criteria-referenced experiential objectives which require that a person experience a specific event without specifying the outcome (Houston, *et al.*, 1971) or as criteria-referenced outcome objectives which require that a specific outcome be demonstrated.

HAWD-3. Underline 2. Say, 4. Enter, 5. Laugh, 6. Touch, 8. Kiss, 10. Turn.

Because criteria-referenced experiential objectives require that a person experience a specific event without specifying the outcome, they are legitimate as long as they are thought to hold promise for significant learning or change even though specific expected outcomes from the experience may not be identifiable in advance. An example of an experiential objective would be "the counselor-in-training will visit the homes of at least two of his clients before mid-semester." The desired result may be the development of a positive attitude toward the parents of his or her clients. However, negative feelings might result if the visitations are extremely unpleasant.

Criteria-referenced outcome objectives may be further classified according to the type of criteria that is applied in determining whether the objective has been achieved. Four types of outcome objectives may be differentiated. The four types are as follows:

1. Cognitive objectives which specify the knowledge and understanding that is to be demonstrated;

2. Affective objectives which describe the awareness and attitudes that are to be displayed;

3. Performance objectives which require that certain actions be performed; and

4. Consequence objectives which specify changes in others or changes in structures which the change agent should be able to accomplish.

HAWD-4.   1. A, P; 3. P, A; 3. A, P; 4. P, A.

HAWD-5.   There are no right answers. What is important is that your entries include statements of observable performance, i.e., behaviors that can be seen, heard, or felt.

Complete the sentences which follow using the information provided previously.

1. Criteria-referenced outcome objectives differ from criteria-referenced _____ objectives in that the latter do not specify expected outcomes.

2. Criteria-referenced outcome objectives may be classified according to the type of criteria that are applied in determining whether the objective has been achieved. The four types of criteria are _____, _____, _____, and _____.

Check your responses with the HAWD - 6 footnote.

Now that you are able to recognize the major difference between outcome-referenced and experience-referenced objectives, you're ready for a more exacting consideration of the four types of criteria-referenced outcome objectives.

Cognitive-Based Objectives specify the knowledge, intellectual abilities, and information or data which the person is expected to demonstrate or somehow show evidence of having acquired. Cognitive-based objectives focus on what the change agent knows about change strategies, not how well the change agent can perform the acts that go into that strategy (e.g., interviewing), nor how successful the change agent is in effecting the desired change through the deployment of the change strategy.

Affective-Based Objectives focus on how the change agent feels about something. Of importance is the "probability that the change agent will perform in a particular way." Said another way, it's what the change agent would like to do or how he/she is likely to perform that counts.

Performance-Based Objectives focus on the change agent's ability to draw upon information, data, knowledge, and understanding in order to demonstrate or use prescribed change agent behaviors under specified conditions, either real conditions or simulated conditions. Three examples follow:

"To use open-end leads in a ten-minute microcounseling situation,"

265

"To interpret accurately to a parent in a parent conference a student's score profile on an academic achievement test," and

"To reward children according to pre-specified contingencies."

In all three situations, it's the "live performance" in which we're interested. The actual question for each is "Did the person in fact use open-end leads to the satisfaction of some pre-specified criterion level?" Was the verbal interpetation of the test score profile an accurate one?" "Did the parent administer and withhold rewards from her child according to the contingency contract (e.g., ten minutes of Monday night football on TV for every ten minutes of practice on the saxophone)?"

In none of the previous examples is the effect of the person's performance upon someone else questioned. This effect is not the focus for performance-based objectives. Rather, performance-based objectives require assessment on the basis of the live performance of the change agent independent of any consideration of the effect of that performance upon someone (e.g., a client, a student, a child) or upon something.

Consequence-Based Objectives focus on the ability of a change agent to bring about change in others. Assessment, therefore, focuses not upon what the change agent knows or can do, but upon the result of his/her knowing and doing, results which are demonstrated through some one other than the change agent. Said another way, consequence-based objectives require assessment on the basis of consumer welfare or consumer performance. In assessment of consequence-based objectives, it's what the receiving person, the client, knows, does or can do that counts. While the change agent by necessity may need to know certain things, "knowing", "being able to do", or "performing" do not guarantee results or consequences. The change agent, in fact, may know everything about a particular change strategy, be able to perform that act to perfection, and may still not be able to promote client welfare or to bring about the desired client change.

HAWD-6.   1. experiential 2. cognitive, affective, performance, and consequence.

In Figure 5.6 is illustrated the focus of assessment for each type of objective (Froehle, 1976). Careful study of this figure will help you pull together what has been described in several previous pages.

What we would like you to conclude from this discussion should be quite obvious, namely, that consequence-based outcome objectives are the key to change agent performance and change agent accountability. If consequence-based outcome objectives are not generated by change agents and if change agents are not held accountable for their achievement, the core of professional accountability is lost.

> **HAWD - 7**
> **How Are We Doing?**

Using the spaces provided write in the type of objective (i.e., cognitive, affective, performance, consequence, or experiential) illustrated in each stated objective. When you finish making your entries, check your answers against the HAWD-7 footnote.

_____ 1. Each student teacher will observe for a minimum of two hours a class of emotionally disturbed children.

_____ 2. Each change agent will list the four types of criteria-referenced outcome objectives.

_____ 3. Following the micro-counseling training session, the counselor trainee will be able to use attending behaviors of eye contact, relaxed posture and verbal communication to the satisfaction of a practicum supervisor

_____ 4. Each teacher will raise by one grade point the average grade level performance for his/her class on the Metropolitan Achievement Test.

OBJECTIVE TYPE	FOCUS FOR EVALUATION
Cognitive-Based Objectives	It's what the person knows and/or the amount of information or data which he/she possesses that counts.
Affective-Based Objectives	It's how the person feels about something that counts. It's the probability that a person will perform in a particular way that counts. It's what the person would like to do that counts.
Performance-Based Objectives	It's how the person performs that counts. It's what the person does with what he/she knows that counts.
Consequence-Based Objectives	It's client welfare that counts. It's what the client knows, how he/she feels, or what he/she can do as a result of the helper's efforts that counts.
Experiential Objectives	It's the experience or the activity that counts. (Gains in knowledge, affect and performance are desired, but not expected specifically or planned in detail.)

Figure 5.6. Assessment Focus for Criteria-Referenced Outcome Objectives and Criteria-Referenced Experiential Objectives.

5. Parents will demonstrate increased appreciation for the value of concrete parent-to-child feedback by increasing by 50% over their pre-workshop baserate the amount of concrete parent-to-child feedback.

Describing Goals in Terms of Criteria-Referenced Objectives

Objectives are a functional necessity for a change agent. Objectives constitute the criteria for determining the effectiveness of "helping." Objectives are an essential safeguard to the client's interests and the change agent's credibility. Objectives stated in performance terms are a benchmark available to both client and change agent to serve as a basis for evaluating current helping procedures or considering alternatives available in the future. Being able to state where they are going, how they will get there, and how they will know they have arrived are evidence that a professional helping relationship exists (Mager, 1962).

Objectives

An objective may be defined as a collection of words or symbols that describe an intention for change. In this Chapter a differentiation is made between the terms "goal" and "objectives" on the basis of their degree of specificity (Ryan, 1969; Armstrong et al., 1970). Within this framework, goals tend to be very broad and general statements open to many interpretations. From goals, objectives can be explicated in clear, precise, and measurable terms.

Specifying objectives in performance terminology is no easy task. Behind all purposeful activity, however, some objectives exist. The fact that one's purpose is to teach the student how to "understand" and "appreciate" classical music does not mean that performance-term objectives are not present. Implied in the evaluation process which the music teacher uses to infer "music appreciation" for Susan and "lack of music appreciation" for Bill are one or more performance-term objectives.

Characteristics of a Performance-Term Objective

The following are the characteristics of performance-term objectives:

1. Identification of the PERSON or thing to be performing.

2. Identification of the PERFORMANCE (one which can be measured or otherwise verified) which must occur.

3. Description of the important CONDITIONS under which the performance must occur.

4. Specification of the CRITERION of acceptable performance, i.e., how much of the behavior is expected or how well it must be performed.

Regardless of the situation, the *first step* in systematic problem-solving is to specify precisely what behavior(s) one wants to establish, under what conditions the behaviors are to occur, and what constitutes a minimum performance level. Said another way, one must establish *who... will do what... under what conditions... and to what extent.* An instructor in Spanish, for example, should specify in advance whether the students' final performance is to be measured in terms of reading or writing or speaking Spanish, and whether the direction of translation should be from Spanish to English, or English to Spanish, or both. Once this has been established, the Spanish instructor is ready to specify how these performances are to be evaluated relative to a criterion (e.g., speed, error rate) and the standard of performance judged to be minimally acceptable. Regardless of the decision, all statements of objectives must contain each of four components:

1. identification of the *who,* the doer (the *"Who"* question)

2. specified *performance* (the *"Will do what"* question)

3. specified *conditions* for attaining the objective (the *"Under what conditions"* question)

4. an indication of the *criterion* of minimum performance (the *"To what extent"* question).

HAWD - 7.   1. Experiential objective; 2. Cognitive objective; 3. Performance objective; 4. Consequence objective; 5. Affective objective.

Second step in a counseling situation, the specified terminal *performance* refers to the behavior you would like your client, the *who,* to be able to demonstrate at the time your influence over him or her ends. This terminal performance describes what the client will be doing as a result of counseling. Again, a vague description of the terminal behavior would not be acceptable since no way would exist to measure it reliably (e.g., "to be motivated").

The *third* step in the same situation is to specify the *conditions* that will be imposed when the client is demonstrating his/her achievement of the performance term objective (e.g., "While studying in the lounge . . . " or "When taking a test . . . " or "During the next week when someone drops by your room . . . " or "When talking to a mixed group of classmates at Nick's . . . ").

Once you have described what the client should be able to do and under what *conditions* or circumstances, then *fourth* specify the criterion for acceptable performance. In a counseling situation the criterion may be total accomplishment of a task or work on the task *for a specified period of time* or *to a given degree.* The criterion is the standard or test for evaluating the achievement of an objective. These four components—who, performance, condition, and performance criterion—are diagrammed in Figure 5.7.

The next section of this Chapter is designed to assist you in analyzing objectives with reference to the four components—who, performance, condition, and criterion—charted in Figure 5.7. As a starter, read carefully the following three objectives and see if you can identify the four components in each objective. When finished, check your results with the suggested ones charted in Figure 5.8.

School Example: During the next month Robert will increase by fifty percent over his last month average the number of words that he spells correctly on the Friday spelling quiz.

Home Example: Without being reminded to do so during the next two weeks, Mildred will be in bed with lights out by 9 p.m. daily.

University Example: Given a thirty-minute audio tape of a counseling interview, the counselor-in-training will correctly classify twenty-seven of the thirty counselor statements as reflection, clarification, or restatement.

271

Doer (who)	Performance (will do what)	Conditions (under what conditions)	Performance Criterion (to what extent)
Who will perform	What the learner or client will be doing when demonstrating his/her achievement. This must be stated as a performance; an abbreviation will not suffice. Use verbs that denote observable action.	Conditions under which the terminal behavior is to occur. a. Physical, situational or temporal circumstances. b. Psychological conditions.	A standard that indicates when the learner or client has successfully demonstrated his/her achievement of the performance. a. Accuracy or correctness of response. b. Response length, rate, and so forth.

Figure 5.7. Components of Performance—Term Objectives.

In Figure 5.8 portions of each of the three performance term objectives are classified according to the three criteria for successfully stated performance term objectives.

```
┌─────────────────────────────┐
│                             │
│ HAWD - 8                    │
│ How Are We Doing?           │
│                             │
└─────────────────────────────┘
```

In the space provided correctly classify according to Mager's criteria the separate components of each of the following four performance term objectives. When you finish making your entries in the spaces provided, check your results with the suggested ones in HAWD-8 footnote.

1. Each group participant will speak first to at least one different girl on my floor each day for the next week.

2. Susan will stop smoking for one month.

3. Anthony will read history for at least sixty minutes between lunch and dinner during each school day for the next two weeks.

	WHO	PERFORMANCE	CONDITION	CRITERION
1				
2				
3				

EXAMPLE	WHO	PERFORMANCE	CONDITION	CRITERION
School	Robert	spells	during the next month ... on the Friday spelling quiz	increase by fifty percent over his last month average the number of words which he spells correctly.
Home	Mildred	will be in bed	without being reminded ... with lights out by 9 p.m.	daily ... next two weeks.
University	Counselor-in-training	will classify counselor statements as reflection, clarification or restatement	given a thirty-minute audio tape of a counseling interview	27 of 30 correctly.

Figure 5.8. Performance Objective Components Classified According to Criteria Specified by Mager (1962).

Clearly, some of the consequences of specifying performance term objectives are discomforting. For one thing, specifying terms takes the "comfortable mystery" out of helping (e.g., teaching, counseling, parenting). In a similar vein, this process is likely to force to our attention some helping strategies which, upon closer inspection, cannot be justified, i.e., where it is not possible to demonstrate a functional relationship between the strategy and future performance of a person on the intended terminal behavior.

Advantages of specifying performance term objectives are numerous. Included among the advantages is the high probability that the identification of specific objectives will enable both the change agent and the client to assess progress continually. Specificity makes measurement of behavior change and feedback possible. Proper feedback throughout the helping process provides the change agent and client with some benchmarks enroute to the client's goal and allows for re-routing. And lastly, objectives can be sequenced to ensure successful accomplishment by the client. Successive approximation through the use of short-term objectives maintains the client's motivation to achieve behaviors or objectives.

HAWD - 8

WHO	PERFORMANCE	CONDITION	CRITERION
Each group participant	will *speak* first to ...	... on my floor each day	... one different girl ... each day for the next week.
Susan	will stop *smoking*	"under all conditions" is implied	for one month ... criterion level is implied (i.e., "cold turkey" or 100% reduction).
Anthony	will *read history*	... between lunch and dinner during each school day	... for at least sixty minutes ... for the next two months.

Because specific performance objectives are not easily stated, your first attempts are not likely to be perfect or even very good. Nevertheless, we know what the ultimate terminal performance is and we can get there through successive approximations.

In the following HAWD-9 are listed four statements of helping intent for which performance-term objectives could be written. As written, the goals (i.e., helping intentions) are subject to many interpretations. Performance term objectives which communicate much more accurately can be written to replace these faulty objectives provided one remembers the following:

A. Statements of performance term objectives include three pieces of information

    1. *Doer*—who will be performing.

    2. *Performance*—what observable behavior or event will be achieved.

    3. *Condition*—when or where the performance will occur.

    4. *Criterion*—how well or how much must be done or performed and for how long.

B. Useful objectives are objectives that permit people to agree when the objective has been met.

HAWD - 9
How Are We Doing?

In the space provided, write at least one performance term objective for each goal using the guidelines which have been considered thus far.

    1. *Goal*—"To teach Jim to be polite on the telephone."
    Performance Term Objective: _____
    _____
    _____

    2. *Goal*—"To help each student develop a sensitivity to cultural differences."
    Performance Term Objective: _____
    _____
    _____

3. *Goal*—"To make Billy see the importance of delivering his papers on time."
Performance Term Objective: _____
_____
_____

4. *Goal*—"To motivate the class."
Performance Term Objective: _____
_____
_____

Before moving on to the next section of this Chapter, you may want to check the comments entered in the HAWD-9 footnote.

PART II
ASSESSMENT PROCEDURES

Assessment is an essential activity in the helping act which appropriately concerns itself with two classes of performance: change agent performance (e.g., a teacher's teaching performance) and client performance or accomplishment (e.g., what a student has learned). Through assessment one attempts to acquire useful information regarding the effectiveness, efficiency, and utility (e.g., relevance) of the endeavor to help. More specifically, assessment may aid our efforts

1. To help determine whether "help" is needed.

2. To help determine what kind of "help" might be helpful.

3. To help determine whether you are able to provide that "help."

4. To help determine whether you wish to "help."

5. To help determine whether your efforts are helpful as planned.

6. To help determine when your helping is no longer needed.

Unfortunately, assessment is seldom viewed or used as an ally in the process of improving our helping strategies. In most situations, assessment activity focuses upon points of entry and exit. In reality, however, assessment should enable us to make better decisions at the many points which lie between entry and exit and thereby improve the overall quality of our helping endeavors. Said another way, assessment also can enable us "... to exercise our essential managerial *control* function, in the sense that it feeds back to us control information regarding the appropriateness of our organization of learning resources (Davies, 1973, p. 209)."

ASSESSMENT: SOME DISTINCTIONS

If assessment is to be our ally, then imperatively one must recognize the junctures which require assessment and evaluation. The fact is, the change agent must monitor the activities of his/her clients continuously in order to insure the appropriateness of the helping strategies which he/she and the client have together selected for implementation. In the most formal sense, this means that the change agent must assume responsibility for three assessment activities: pre-assessment, process assessment, and post-assessment. The assessment junctures and the assessment questions relevant to each juncture are illustrated in Figure 5.9.

Pre-assessment

Pre-assessment enables the change agent and the client to determine need (i.e., to identify discrepancies between "the way it ought to be" and "the way it is") and to determine the advantages and disadvantages of alternative change strategies available to the change agent and the client. These data become the beginning point and serve as the point from which all future progress will be gauged to determine gains and losses. These data also can have a motivating effect since they permit recognition of success. They help to demonstrate when and how much change has taken place.

HAWD - 9. There are, of course, no single correct statements of objectives. What is critical is that each statement describes a specific performance, the conditions under which it will occur, and the amount of minimum performances expected.

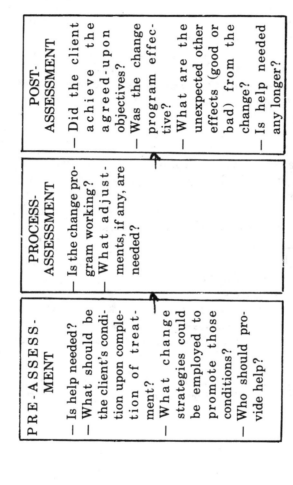

PRE-ASSESS-MENT

— Is help needed?
— What should be the client's condition upon completion of treatment?
— What change strategies could be employed to promote those conditions?
— Who should provide help?

PROCESS-ASSESSMENT

— Is the change program working?
— What adjustments, if any, are needed?

POST-ASSESSMENT

— Did the client achieve the agreed-upon objectives?
— Was the change program effective?
— What are the unexpected other effects (good or bad) from the change?
— Is help needed any longer?

Figure 5.9. Assessment Functions and Questions Associated with Each Function.

279

Process Assessment

In order to ensure the appropriations of the helping strategies selected by the change agent and client, one needs to monitor the activities of the change agent continuously. Sometimes monitoring will reveal some ways in which the change strategy is not being implemented as originally planned. This suggests a need to get the change strategy on target or to select an alternative strategy. On the other hand, if monitoring reveals that the strategy is being followed according to design, but that the client's goal is not being approximated, then the need to select an alternative change strategy should be quite apparent. In summary, process assessment permits validation of the change agent's assumptions and hypotheses (i.e., "if-then" statements made in selecting the change strategy from a number of possibilities) and program modification based on the confirmation or disconfirmation of these hypotheses.

Post-assessment

The main function of post-assessment, of course, is to determine whether or not the objectives negotiated previously between the change agent and the client have been accomplished. This assessment properly focuses upon the terminal condition of the client in relation to the objectives negotiated.

```
HAWD - 10
How Are We Doing?
```

In the space provided indicate the kind of assessment which best completes each statement (pre-assessment, process assessment, post-assessment). You may want to check your answers against those in HAWD-10 footnote.

1. _____ *assessment* is used to determine whether the intervention (change program) is being administered and whether it is working.

2. _____ *assessment* compares the terminal condition of the client with the objectives previously negotiated between the client and the change agent.

3. _____ *assessment* focuses upon the identification of client need and of high probability means for satisfying that need.

280

EVALUATIVE ASSESSMENT VERSUS
DIAGNOSTIC ASSESSMENT

The second distinction to make is between *evaluative assessment* and *diagnostic assessment.* In all too many situations, especially in education, assessment has been implemented in order to rank persons on one or more criteria. Under these conditions, some persons are rejected and others selected; some pass and some fail. In such situations, tests and other measurement procedures are designed to be filtering or screening devices which permit passage or continuation only to those who can demonstrate certain knowledge or ability. Although such information is useful, especially for administrative purposes, it often fails to tell persons very much about their own competence since the feedback is primarily on completed performance. All that the persons under such conditions learn from this information is the fact that they have done some things wrong (and failed) or did some things right (and passed). This gives the change agent little specific information regarding an individual's present level of competence.

END-POINT ASSESSMENT VERSUS
PERIODIC ASSESSMENT

A third distinction to be made is between *end-point assessment* (i.e., summative evaluation) and *periodic assessment* (i.e., formative evaluation). Traditionally, when assessment of some sort is used to select or reject persons for something, the assessment procedures are executed at a specific point in time. The emphasis generally is upon complete performance. Scoring an achievement test in terms of an overall score is an assessment of complete performance. Contrast this with the swimming or diving coach who on a daily basis scores and subsequently provides feedback on the performance of a team member preparing for a regional contest. The latter situation is a good example of formative or periodic assessment; the purpose is to diagnose and to give response guidance as well as to evaluate.

Collective on-going data permits improvement in client performance. In the case of the swimming/diving coach, such observations are made frequently. Because both are complex processes, components of the performance must be observed as carefully as the completed performance itself. Formative or periodic assessment permits more clear recognition of which elements of the final performance are demonstrated satisfactorily, which ones need modification and which ones need to be added. In most cases, the assessment must look at more than the final element of performance (e.g., diver entering the water). Observing only the terminal element of performance generally does not permit detection of the source of difficulty, i.e., the point which precipitated the poor entry into the water. This situation is like the child doing hand-calculated long division: the same wrong answer may be due to one child's not being able to subtract and a second child's having forgotten to indent. The same holds with respect to a diver's poor entry into the water. In summary, only if one observes the component performances can one diagnose the difficulties and prescribe interventions or change programs. Formative assessment makes precise diagnosis and appropriate remediation more likely.

Continuous or periodic data gathering allows the change agent to intervene long before the terminal (and often incorrect) performance by the person with the problem. Catching early the substandard performance permits early modification or correction by the person. Lastly, formative assessment and data gathering allow one to see the effect on the person and to adjust the strategies on the basis of the feedback one gets.

> HAWD - 11
> How Are We Doing?

1. Assessment distinctions made thus far are between _____ assessment and "diagnostic assessment" and
2. between "end point assessment" and _____ assessment."

See HAWD-11 footnote to check your response.

HAWD - 10. 1. Process assessment, 2. Post-assessment, 3. Pre-assessment.

CRITERION-REFERENCED ASSESSMENT VERSUS NORMATIVE-REFERENCED ASSESSMENT

A fourth distinction might be made between normative-referenced assessment and criterion-referenced assessment. One of the more frequently used examples of normative-referenced assessment is the use of grades in public education. Grades typically compare students with other students. Group norms are used then to determine where a student is in relation to the average, i.e., whether the student's performance is "below average" or "above average" or "just average" for the group. Each of us has had, no doubt, some past experience with grading curves. For example, you might recall the high school teacher(s) who would consistently curve the grades across class sections to insure that a certain number of A's, B's, C's, D's, F's, are found at each grade level. The teacher who grades on the normal curve would sort out a class of one hundred students on a curve approximating the one presented in Figure 5.10. On the other hand, you also might recall the teacher who had a reputation for being an easy grader. A typical curve for that teacher is presented in Figure 5.11. In Figure 5.12 is illustrated a contrasting grade curve, the kind of curve that "really tough" instructors might use. Regardless of the specific norm, regardless of whether the norm was set before or after performance was assessed, and regardless of the shape of the curve used, this approach to assessment compares students to the "average" students and the "below" and the "above" average students. Because of the reliance upon some kind of norm this approach to assessment is called *normative referencing.*

Norm-referenced tests are used correctly when the primary purpose of measurement is to establish the relative standing of the person being tested. A common example of this in practice is the quite regular and systematic administration of academic achievement tests. In most such situations the purpose is not to assess individual student attainment of specified curriculum objectives; rather, the results permit reliable ordering of students in a class or

---

HAWD - 11. 1. Evaluative, 2. Periodic.

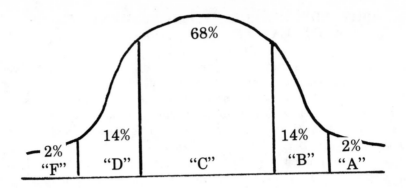

Figure 5.10. Normal (Bell-shaped) Grading Curve with Percentages of Students Receiving Different "A" to "F" Letter Grades.

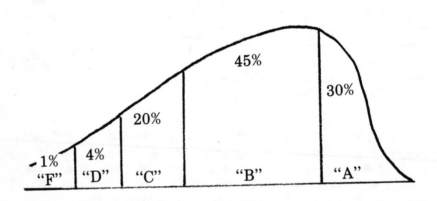

Figure 5.11. Negatively Skewed Grading Curve with Percentages of Students Receiving Different "A" to "F" Letter Grades.

school. The result is a distribution where a few students do very well, a few do quite poorly, and a majority cluster around the average. Although this practice of ordering students may be the prevailing one, the suggestion is not that it is a desirable practice.

Under *criterion referencing,* student performance is interpreted relative to predetermined criteria or performance standards. With criterion referencing, one person's performance is not compared with other persons. Consequently, no person is ever at the bottom or at the top of a distribution, because performance is not distributed over a range. The range is restricted to a "yes" or "no" kind of thing. Either the person reached or did not reach predetermined criterion level.

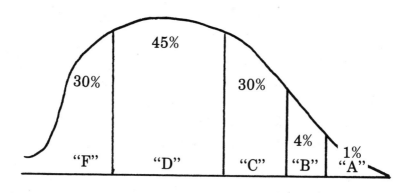

Figure 5.12.   Positively-Skewed Grading Curve with Percentages of Students Receiving Different "A" to "F" Letter Grades.

Criterion-referenced tests are used correctly when the purpose is to "provide information as to the degree of competence obtained by a particular student which is independent of reference to the performance of others (Glaser, 1963, p. 52)." Criterion referencing permits the individual learner to determine where he/she is in relation to own goals without references to where he/she stands in relation to other members of the group to which he/she is categorized. Under criterion testing, the resulting distribution is skewed negatively, i.e., most of the test scores will cluster in the upper regions. Also unlike normative measurement, such a negatively skewed distribution says nothing about the overall soundness of the measurement device.

> HAWD - 12
> How Are We Doing?

In the following space provided, describe the use of assessment in criterion-referenced instruction and normative-referenced instruction.

_____
_____
_____
_____

You may like to compare your comments against our comments which are provided in HAWD-12 footnote.

SYSTEMATIC OBSERVATION AND ASSESSMENT

Having briefly discussed some basic assessment distinctions, consideration of some specific observation, measurement, and data reporting techniques is needed. Once a decision is made to assess, one must consider "what" should be assessed, "where" should the assessment be made and "when." This section of the Chapter concerns thse questions.

What To Assess

Measurable Attributes of Human Performance. With respect to the "what to assess" question, three attributes of human performance can be measured:

1. Frequency—the number of times the performance occurs.

2. Duration—the length of time over which the performance occurs.

3. Intensity—the force with which the performance occurs.
These attributes differ on at least three accounts: how measurement is made, where it is taken, and by whom measures can be obtained (Lauver, 1971). In Figure 5.13 is illustrated these differences.

ATTRIBUTE	INSTRUMENT (How)	PLACE (Where)	PERSON (By Whom)
Frequency: (How often?)	none needed	anywhere	most anyone
Duration: (How long?)	stop-watch, timers, chronographs	anywhere	most anyone
Intensity: (How much?)	meters, electronics, etc.	laboratory conditions	trained person

Figure 5.13. Measurement Dimensions of Three Attributes of Performance.

In Figure 5.13 is clearly illustrated a progression with respect to ease or simplicity of measurement for the three attributes of performance. Most complicated and demanding is the measurement of intensity. Some sort of apparatus (e.g., a mouth thermometer, an audiograph, a polygraph machine) is required and a person skilled in using that apparatus is needed. Further, generally the subject is required to be put into direct contact with the apparatus or with at least one component of that apparatus. Measurement of duration, on the other hand, requires the use of some sort of timing device which need not be in contact with the subject. Furthermore, the operation of the timing apparatus generally does not require any particular skill. Measurement of the frequency attribute requires neither a special instrument nor a skilled operator, and measurement may be made indirectly, i.e., the subject is not put into direct contact with the measurement procedure. Frequency is the simplest measure to acquire since it involves only counting and therefore can be made any place by most anyone.

In spite of the ease with which frequency is measured it has proven to be the attribute of most importance in problem situations. A good example is bed wetting. The *number of times* Wilbur wets the bed, not *how wet* or *how long,* is of primary interest. Problem situations are most often situations where a performance doesn't occur often enough (this may be referred to as performance deficit) or where a performance occurs too frequently (performance excess).

Derived Indices of Frequency, Duration, and Intensity. Frequency, duration, and intensity may be recorded and expressed in three ways: as a total amount, as an amount per unit of variable time (rate), or as an amount per unit of fixed opportunity (percentage).

HAWD 12. Under criterion-referenced instruction, assessment is used to ascertain student performance with respect to an established criterion or performance standard. This contrasts with assessment under normative-referenced instruction where the purpose is to ascertain student performance in relation to the performance of other students.

1. As a total amount
   Examples
   Frequency: Wilbur wet the bed fifteen times.
   Duration: Kimberly was "on-task" for fourteen minutes.
   Intensity: Bert drove the weight to the 120 pound marker on the column.

2. As an amount per unit of variable time (rate)
   Examples
   Frequency: On the average, Wilbur wet the bed three times a week.
   Duration: On the average, Kimberly was on-task seven minutes each classroom hour.
   Intensity: On the average, Bert maintained 92.7 pounds of force on the bar over the three-minute time period.

3. As an amount per unit of fixed opportunity (percentage).
   Examples
   Frequency: Ralph struck out half of the time (i.e., fifty percent).
   Duration: Kimberly was on-task seventy-five percent of the time.
   Intensity: Bert drove the weight two-thirds of the distance to the bell.

Experience has taught us that rate or percentage are the usual choices because they best describe problem situations. People who talk about doing things too much (like smoking), or not enough (like studying), are dissatisfied with the rate of a particular behavior. Failing to remember birthdays or names that go with faces and similar limited occasion events may be best expressed as a percentage. Ultimately, the decision as to which attribute to measure and how to express the measure is influenced by the problem.

HAWD - 13
How Are We Doing?

---

1. The three measurable attributes of human performance are _____, _____, and _____.

2. Which of the three attributes has proven to be the most useful? _____.

Answers are presented in the HAWD-13 footnote, appearing later.

Low-rate and High-rate Performance. As indicated previously, one of the most useful ways to consider human performance is in terms of the rate at which it occurs. Performance which is virtually continuous may be referred to as high-rate performance. Examples are whispering, talking, gesturing, studying, and playing with others. Low-rate performance, on the other hand, includes behaviors such as dating and mowing the lawn. In a case of low-rate performance, the event may be tallied as a complete unit but with high-rate performance this is not the case. Under high-rate conditions any determination of when one behavior ends and another begins is impossible. In such cases one might choose to make one observation per unit of time (e.g., on the minute) and simply record yes or no to indicate whether or not the performance was underway at a specific observation point.

In Figure 5.14 is presented an example for "gesturing with hand" performance. The unit of time is the first three seconds in each minute.

Hand Gesturing

Time	1	2	3	4	5	6	7	8	9	10	11	12
Yes	X	X		X	X			X	X	X		X
No			X			X	X				X	

Figure 5.14. Observation Record of Hand Gesturing Behavior.

Based on data presented in Figure 5.14, during eight of the twelve observation periods some form of hand gesturing was occurring. From this sampling one can be reasonably sure that the person's hands are in some gesturing movement about two-thirds of the time. If the objective is to decrease the hand gesturing by fifty percent (i.e., by one-half), then the frequency of gestures during the subsequent criterion sampling would have to total four or fewer over the twelve-minute period.

Before moving on to the "where to observe question," emphasis should again be given the point that accurate quantification is possible only after units of observable performance have been defined (recall previous section on performance terminology). Precision of definition increases by naming the physical movements or actions of interest. Examples of target performance might be "raising-hand," "sitting-on-bed," "head-nodding," and the like. Definitions can vary in precision as the performance class of interest is analyzed into smaller and smaller components. Eating, for example, involves a number of movements and actions, such as "chewing-with-your-mouth-closed." Also one should remember that the criterion for success in accurately defining the unit of performance is agreement among observers. The definition must insure that the same performance is counted on each occurrence and by each observer. Clear definition of the *onset* of the behavior (such as "lips-part) and the *termination* of the behavior (such as "lips-come-together") help observers agree that a unit of the performance has occurred.

Where to Assess

The place to assess (observe) is where the problem is—the lunchroom, the playground, the theatre lobby, or around the dinner table. At times the question "Where to Observe" gets tricky because a particular behavior may be problematic under a specific set of circumstances and non-problematic during a social studies period. Where to observe in such cases is quite obvious.

When to Assess

Obviously, around the clock assessment (observation) seldom is possible and even if it were possible, it is usually not needed. The

---

HAWD - 13.   1. frequency, duration, intensity; 2. frequency.

criterion of efficiency requires that one expend only those resources (time and energy) which reliable measurement requires. What is needed is representative measurement with respect to time of observation. The ultimate criterion is comparability between the data collected under a particular schedule of observations and the data obtained if around the clock observation were to be made. To insure such comparability, consideration of possible fluctuation in the performance because of temporary and cyclical events is essential. For example, a temporary event such as icy road conditions during early November in Kentucky may distort data regarding tardiness for kindergarten children in the Louisville public schools. To the extent that icy roads are related to the time taken to get from home to school, to that extent will tardiness data collected under their temporary conditions differ from tardiness data collected under the more usual non-icy conditions.

Pending week-ends and holidays are examples of cyclical events which may generate non-representative data on a specific performance. For example, a fifth grade teacher who wants to collect data on the on-task behavior of the class should not anticipate representative data if the teacher makes observations over four consecutive Friday afternoons or over the entire week just preceding Christmas vacation. In both cases, on-task behavior is likely to vary from the usual level because of the upcoming event—vacation from school. Therefore the conclusion that the observation data will reflect this deviation from the usual and will *not* be "representative of what is."

REPORTING DATA WITH GRAPHS

One of the easiest ways to get the big picture, to see what has happened and what is happening, is to present data on a graph. Stated another way, on a graph can be presented a condensed picture of a large number of events. Graphs have the following characteristics:

1. Identification of the behavior being measured

2. A unit of measurement

3. Measurement over a period of time

292

In most textbooks is described a standard graphing procedure where frequency or percentage is shown on the vertical axis and a score or some other measure is shown on the horizontal axis. Baseline and intervention data are typically not plotted this way. The unit of measurement (frequency, duration or intensity) is placed on the vertical axis of graphs and the days or times at which the behavior is measured are placed on the horizontal axis as illustrated in Figure 5.15.

HAWD - 14
  How Are We Doing?

---

1. In the space provided, indicate with an "X" three characteristics of a performance graph.

   a. _____ A unit of measurement
   b. _____ A description of the measurement device
   c. _____ Measurement over a period of time
   d. _____ Behavioral identification

2. What performance does Figure 5.15 describe? _____
3. What is the unit of measurement in the graph presented in Figure 5.15? _____
4. What is the length of time over which data in Figure 5.15 were taken? _____

To check your responses against ours, check the HAWD-14 footnote.

Advantages of Graphic Representation

As indicated previously, one advantage of graphic representation of data is that it tells you at a glance what is being observed and what is happening to the behavior that is being measured. In most situations graphic representation permits the most emphatic illustration of increasing, decreasing or stable behavior rates.

A second advantage, and in some ways a more important advantage to the would-be change agent, is the fact that graphic representation will often reveal patterns that are not always apparent in narratives or in columns of numbers. This point is well illustrated in Figure 5.16. In this situation an appropriate question would be "is the frequency of Kim's tattling on classmates consis-

Frequency

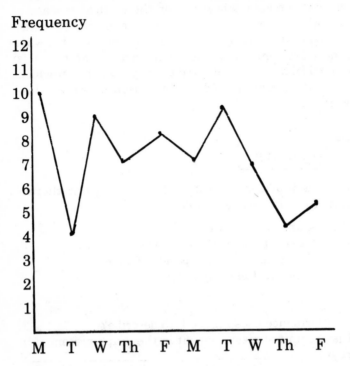

Figure 5.15. Trips Tony Takes to the Restroom.

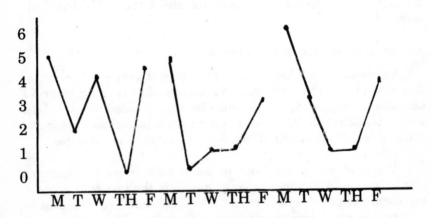

Figure 5.16. Kim's Tattling Episodes Over a Three-Week Period.

tently higher on certain days of the week?" If so, then one might want to discover what about those particular days of the week or about the days just prior to the "problem days" might be influencing the behavior.

In applied behavioral analysis, a single graph often is used to represent an entire intervention history. Such a history includes information about pre-intervention conditions, about conditions during intervention, and about post-intervention conditions. Such an intervention history may be observed in the graph presented in Figure 5.17.

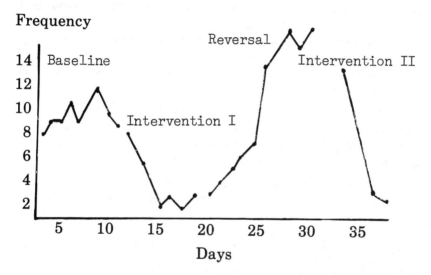

Figure 5.17. The Effects of Two Intervention Strategies Upon the Number of Target Behaviors Observed Each Day.

HAWD - 14.   1. a, c, d, 2. trips to the restroom, 3. sample frequency, 4. two weeks.

Data regarding each of these conditions are useful in the execution of four critical functions:

1. Defining the problem,
2. Setting up objectives for intervention,
3 Monitoring the implementation of the intervention procedures, and
4. Evaluating the success of the intervention procedures.

Each of these functions and implications for graphing are discussed in the section which follows.

Baseline Measures

A "baseline" may be defined as "a measure of the behavior as it is." Stated another way, a measure of what presently is happening is called a baseline. A baseline has the following characteristics:

1. A definition of the behavior being observed/measured
2. A unit of measurement
3. A series of observations taken over a *period of time prior to intervention*

EXAMPLE: Ms. Tinkle, a first grade teacher, feels that one of her pupils, Tony, simply "makes too many trips to the restroom" and has decided to do something about this "behavioral excess." Two different types of baseline data might be collected.

1. Frequency or the number of times each day Tony goes to the restroom. The unit being measured is the event of going to and leaving the restroom.
2. Duration or the amount of time Tony spends in the restroom each day. The unit being measured is the length of time in minutes which Tony spends in the restroom.

Both types, i.e., frequency and duration, produce specific data about the behavior that concerns the teacher. Whichever attribute is used in acquiring a baseline measure must be used to evaluate the tentative intervention strategy selected and implemented. If Ms. Tinkle uses the number of times Tony goes to the restroom as a baseline, frequency of going to the restroom after the tentative solution has been implemented must be used to evaluate the tentative solution.

In the spaces provided, describe briefly the three things which a baseline measure must do:

1. _____
2. _____
3. _____

For a check on your answer, see the HAWD-15 footnote.

Why Baseline?—For several reasons, baseline data are essential to the "designing," "implementing," and "evaluating" functions of systematic problem solving. More specifically, baseline data are critical in any attempt to

1. formulate an operational definition of the presenting problem,
2. complete a motivational analysis in order to determine factors controlling behavior, and
3. set up benchmarks against which to monitor and to evaluate any intervention attempts.

Baseline Reliability. The critical question regarding reliability of baseline data may be posed as follows: "After a solution has been attempted, will it be possible to compare the baseline data with later data and show with reasonable certainty that the problem as described has been solved or is well on the way toward solution or that the problem situation is unchanged?" The conclusion is that one of the features of a baseline is that it is taken over a period of time since a "one-shot" measure might give an inaccurate picture. For example, one might measure the number of times Tony "makes a trip to the restroom" on a particular day but that might be one of his "good days" or "bad days." No absolute time limit for observation exists. The objective, or course, is to get as accurate a picture of the present performance as is economically possible and this accuracy will be influenced by the seriousness of the problem and the cost of observing the problem behavior.

The Obtrusive Baseline. If a baseline is to be a "measure of the behavior as it is," it is essential that the observer and his/her measurement procedure be as unobtrusive as possible. Two conditions militate against unobtrusive observation and recording of baseline data:

1. When the object of measurement is aware that he/she has been singled out for observation.
2. When taking the baseline actually introduces changes in the environment which might affect the behavior.

To insure an accurate baseline measure, one wants the subject to behave naturally.

HAWD - 16
How Are We Doing?

In the space provided indicate with the letter "U" the two baseline examples which are most unobtrusive; indicate with the letters "OM" the baseline example where the object of measurement might bias the observation.

1. _____ Once every hour Ms. Crimple casually looks over the class and if Tommy is talking to his neighbor or out of his seat she makes a mark on a tally sheet at her desk.

2. _____ Mr. Henderson is bothered by Bill's talking out of turn. Every time Bill starts talking without raising his hand, Mr. Henderson walks over to the class "Blooper" chart and puts an "X" next to Bill's name.

3. _____ Ms. Dick is trying to decide if Hal still belongs to the slow reading group. She records the number of words each student does not recognize in each sentence.

Answers are presented in the HAWD-16 footnote.

The Baseline Treatment. In the previous section the focus was upon subject awareness as a source of bias in the data which an observer gathers. One should note, however, that even if the observee has no idea of what the observer is doing, the observation will not necessarily be an accurate measurement. The measurement will be accurate to the extent that no changes occur in the observee's environment that could influence the behavior being measured.

HAWD - 15
1. State what behavior is being measured.
2. State the unit of measurement.
3. Take the measure of the behavior over time.

EXAMPLE: Ms. Jones was interested in getting Sam to stay in his seat. She constantly was telling him to return to his desk and to get back to work. When she started to take a baseline, she decided she would stop telling him to return to his desk and work, but would just keep a frequency count of the number of times he was out of his seat. Apparently she must not have been as unobtrusive as she thought, or else something outside Ms. Jones' knowledge was happening to Sam, because she obtained in a ten-day period the data presented in Figure 5.18.

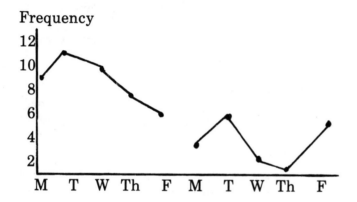

Figure 5.18. Time Days Sampling of Sam's Out-of-Seat Behavior Over a Two-Week Period.

HAWD - 16. 1. U, 2. OM, 3. U.

How might Ms. Jones have influenced the baseline she was trying to get? Write some possibilities in the space provided.

_____

_____

_____

Some possibilities are suggested in the HAWD-17 footnote.

Often other environmental events occur over which one has no
control and which may affect the behavior that is being measured.
For example, fighting and other aggressive acts may increase on
days when it rains or snows heavily and the students must be kept
inside. A substitute or other visitor may interrupt the regular
classroom procedure. Baseline observations will be more meaningful if such events are noted and entered with the data obtained.

For many problems unobtrusive measurement will help both
for giving the most accurate basis for designing a helping strategy
and for deciding if your strategy or solution has been effective.

Success Gradients

A use of the frequency polygon or graph is to formulate and
chart objectives for intervention in relation to the baseline data
previously collected and graphed. This action assumes, of course,
that after monitoring the occurrence of the target behavior for the
predetermined units of time, an agreement exists that the rate of
occurrence of the behavior is not satisfactory. Once this decision is
reached, the desired rate must be determined. For example, let's
assume that Ms. Tinkle has monitored the number of trips Tony
takes to the restroom (see Figure 5.15) and has determined that an
average of seven or eight trips to the restroom each day was
excessive and that this number should be cut by one-half or down to
four or fewer times each day. In Figure 5.18 the baserate data have
been reproduced and a success or achievement bar for intervention
during the following week has been charted. One should note that
the success gradient has been charted at a frequency of four to indicate the level below which the data must remain if the intervention

300

is to be regarded as successful and complete. The distinct advantage of charting a success gradient is that it permits all parties involved to recognize immediately when the objective has been reached or the degree of progress made toward reaching the objective.

MONITORING AND EVALUATING THE INTERVENTION STRATEGY

To an unfortunate extent in the past, persons involved in helping strategies have acted as if quantifying or measuring behavior was either an early step or a late step in the problem-solving process. More recently, change agents are beginning to regard periodic measurement of behavior as a critical basis for determining if the intervention procedure is being carried out according to design and if it is moving the target behavior in the desired direction. This trend toward "periodic measurement" derives considerable support from the current emphasis upon change agent accountability through the systems approach which manifests itself in continuous monitoring and ongoing evaluation as to what is and what is not being accomplished.

As indicated in a previous section of this Chapter, the advantages of periodic measurement are many. The measurement may strongly suggest, for example, that whatever was being done during the intervention period was done in the direction of the agreed-upon objective, but that considerable distance still separates the present level of the behavior from the desired level. This decision might

---

HAWD -17—Ms. Jones *may* have inadvertently implemented a solution. Either stopping paying attention to Sam, or the fact that her tallying his out-of-seat behavior was so obvious it may have changed the situation. You might comment at this point, "The boy is not getting out of his seat as much and that is what the teacher wants, so what's wrong with that?" Nothing, as long as you realize that the "baseline" became an attempted solution, instead of a baseline. If, when the teacher stops making these observations, the undesirable behavior does not resume, there is no problem. If it appears to resume, however, you are back to where you started.

suggest several alterations, one of which might be to set objectives lower but in a graduated fashion. For example, based on the intervention data reported for one week (see Figure 5.19), Ms. Tinkle might be advised to reduce her original terminal objective to a lesser level for the following week and to then increase it by a given percentage for each of a finite number of future weeks. Such an alteration has been introduced in Figure 5.19 and is represented by the success gradient which graduates over two successive weeks and then levels off.

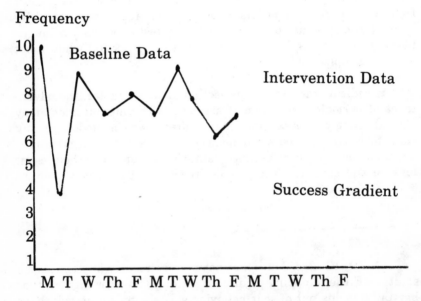

Figure 5.19. Baseline and Intervention Data on Trips Tony Makes to the Restroom.

On the other hand, the criterion of efficiency may suggest a second alternative. Ms. Tinkle may decide after using the first intervention procedure for one week that a less time-consuming or less-expensive procedure should be considered. Making such a decision clearly requires reliable data on the effects of the current intervention procedure as well as projected data for the less costly alternatives.

> **HAWD-18**
> **How Are We Doing?**

In the space provided, indicate with a T or F whether the statement is True or False.

     _____1. Success gradients are charted following the baseline period to indicate a desired rate of change.

     _____2. Success gradients are used appropriately in behavioral excess conditions as well as in behavioral deficit conditions.

     _____3. Success gradients should never be changed once they are established.

     _____4. Success gradients could be viewed as a graphic representation of a performance objective.

When you finish, you may want to check your answers against those reported in the HAWD-18 footnote.

In the previous section of this Chapter some fundamental observation and assessment procedures were considered. Highlighted in that discussion were data-collection and reporting techniques which may be used in defining the problem, in setting up objectives for intervention, in monitoring the implementation of the intervention procedures, and in evaluating the success of the intervention procedures.

The techniques described in this Chapter are believed to be essential to quality control in helping. The deliberate and responsible use of these techniques should better enable you, the change agent, to respond to questions about what you are trying to do, how to go about doing it, and how to gauge your successes or failures (Mager, 1970).

SUMMARY

This Chapter contains discussions on what are thought to be essential considerations in the planning, monitoring, and evaluating of "helping" efforts. This includes the systematic assessment of client needs, the translation of needs into statements of goals and objectives, the gathering of data on the helping process and the analysis of these data in relation to helping intent.

In this Chapter a NEED is defined as a discrepancy between "THE WAY IT IS" and "THE WAY IT OUGHT TO BE" as perceived by the client, the client being the person, organization, or institution to whom the change agent has contracted services. From this perspective then, the ability to reduce these discrepancies is the mark of change agent competence.

In the "goal analysis" section of this Chapter, the reader was encouraged to generate goal statements which describe outcomes rather than procedures or procedures designed to achieve particular outcomes. Under the "objectives" section, on the other hand, both outcome and process objectives were considered. Although the focus of evaluation is different for each type of objective, both types benefit through the use of criterion referencing and performance terminology. Objectives so charaterized specify in performance language *who will do what under what conditions and to what extent.*

In the assessment section of this Chapter the value of diagnostic assessment as well as evaluative assessment and the need for periodic assessment as well as end-point assessment were stressed. Similarly, the advantages and disadvantages of criterion-referenced assessment as well as normative-referenced assessment were considered.

In the final section of this Chapter are described some observation and data collection and reporting techniques which may be used in defining the problem, in setting up objectives for intervention, in monitoring the implementation of the intervention procedures, and in evaluating the success of the intervention procedures.

HAWD-18.   1.T 2. T 3. F 4. T

The techniques described in this Chapter are, we believe, essential to quality control in helping. The deliberate and responsible use of these techniques should better enable you, the change agent, to "respond to inquiries about what we are trying to do, how we go about it, and and how we gauge our successes or failures" (Mager, 1973).

REFERENCES

American Personnel and Guidance Association. *The counselor: Professional preparation and role.* Washington, D.C.: American Personnel and Guidance Association, 1962.

Armstrong, R.J., Cornell, T.D., Kraner, R.E. and Robertson, E.W. *The development and evaluation of behavioral objectives.* Belmont, California: Wadsworth Publishing Company, 1970.

Banathy, B.H. *Instructional systems.* Palo Alto: Fearon Publishers, 1962.

Davies, I.K. *Competency based learning: Technology, management, and design.* New York: McGraw-Hill, 1973.

Froehle. T.C. Some assessment dimensions in competency-based counselor education. In Froehle, T.C. (Ed.) *Competency-based counselor education: Designing, implementing and evaluating criterion referenced instruction.* Bloomington, Indiana: Indiana University, 1976.

Glaser, R. Instructional technology and the measurement of learning outcomes: Some questions. *American Psychologist,* 1963, *18,* 519-521.

Houston, W.R. et al. Developing instructional modules. (Work Text, Director's Guide), University of Houston, 1971.

Kibler, R.J., Barker, L.L., and Miles, D.T. *Behavioral objectives and instruction.* Boston: Allyn and Bacon, Incorporated, 1970.

Lauver, P. Developing and using behavioral data. Unpublished manuscript. Indiana University, 1971.

Mager, R.F. and Pipe, P. *Analyzing performance problems: You really oughta wanna.* Belmont, California: Fearon Publishers, 1970.

Mager, R.F. *Preparing instructional objectives.* Palo Alto: Fearon Publishers, 1962.

Mazer, G. (Ed.) *Preparation of guidance associates and professional counselors within the framework of a competency-based program.* Washington, D.C.: American Personnel and Guidance Association, 1973.

Mueller, D.J. The mastery model and some alternative models of classroom instruction and evaluation: An analysis. *Educational Technology,* 1973, *13,* 5-10.

Nunnally, J.C., Jr. *Introduction to psychological measurement.* New York: McGraw-Hill, 1970.

Ryan, T. Antoinette. *Defnining behavioral objectives.* Paper presented at the AERA 1969 pre-session, Los Angeles, February 2, 1969.

INDEX

INDEX

Index

A

Abbreviations 258
Acceptance 40
Access 39
Action
  course 24
  sociogram 191
  team 29-30
Active inquiry 8
Activities
  criteria-referenced 255
Activity guide 116
Adlerian concern 81
Administrators 9
Alternative behavior 85
American Personnel and
  Guidance Association 258,
  306
Analysis 19, 24, 32
  problem 24
Anxiety 190
Approach
  differential 53
Approaches
  collaborative 7-11
    implementing 21-32
  systematic 7-17
    implementing 21-32
Armstrong, R 254, 269, 306
Assessment 19, 23, 32
  criterion-referenced 283
  diagnostic 281
  distinctions 278
  end-point 281
  evaluative 281
  normative-referenced 283
  periodic 281
  procedures 277
  process 280
  systematic 286
Audience sharing 205
Auxiliary ego 183-184, 196

Awareness 117-119
  interchange units 120
  program category 111
  topics 164

B

Bain, R 219,240
Ball, G 103,104,106,108,
  112, 131
Banathy, B 306
Bank, A 46
Barbour, A 205,240
Barker, L 306
Baseline 86
  measures 296
  obtrusive 297
  reliability 297
  treatment 298
Beam, P 172, 240
Beatings
  physical 57
Beethovan 118
Behavior
  attending 65
  attention-getting 81
  awareness 58
  classifying 58
  desirable 58
  evaluation 118
  expected 12-13
  modeling 130
  operant 78
Behavior change
  awareness 52
  planning 78-81
  theoretical framework 53
Behavior system
  classification 58
Behavioral abbreviation 261
Bell, R 97,98
Berenson, B 98
Berne, E 240

311

Bessell, H 114, 124, 165
Blocking forces 26, 28
Borton, T 165
Brainstorming 29
Braybrooke, D 15, 46
Brown, G 165
Brubaker, J 46
Bunche, R 118
Business people 107

C

Carkhuff, R 98
Castan, F 116,126,165
Catharsis 184
  abbreaction 184
  integration 184
Challenges
  economic 7
  personal 7
  social 7
Change agents 249
Change
  environmental 9-81
    exercise 81
    worksheet 82
Changes
  blocking 26
  creative 8
  resistence 13-16
  organizational 8
Child beating 57
Child behavior
  effective influence 53
Child's esteem
  bolstering 83
  exercise for bolstering 83
Child-rearing practices 52
Children
  behavior 57-59, 63-64
  negative attitudes 52
  changing 78
  goals 59-63
Christie, S 5-6, 7, 29, 46, 85
Circle Sessions 109-111
  analyzing 150
  Ball critique 148
  evaluation 149
  format 109-112
  frequency 158
  leading 129

Circle Sessions (cont)
  objectives 110-111
  participation phase 111
  process 110-111
  space 157
  teacher critique 147
  theoretical base 110-111
  time 157
  transcript 131-146
Circumstances
  definition 214
Clapp, W 52, 98
Classroom
  self-contained 156
Classrooms 211
Client welfare 249
Climate
  home, emotional 52
  school 11
Climax 200
Closure 205
Cognitive change 81
Collaborative group problem
  solving 20-21
Communication systems 52
  effective 51
Communications
  among system members 11
  children 65
  positive modes 126
  interpersonal 126
  school-community 51
Conditions 270
  resistance to change 13-16
  specified 270
Conflict
  understanding 33-36
  utilizing 33-36
Confusion 66
Consumers 107
Contingency contracting 88-89
  exercise 90
Cooley, C 222, 240
Coopersmith, S 165
Cordova, H 166
Cornell, T 307
Counselors 9
Creative process
  learning 177-182
Creativity 189,234

Criteria-referenced objectives
  classification 263-277
Criterion 270
Cue
  behavior 86
Culture
  values 12
  conserve 234
  crises 210
Culver, C 46
Curriculum
  development 108

D

Data
  gathering 72
  reporting, graphs 292
Davies, I 306
Depression 260
Decision making 19, 24, 32
Decisions
  feedback 11
Delphi Technique 43-45
  application 43
Detweiler, J 232, 241
Dialogue 205
Dinkmeyer, D 59,81, 98
Director 184
Dix, D 118
Dodson, L 2
Ducasse, C 172
Dyad exercise 76

E

Education
  conditions 7
  expense 16
  religious courses 113
  practitioners, goal v
Education program
  bilingual 112
Education trainers
  goal v
Elbert, W 128,165
Emotional continuum 188
Encounter 189
Environmental change 79-81
  exercise 81
  worksheet 82

Ergo 176-177, 180
Evaluation
  cooperative 55
Evaluation systems 96-97
Experiences
  types 174

F

Family conferences
  exercise 76
Family Life Attitude Inventory
  97
Fantina, M 166
Feedback 36-38
  deserved 122
  positive 122
Feelings 181
  student 118
  understanding 67
Fel's Rating Scale 152
Force Field Analysis 25-27
  steps 26-27
Froehle, T 96, 245-248,254,306

G

Glaser, R 286,306
Goal analysis 254-257
Goal descriptions
  analyzing 257
Goal orientation 83
  exercise 81
Goals
  ambiguity 13,15
  assessing human growth 252
  describing 269
  discrepancy 7
  honorable 60-61
  of education v
  man 8
Goals as needs 8-9
Goodlad, J 6
Grades 13
Grading Curve 284
Graphic representation
  advantages 293
Graphs
  data reporting 292

Group
  dynamics 205
  membership 14
Group problem solving
  systematic 18
Growth
  human 10
Guitar phenomenon 178

H

Handbook of Structured
  Experiences for Human
  Relations Training 70
Helfat, L 113, 165
Hess, R 53, 98
Hollander, C 170, 171, 186,
  240
Hollander, S 210,212, 219,
  240
Hollander Psychodrama Curve
  186-189,206,209
Home
  emotional climate 52
Home environment
  child 52
  influence on learning 53
Houston, W 306
Human development group
  composition 156
  size 156
Human development
  profile
  self-contained classroom
    156
Human development program
  108-164
  categories 111
  curriculum sequence 113
  goals 111
  total content 111-112
  ways of evaluating 151-153
Human growth 10
  assessing 249-306
Human interaction 17-18
Human performance
  measurable attributes 286

I

Ideals 118
Ideas
  trading 13
Incrementalism, disjointed
  elements 15
Individual
  group relationship 33
  orientation 16
  role types 13
  troubled 115
Independence
  child 52
Information
  sources 77-78
Inquiry
  active 8-9
  common 18
  problem solving 9
  process 9
  scientific method 8
Integration 184, 203
Interaction
  human 17,18
  positive 109
  social 124-127
  structure 109
Interchange
  awareness units 120
  mastery units 123
Interchange program 108-112
  content 112
  issue range 112
  target population 112
Intercommunication
  lack 13-14
Internal processes
  individual 74
  sequence 74
Interpersonal encounter 74
Intervention strategies 295
  evaluating 301
  monitoring 301
Intolerable behavior 58
Involvement
  community 163
  parents 163

J

Jackins, H 125, 165
Jones, J 70, 98
Judson, S 116

K

Kibler, R 306
Kluckhorn, C 240
Kraner, R 306
Krumboltz, H 98
Kurpius, D viii, 2-4, 7,
25, 36, 46, 85

L

LaChapelle, D 113, 165
Lauver, P 258, 306
Leaders
education 9
responsibilities 129
Leadership training
student 130
Learning 219
environmental change 108
optimal environmental
conditions 54-55
self-improvement v
Learning environments
characteristics v
cooperativeness 55
productive 52
Learning process
children 52
teacher contribution 51
Learning teams
children 51
communication system 51
parents 51
Leman, S 209,240
LeShan, E 98
Lewin, K 25
Life-process curve 233
Lindbloom, C 15,46
Linkage 39
Listener
behaviors 66
involvement 66
Listening skills 73
Lovemaking 188

Loving 64

M

Mager, R 269, 274, 305, 306
Magic Circle 108-113
awareness topics 119-120
mastery tasks 122
mastery topics 123
program 112-113, 119-121
program units 119-121
student involvement 162
Man
goals 8
Mann, C 218, 240
Mann, J 218, 240
Maslow, A 8, 46
theory of motivation 8
Mastery 121-124
program category 111
topics 164
Mastery sessions
first graders 122
kindergarten 122
pre school 122
Mastery tasks
magic circle 122
Mastery topics
ages seven to twelve 123
Mastery units
junior-senior high 123
Mazer, G 307
McCann, G 46
McIntire, R 59, 98
McKay, G 59, 81, 98
Measurement dimensions 287
Meetings
organizing 41-42
Mental health 114
Merton, R 12, 46
Michelangelo 118
Miles, D 306
Miller, P 46
Mind
inquiring 9
Misbehavior 61
Model
systematic-collaborative 1-
45

Modeling
  listening skills 73
Moreno Institute 170
Moreno, J 182, 185, 189, 190,
  191, 200, 212, 232, 240, 241
Mueller, D 307

N

National Science Foundation 5
Needs
  assessment 55-57
  basic 8
  definition 250
Negative reinforcement 87
Newberg, N 126
Non-possessive warmth 54
Norms
  collaborative 15
  separatist 15
Northway, M 232, 241
Nunnally, J 307

O

Objectives
  affective 264-268
  assessing human growth 252
  classifying exercise 75
  cognitive 264-268
  consequence 264-268
  criteria-referenced
    classification 263-277
  evaluation 256
  experiential 256
  foundation 55-56
  performance 264-268
  performance-term 270
Observation
  systematic 286
Opportunities
  behavior change 80
Orientation
  individual 13, 16
Osgood, C 97,98
Outcomes
  criteria-referenced 255
  evaluation 31, 256
  objectives 256

P

Palomares, U 103-104, 106,
  108, 112, 116, 165-166
Paraphrasing 67
Parent attitude
  change 52
  research 97
Parent Teacher Association 15
Parents
  dreams 15
  training 51
Patterson, G 78, 98, 166
People
  child sees worthwhile 54-55
People-helping 177
Perception check 67
Performance 259, 290
  high rate 290
  low rate 290
  minimum 270
  specified 270
  terminology 252
Performance-term objectives
  components 272
Person 270
  worthwhile 54
Pfeiffer, J 70, 98
Physical beatings 57
Play experiences 209
Positive learning
  environments v, vi
Positive reinforcement 87
Post-assessment 280
Post-treatment
  condition 250
Power 81
Pre-assessment 278
Preventive measures
  training programs 53
Prince, J 46
Principal 13
Priorities 43
Problem
  assessment 23-24
  defining 22
  sensing 21-22
Problem solving 7-8
  beginning point 38
  collaborative 1-45
  elements 25

Problem solving (cont)
  group 18
  inquiry-based 7
  processes of group 19
  systematic 1-45
Products
  education 107
Process, evaluating 32
Profile, developmental 152,
  153-155
Protagonist 185, 193
Psychodrama 171-239
  as an art 172
  goals 183
  language 183
  power 177
Psychodramatic enactment 191
  process 185-186
Public school
  criticism 15
Punishment 87
  alternatives 93
  problems of using 92

Q

Questioning 66

R

Racial integration 112
Rasmussen, R 46
Rating Scale
  Fel 152
Reality 200
  level 196
Rector, W 99
Reinforcement 86
Reorientation 80
Resistance 198
Reaction form 56
Respect
  individual 113
Respondent 78
Restriction
  children 80
Revenge 81
Rewards 86
Rivera, F 166
Robertson, E 306
Robinson, S 44, 46
Rogers, C 118, 125, 166

Rogers, E 46
Role performance
  boundaries 11
Role playing 60, 75, 171-239
  audience 183, 203
  implementation 213
  situations 215-217
  structure 213
Rose, S 98
Rubini, L 116, 166
Ryan, T 254, 269, 307
Saavedra, C 112, 116
Satir, V 52, 60, 98

S

S-C see S-C Model
S-C see Approaches,
  systematic
  collaborative
S-C Model 17, 20-45
  inqiury objectives 20
  introduction 18-21
  objectives 20
  six steps 19
Scene setting 213
Schaefer, E 97, 98
Schein, E 38, 46
Schmuck, P 98
Schmuck, R 46, 98
Schmidt, W 46
School Boards 14
Schools
  as biological systems 11
  as social systems 11
  as systems 11
  decisions 11
  existing conditions 13-16
  goal ambiguity 15
  resistance to change 13-16
  social system 12
  structure of system 11
  traditional 15
  vulnerability 15
School staff
  low interdependence of 13-14
School system
  vulnerability 14-15
Schutz, W 241
Selecting strategy 24-25
Self confidence
  program category 111

Self-directed discovery 182
Self discovery 54
Sensing problems 21-22
Semantic differential 97
Services
   educators 107
Shakespeare 118
Shaw, C 53, 99
Shaw, M 97, 99
Shipman, V 53, 98
Significant persons 51
Simpson, E 166
Skills
   child decision making 84
Smoking 12
Social atom
   collective 221
   individual 223
   principles 225
   psychological 220
Social interaction 124-127
   innerchange units 127
   program category 111
   topics 164
Social learning 78-79
Social systems
   boundaries 12
   norms 12
   schools vi
   role expectations 12
Sociometric choices 231
Sociometric placement 194
Sociometric process 189
Sociometry 170-239
   as an art 172
Socrates 118
Solution definition 252
Sollutions
   suggestions 20
Spontaneity 113, 189, 233
Spontaneous involvement 182
Stachowiak, J 98
Staff
   development 17
   low interdependence 13
   members 16
Stimulus 86
   reduction 80
Stage 185
Strategy implementation 29-30
Structure 11

Student
   actors 214
   feelings 130
   ideas 130
   participation 129
   responsibility 130
Student leadership
   importance 162
   training 130
Students 13, 16
Success gradients 300
Suci, G 98
Summarizing 66
Supporting forces 26, 28
Surplus reality 200-201
Synthesis 19, 24, 32
   problem 24
System members
   behavior 12
Systematic and Collaborative
   Approach see S-C Model
Systematic-Collaborative Model
   1-45
Systematic group problem
   solving, processes 19
   six steps 19
Systematic problem solving 251
Sze, W 52, 99

T

Tannenbaum, P 98
Taschman, H 98
Teacher
   role 127
   artists 128
Teachers 9, 13, 16, 111
   interventions 229
   natural behaviors 128
   training 51-52
Teaching 188
Technical assistance
   problem solving 23-24
Temporal continuum 188
Terminal performance 271
Termination 41
Terms
   non-performance 260
   performance 260

Theoretical framework
  behavior change 53
Time
  setting 214
Time lines 43
Tolerable behavior 58
Topics
  social interaction 126-127
Transaction
  interpersonal 125-126
Trist, E 8, 46

U

Undesirable behavior 58
United States Government
  Education, office 2
University
  coursework 17

V

Values
  culture 12
  set 11
Value differences 26
Value systems
  personal 7
Vargas, J 64, 79, 99
Viewing life 175
Vockell, E 87, 91, 99
Vulnerability 13

W

Warm-up 185
  period 192
  phase 190
Weaver, L 43, 46
Weigand, J 63, 99
Weinstein, G 166
Wolff, S 52, 99
Worksheet
  environmental change 82